CIMA's CGMA® Professional Qualification

Management Level

F2 Advanced Financial Reporting

Exam Practice Kit

For exams from January 2025

Eleventh edition 2024

ISBN 9781 0355 1835 7

e-ISBN 9781 0355 1884 5

British Library Cataloguing-in-Publication Data
A catalogue record for this book
is available from the British Library

Published by

BPP Learning Media Ltd
BPP House, Aldine Place,
142/144 Uxbridge Road
London W12 8AA

learningmedia.bpp.com

Printed in the United Kingdom

> Your learning materials, published by BPP Learning Media Ltd, are printed on paper obtained from traceable, sustainable sources.

All rights reserved. No part of this publication may be reproduced, stored in a retrieval system or transmitted, in any form or by any means, electronic, mechanical, photocopying, recording or otherwise, without the prior written permission of BPP Learning Media Ltd.

BPP Learning Media is grateful to the IASB for permission to reproduce extracts from IFRS® Accounting Standards, IAS® Standards, SIC and IFRIC. This publication contains copyright © material and trademarks of the IFRS Foundation®. All rights reserved. Used under license from the IFRS Foundation®. Reproduction and use rights are strictly limited. For more information about the IFRS Foundation and rights to use its material please visit www.IFRS.org.

Disclaimer: To the extent permitted by applicable law the Board and the IFRS Foundation expressly disclaims all liability howsoever arising from this publication or any translation thereof whether in contract, tort or otherwise (including, but not limited to, liability for any negligent act or omission) to any person in respect of any claims or losses of any nature including direct, indirect, incidental or consequential loss, punitive damages, penalties or costs.

Information contained in this publication does not constitute advice and should not be substituted for the services of an appropriately qualified professional.

©
BPP Learning Media Ltd
2024

A note about copyright

Dear Customer

What does the little © mean and why does it matter?

Your market-leading BPP books, course materials and e-learning materials do not write and update themselves. People write them: on their own behalf or as employees of an organisation that invests in this activity. Copyright law protects their livelihoods. It does so by creating rights over the use of the content.

Breach of copyright is a form of theft – as well as being a criminal offence in some jurisdictions, it is potentially a serious breach of professional ethics.

With current technology, things might seem a bit hazy but, basically, without the express permission of BPP Learning Media:

- Photocopying our materials is a breach of copyright
- Printing our digital materials in order to share them with or forward them to a third party or use them in any way other than in connection with your BPP studies is a breach of copyright.

You can, of course, sell your books, in the form in which you have bought them – once you have finished with them. (Is this fair to your fellow students? We update for a reason.) Please note the e-products are sold on a single user licence basis: we do not supply 'unlock' codes to people who have bought them second-hand.

And what about outside the UK? BPP Learning Media strives to make our materials available at prices students can afford by local printing arrangements, pricing policies and partnerships which are clearly listed on our website. A tiny minority ignore this and indulge in criminal activity by illegally photocopying our material or supporting organisations that do. If they act illegally and unethically in one area, can you really trust them?

NO AI TRAINING. Unless otherwise agreed in writing, the use of BPP material for the purpose of AI training is not permitted. Any use of this material to 'train' generative artificial intelligence (AI) technologies is prohibited, as is providing archived or cached data sets containing such material to another person or entity.

Copyright © IFRS Foundation

All rights reserved. Reproduction and use rights are strictly limited. No part of this publication may be translated, reprinted or reproduced or utilised in any form either in whole or in part or by any electronic, mechanical or other means, now known or hereafter invented, including photocopying and recording, or in any information storage and retrieval system, without prior permission in writing from the IFRS Foundation. Contact the IFRS Foundation for further details.

The Foundation has trade marks registered around the world (Trade Marks) including 'IAS®', 'IASB®', 'IFRIC®', 'IFRS®', the IFRS® logo, 'IFRS for SMEs®', IFRS for SMEs® logo, the 'Hexagon Device', 'International Financial Reporting Standards®', NIIF® and 'SIC®'.

Further details of the Foundation's Trade Marks are available from the Licensor on request.

Contents

Question and Answer index	iv
Using your BPP Exam Practice Kit	v
Examination structure	viii
How to pass	xi

Questions and answers

Questions	3
Answers	135

Practice mock

Questions	242
Answers	264

Mathematical tables and exam formulae 286

Question and Answer index

Objective test questions	Question (Page)	Answer (Page)
1 Types and sources of long-term funds	3	135
2 Cost of long-term funds	8	139
3 Revenue	14	145
4 Leases: Lessor accounting	21	153
5 Provisions, contingent liabilities and contingent assets	28	159
6 Financial instruments	34	163
7 Intangible assets	41	169
8 Income taxes	47	174
9 Consolidated statement of financial position I	53	180
10 Consolidated statement of financial position II	61	185
11 Consolidated statement of profit or loss and other comprehensive income	68	190
12 Associates and joint arrangements	76	196
13 Foreign transactions and foreign subsidiaries	82	201
14 Consolidated statement of changes in equity	92	208
15 Consolidated statement of cash flows	99	213
16 Disclosure standards	108	219
17 Integrated reporting and Sustainability Reporting	113	226
18 Working with financial statements I	118	229
19 Working with financial statements II	125	234
Practice mock	242	264

Using your BPP Exam Practice Kit

One of the key criteria for achieving exam success is question practice. There is generally a direct correlation between candidates who study all topics and practise exam questions and those who are successful in their real exams. This Kit gives you ample opportunity for such practice throughout your preparations for your Objective Test exam.

All questions in your exam are compulsory and all the component learning outcomes will be examined so you must **study the whole syllabus**. Selective studying will limit the number of questions you can answer and hence reduce your chances of passing. It is better to go into the exam knowing a reasonable amount about most of the syllabus rather than concentrating on a few topics to the exclusion of the rest.

Practising as many exam-style questions as possible will be the key to passing this exam. You must do questions under **timed conditions**.

Breadth of question coverage

Questions will cover the whole of the syllabus so you must study all the topics in the syllabus.

The weightings in the table below indicate the approximate proportion of study time you should spend on each topic, and is related to the number of questions per syllabus area in the exam.

F2 Advanced Financial Reporting Syllabus topics	Weighting
A Financing Capital Projects	15%
B Financial Reporting Standards	25%
C Group Accounts	25%
D Integrated Reporting and Sustainability Reporting	10%
E Working with Financial Statements	25%

www.aicpa-cima.com/resources/landing/exam-blueprints

Blueprint index

Listed below are the lead syllabus outcomes and component outcomes from the CIMA CGMA® Official Blueprint along with the numbers of the questions (excluding the mock exams) covering those topics. If you need to concentrate your practice and revision on certain topics, or if you want to attempt all available questions that refer to a particular component outcome, you will find this index useful.

Lead outcome		Component outcome		Questions	Completed
A1	Types and sources of long-term funds	a–b.	Long-term debt and equity finance	1.2, 1.3, 1.5, 1.6, 1.7, 1.8, 1.9, 1.10, 1.12, 1.14, 1.15, 1.16	
		c.	Markets for long-term funds	1.1, 1.4, 1.11, 1.13, 1.17, 1.18, 1.19, 1.20	
A2	Cost of long-term funds	a.	Cost of equity	2.2, 2.7, 2.8, 2.16, 2.17, 2.18, 2.19	

Lead outcome		Component outcome		Questions	Completed
		b.	Cost of debt	2.1, 2.4, 2.5, 2.6, 2.9, 2.12, 2.13, 2.14, 2.15, 2.20, 2.21	
		c.	Weighted average cost of capital	2.3, 2.10, 2.11, 2.22	
B1	Relevant financial reporting standards for revenue, leases, financial instruments, intangible assets and provisions	a.	Revenue	3.1–3.20	
		b.	Leases	4.1–4.20	
		c.	Provisions	5.1–5.20	
		d.	Financial instruments	6.1–6.20	
		e.	Intangible assets	7.1–7.20	
		f.	Income taxes	8.1–8.20	
		g.	Changes in foreign currency rates	13.1–13.20	
B2	Relevant financial reporting standards for group accounts	a.	Relevant IFRS's for group accounts	9.1–9.20	
C1	Group accounts based on IFRS	a–d.	Statement of financial position, statement of profit or loss and other comprehensive income, statement of changes in equity and statement of cash flows	10.1–10.20 11.1–11.20 12.1–12.20 14.1–14.20 15.1–15.20	
C2	Additional disclosure issues related to the group accounts	a.	Transaction between related parties	16.1–16.10	
		b.	Earnings per share	16.11–16.20	
D1	The integrated reporting framework	a.	Understand the purpose and benefits of integrated reporting and of accounting for sustainability	17.1	
		b.	Integrated thinking	17.3, 17.4, 17.9	
		c.	The Integrated Reporting Framework	17.5, 17.6, 17.7, 17.8, 17.10, 17.13, 17.14, 17.16, 17.18, 17.19, 17.20	
D2	The six capitals of integrated reporting	a.	The measurement and disclosure issues of financial capital, manufactured capital, intellectual capital, human capital, social and relational capital and natural capital	17.8, 17.11, 17.12	
D3 Sustainability		a.	IFRS Sustainability Disclosure	17.2, 17.15,	

Lead outcome		Component outcome		Questions	Completed
	reporting		Standards	17.17	
E1	Financial statements	a.	Performance, position, adaptability and prospects	18.1–18.20 19.15–19.19	
E2	Actions based on insights from the interpretation of financial statements	a.	Recommended actions	19.1, 19.2, 19.3, 19.4, 19.6, 19.7, 19.8, 19.9, 19.10, 19.11, 19.12	
E3	The limitations of the tools used for interpreting financial statements	a–b.	Data limitations and limitations of ratio analysis	19.5, 19.13, 19.14, 19.20	

Examination structure

The Objective Test exam

Pass mark	70%
Format	Computer-based assessment
Duration	90 minutes
Number of questions	60
Marking	No partial marking – each question marked correct or incorrect All questions carry the same weighting (ie same marks)
Weighting	As per syllabus areas All representative task statements from the examination blueprint will be covered
Question Types	Multiple choice Multiple response Drag and drop Gap fill Hot spot
Booking availability	On demand
Results	Immediate

What the examiner means

The table below has been prepared by CIMA to further help you interpret the syllabus and learning outcomes and the meaning of questions.

You will see that there are five skills levels you may be expected to demonstrate, ranging from Remembering and Understanding to Evaluation. CIMA Certificate subjects only use levels 1 to 3, but in CIMA's CGMA® Professional Qualification the entire hierarchy will be used.

	Skills level	Verbs used	Definition
Level 5	Evaluation *The examination or assessment of problems, and use of judgment to draw conclusions*	Advise	Counsel, inform or notify
		Assess	Evaluate or estimate the nature, ability or quality of
		Evaluate	Appraise or assess the value of
		Recommend	Propose a course of action
		Review	Assess and evaluate in order, to change if necessary
		Select	Choose an option or course of action after consideration of the alternatives

	Skills level	Verbs used	Definition
Level 4	**Analysis** *The examination and study of the interrelationships of separate areas in order to identify causes and find evidence to support inferences*	Align	Arrange in an orderly way
		Analyse	Examine in detail the structure of
		Communicate	Share or exchange information
		Compare and contrast	Show the similarities and/or differences between
		Develop	Grow and expand a concept
		Discuss	Examine in detail by argument
		Examine	Inspect thoroughly
		Monitor	Observe and check the progress of
		Prioritise	Place in order of priority or sequence for action
		Produce	Create or bring into existence
Level 3	**Application** *The use or demonstration of knowledge, concepts or techniques*	Apply	Put to practical use
		Calculate	Ascertain or reckon mathematically
		Conduct	Organise and carry out
		Demonstrate	Prove with certainty or exhibit by practical means
		Determine	Ascertain or establish exactly by research or calculation
		Perform	Carry out, accomplish, or fulfil
		Prepare	Make or get ready for use
		Reconcile	Make or prove consistent/compatible
		Record	Keep a permanent account of facts, events or transactions
		Use	Apply a technique or concept

Skills level		Verbs used	Definition
Level 1/2	**Remembering and understanding** *The perception and comprehension of the significance of an area utilising knowledge gained*	Define	Give the exact meaning of
		Describe	Communicate the key features of
		Distinguish	Highlight the differences between
		Explain	Make clear or intelligible/state the meaning or purpose of
		Identify	Recognise, establish or select after consideration
		Illustrate	Use an example to describe or explain something
		List	Make a list of
		Recognise	Identify/recall
		State	Express, fully or clearly, the details/facts of
		Outline	Give a summary of
		Understand	Comprehend ideas, concepts and techniques

CIMA's CGMA® Exam Blueprint 2024/25

How to pass

Good exam technique

The best approach to the computer-based assessment (CBA)

You're not likely to have a great deal of spare time during the CBA itself, so you must make sure you don't waste a single minute.

You should:

1. Click 'Next' for any that have long scenarios or are very complex and return to these later.
2. When you reach the 60th question, use the Review Screen to return to any questions you skipped past or any you flagged for review.

Here's how the tools in the exam will help you to do this in a controlled and efficient way.

The 'Next' button

What does it do? This will move you on to the next question whether or not you have completed the one you are on.

When should I use it? Use this to move through the exam on your first pass through if you encounter a question that you suspect is going to take you a long time to answer. The Review Screen (see below) will help you to return to these questions later in the exam.

The 'Flag for Review' button

What does it do? This button will turn the icon yellow and when you reach the end of the exam questions you will be told that you have flagged specific questions for review. If the exam time runs out before you have reviewed any flagged questions, they will be submitted as they are.

When should I use it? Use this when you've answered a question but you're not completely comfortable with your answer. If there is time left at the end, you can quickly come back via the Review Screen (see below), but if time runs out at least it will submit your current answer. Do not use the Flag for Review button too often or you will end up with too long a list to review at the end. Important note –studies have shown that you are usually best to stick with your first instincts!

The Review Screen

What does it do? This screen appears after you click 'Next' on the 60th question. It shows you any incomplete questions and any you have flagged for review. It allows you to jump back to specific questions or work through all your incomplete questions or work through all your flagged for review questions.

When should I use it? As soon as you've completed your first run through the exam and reached the 60th question. The very first thing to do is to work through all your incomplete questions as they will all be marked as incorrect if you don't submit an answer for these in the remaining time. Importantly, this will also help to pick up any questions you thought you'd completed but didn't answer properly (eg you only picked two answer options in a multi-response question that required three answers to be selected). After you've submitted answers for all your incomplete questions you should use the Review Screen to work through all the questions you flagged for review.

The different Objective Test question types

Passing your CBA is all about demonstrating your understanding of the technical syllabus content. You will find this easier to do if you are comfortable with the different types of Objective Test questions that you will encounter in the CBA, especially if you have a practised approach to each one.

You will find yourself continuously practising these styles of questions throughout your Objective Test programme. This way you will check and reinforce your technical knowledge at the same time as becoming more and more comfortable with your approach to each style of question.

Multiple choice

Standard multiple choice items provide four options. One option is correct and the other three are incorrect. Incorrect options will be plausible, so you should expect to have to use detailed, syllabus-specific knowledge to identify the correct answer rather than relying on common sense.

Multiple response

A multiple response item is the same as a multiple choice question, except more than one response is required. You will normally (but not always) be told how many options you need to select.

Drag and drop

Drag and drop questions require you to drag a 'token' onto a pre-defined area. These tokens can be images or text. This type of question is effective at testing the order of events, labelling a diagram or linking events to outcomes.

Gap fill

Gap fill (or 'fill in the blank') questions require you to type a short numerical response. You should carefully follow the instructions in the question in terms of how to type your answer – eg the correct number of decimal places.

Hot spot

These questions require you to identify an area or location on an image by clicking on it. This is commonly used to identify a specific point on a graph or diagram.

A final word on time management

Time does funny things in an exam!

Scientific studies have shown that humans have great difficulty in judging how much time has passed if they are concentrating fully on a challenging task (which your CBA should be!).

You can try this for yourself. Have a go at, say, five questions for your paper, and notice what time you start at. As soon as you finish the last question try to estimate how long it took you and then compare to your watch. The majority of us tend to underestimate how quickly time passes and this can cost you dearly in a full exam if you don't take steps to keep track of time.

So, the key thing here is to set yourself sensible milestones, and then get into the habit of regularly checking how you are doing against them:

- You need to develop an internal warning system – 'I've now spent more than three minutes on this one calculation – this is too long and I need to move on!' (less for a narrative question!)

- Keep your milestones in mind (eg approximately 30 questions done after 45 mins). If you are a distance from where you should be then adjust your pace accordingly. This usually means speeding up but can mean slowing down a bit if needs be, as you may be rushing when you don't need to and increasing the risk of making silly mistakes.

A full exam will be a mix of questions you find harder and those you find easier, and in the real CBA the order is randomised, so you could get a string of difficult questions right at the beginning of your exam. Do not be put off by this – they should be balanced later by a series of questions you find easier.

Errata

BPP Learning Media do everything possible to ensure the material is accurate and up to date when sending to print. In the event that any errors are found after the print date, they are uploaded to the following website: www.bpp.com/learningmedia/Errata

Objective test questions

1 Types and sources of long-term funds

1.1 Which THREE of the following statements are true?

☐ Bonds and shares are both securities which can be traded in the capital markets.

☐ Holders of both bonds and shares will have a right to a cash payment from the issuing entity.

☐ Both bonds and shares will normally be redeemable at any point in time.

☐ The ability to sell bonds on the capital markets enhances their attractiveness to bondholders.

☐ Bondholders will normally be paid a fixed return known as the coupon rate.

1.2 Complete the following sentences by selecting the correct options from the pull down list.

Ordinary shares carry voting rights and [ ] to any declared dividend.

They are a [ ] form of finance from the company's perspective.

Pull down list:

entitlement
no entitlement
flexible
risky

1.3 A bank loan that restricts the recipient of the loan by placing limits on its ability to borrow in future is said to contain which of the following?

○ A positive loan covenant

○ A fixed charge

○ A floating charge

○ A negative loan covenant

1.4 Which THREE of the following are most likely to be associated with a bond issue?

☐ Underwriters are paid a fee for guaranteeing that the bonds will be purchased.

☐ The company issuing the bonds reduces its reliance on bank lending.

☐ Interest costs are often lower than an equivalent bank loan because the bonds can be sold by investors.

☐ Finance can be raised more quickly than an equivalent bank loan.

☐ Underwriters will guarantee to the investors that the company can pay the interest on the bond.

1.5 Which THREE of the following are characteristics of non-cumulative preference shares?

☐ They rank before ordinary shares in the event of liquidation.
☐ They carry limited voting rights when dividends are in arrears.
☐ If the issuing entity makes higher profits than expected, the dividend will not rise.
☐ Arrears have to be paid before ordinary dividends can be paid.
☐ The issuing entity cannot claim tax relief on the dividends paid.

1.6 Which TWO of the following are most likely to be associated with a share issue that is required in order to finance an investment in a long-term construction project?

☐ Underwriters are paid a fee for guaranteeing that the shares will be purchased.
☐ There will be lower gearing.
☐ Finance can be raised more quickly than an equivalent bank loan.
☐ There will be higher interest cover.
☐ The providers of finance will not be owners of the business.

1.7 Complete the following sentence selecting the correct options from the pull down list.

Investors in preference shares require a [   ] level of return than ordinary shareholders because they face less [   ] over the level of their return, and therefore face [   ] risk.

Pull down list:

less
more
higher
lower
certainty
uncertainty

1.8 Which of the following is true in respect of raising equity finance using a rights issue?

○ If an entity is not listed on a stock market it cannot initiate a rights issue.
○ A rights issue will be at the existing market price of an entity to avoid a dilution in its share price.
○ A rights issue occurs when equity shares are available to be purchased by institutional shareholders only.
○ A rights issue allows shareholders the right to ensure that their existing shareholding is not diluted.

1.9 Which of the following is correct in relation to convertible bonds?

○ They normally have a lower coupon rate than redeemable bonds.

○ The issuing company is entitled to choose between redemption and conversion.

○ Security is never offered by the issuing company.

○ They are always issued at a large discount to their nominal value.

1.10 According to the creditor hierarchy, rank the following from high risk to low risk (from the viewpoint of the investor):

1. Ordinary share capital
2. Preference share capital
3. Trade payables
4. Bank loan with fixed and floating charges

○ 1, 2, 3, 4

○ 1, 3, 2, 4

○ 4, 3, 2, 1

○ 4, 2, 3, 1

1.11 Which of the following is an advantage of an initial public offer compared to a placing?

○ Lower issue costs

○ Higher issue price

○ Speed

○ No dilution of control

1.12 Complete the following sentences by selecting the correct options from the pull down lists.

A rights issue is an offer to [⬅1] shareholders enabling them to buy shares, usually at a price [⬅2] the current market price, and in proportion to their existing shareholding.

Pull down list 1:

existing
preference
new

Pull down list 2:

equal to
higher than
lower than

1.13 Which of the following is the adviser who reviews a company's listing documents and reports on the company's readiness for listing?

- ○ Sponsor
- ○ Bookrunner
- ○ Reporting accountant
- ○ Lawyer

1.14 Which of the following is a characteristic of a conventional bond?

- ○ Bondholders will never require security in the form of a fixed or floating charge on the issuer's assets.
- ○ Bondholders are owners of the business.
- ○ Bondholders face higher risk than investors in ordinary shares and therefore will expect a higher return.
- ○ Bondholders have the ability to sell the debt on the secondary markets.

1.15 Which of the following is a characteristic of a bank loan?

- ○ Bank loans are typically irredeemable.
- ○ The interest rate charged by the bank may be fixed, variable or capped.
- ○ Banks face lower risk than investors in ordinary shares and therefore will expect a higher return.
- ○ Bank loans are fixed rate IOUs.

1.16 Which TWO of the following are characteristics of deep discount bonds?

- ☐ They do not have a par value.
- ☐ They carry a much lower coupon rate of interest than conventional, fixed rate redeemable bonds.
- ☐ They carry a much higher coupon rate of interest than conventional, fixed rate redeemable bonds.
- ☐ They are often referred to as convertible bonds.
- ☐ They are redeemable at a higher amount than the price at which they are issued.

1.17 Complete the following sentence by selecting the correct options from the pull down list.

The [_____] markets enable organisations to raise new finance by issuing new securities whereas [_____] markets enable existing investors to sell their investments.

Pull down list:

primary
secondary
capital
financial

1.18 Which TWO of the following are true of an introduction as a method of obtaining a listing?

☐ New shares are issued.
☐ The issuing house will underwrite the issue.
☐ It will improve the marketability of the shares.
☐ New cash is raised for the company.
☐ It is appropriate for a large private company whose shares are widely held.

1.19 Which of the following correctly describes the role of the sponsor when a company is raising finance on the capital markets?

○ Co-ordinates the overall initial public offer (IPO) process and advises the board of directors of the company
○ Underwrites the issue and raises finance from investors on behalf of the company
○ Performs financial due diligence and provides tax advice
○ Performs legal due diligence, drafts the prospectus and provides legal opinions

1.20 Which of the following is an advantage of an initial public offer (IPO) compared to a placing?

○ It is often quicker to arrange and implement.
○ It is likely to be cheaper because there will be no need for underwriting and advertising the issue.
○ It could lead to a higher issue price and therefore could raise more capital for the company.
○ It involves less disclosure of information to the public.

2 Cost of long-term funds

2.1 MR has 4% bonds in issue that are redeemable in three years' time. Interest is paid annually, and an interest payment has just been made. The current market price of the bonds is $92.40 per $100 nominal value and the rate of tax is 25%.

The net present value of the cash flows relating to the bonds has been assessed as follows:

NPV at 4% = +4.91

NPV at 7% = -2.54

What is the post-tax cost of MR's bonds? Give your answer as a percentage to one decimal place.

☐ %

2.2 TR has just paid an ordinary dividend of 20c per share; as a result the shares are trading at $5.30.

Dividend growth is expected to be 4% per annum.

What is TR's cost of equity?

○ 6%

○ 7%

○ 8%

○ 9%

2.3 TX has the following capital structure.

	$m
80 million ordinary shares of 50c	40
Reserves	240
11% bonds	30
	310

The bonds are irredeemable and are trading at their par value. The company's rate of tax is 40%.

TX's cost of equity has been estimated at 18% per annum. The current market price per share is $1.00 ex div.

What is TX's weighted average cost of capital?

○ 14.4%

○ 14.9%

○ 17.0%

○ 16.3%

2.4 Company B has a 2% convertible bond that is either redeemable in five years' time at a premium of 10% to its par value of $100 or convertible into 20 shares. B's share price is currently $4 and is expected to rise by 10% per year. The rate of corporate income tax is 25%.

Which TWO of the following are cash flows that will be used to calculate the cost of B's convertible bonds?

☐ 2 × (1 – 0.25)
☐ 100
☐ 128.8
☐ 110
☐ 80

2.5 AL has $250 million 4% irredeemable bonds in issue. This debt was originally issued at its par value of $100 and is now trading at 125% of this value. AL pays tax at 25%.

What is AL's post-tax cost of debt? Give your answer as a percentage to one decimal place.

[ ] %

2.6 XN has $300 million 6% irredeemable bonds in issue. This debt was originally issued at its par value of $100 and is now trading at 95% of this value. XN pays tax at 25%.

What is the yield to maturity on XN's bonds? Give your answer as a percentage to one decimal place.

[ ] %

2.7 KW has issued 6% irredeemable preference shares of $1 each. The current market value of the preference shares is $0.75 each. The rate of tax is 30%.

What is the cost of KW's irredeemable preference shares?

○ 6.0%
○ 4.2%
○ 8.0%
○ 5.6%

2.8 XC has a policy of increasing its dividend at a rate of 10% per year. XC's shares are currently trading at $4.20 cum div, and a dividend payment of $0.20 is due to be paid.

Using the dividend growth model, what is the cost of equity for XC? Give your answer as a percentage to one decimal place.

[ ] %

2.9 FX has 6% irredeemable debentures in issue which are currently quoted at 90% of their nominal value of $100. FX pays tax at a rate of 25%.

What is the post-tax cost of debt of FX's irredeemable debentures?

○ 4.1%

○ 4.5%

○ 6.7%

○ 5.0%

2.10 **Complete the following sentences by selecting the correct option from the relevant pull down list.**

The weighted average cost of capital (WACC) is the [____1] of the company's finance (equity, bonds, bank loans) weighted according to the proportion each element bears to the total pool of capital. The weighting is based on [____2] current yields and costs after [____3].

Pull down list 1:

actual cost
historic cost
standard cost
average cost

Pull down list 2:

book valuations
market valuations
dividend valuations
profit-based valuations

Pull down list 3:

ordinary dividends
interest
tax
preference dividends

2.11 LL is a listed company experienced in the provision of training courses. The directors of LL are looking to expand the business by building hotels which are located near its training centres. LL is planning to undertake a substantial share issue to raise enough capital to finance this new project. LL's gearing ratio (calculated as debt over debt + equity) is currently 40% and its weighted average cost of capital (WACC) is 9%.

Which TWO of the following statements are true?

☐ LL can use its current WACC to appraise the new project by discounting the project's cash flows at the current WACC to ascertain whether or not to proceed.

☐ LL cannot use its current WACC to appraise the new project because it carries a different business risk profile from the training industry it currently operates in.

☐ LL cannot use its current WACC to appraise the new project because the capital structure will change as a result of undertaking the new project, meaning the WACC will also change.

☐ LL cannot use its current WACC because the investment is marginal to them as only a small investment is required.

☐ LL can use the current WACC to appraise the new project because the business risk profile will remain constant and the change in capital structure is irrelevant to using WACC in project appraisal.

2.12 An 8% $100 bond is redeemable at par in five years' time, or convertible into ten shares at that time. The current share price is $8 and it is expected to increase at 6% per year. The current market value of the bond now is $90 and the tax rate is 30%.

What is the post tax cost of the convertible bond? (Give your answer to the nearest whole percentage.)

☐ %

2.13 AB has a 5% redeemable bond in issue with a par value of $100. The bond is redeemable in five years' time at a 10% premium. The bond is currently trading at 95% of its par value. AB pays tax at a rate of 30%.

Which THREE of the following are cash flows that will be used to calculate the cost of AB's redeemable bonds?

☐ $5
☐ $5(1 – 0.3)
☐ $95
☐ $100
☐ $100(1 – 0.3)
☐ $110

2.14 MJ has in issue 8% $100 par value bonds, redeemable in three years' time at premium of 15%. They have a current market value of $105 per bond. MJ pays tax at 25%.

The net present values of the relevant post-tax cash flows for one bond calculated at discount factors of 5% and 10% respectively are $10.70 (positive) and $3.71 (negative).

What is the post-tax cost of the redeemable bond to MJ?

○ 5.7%

○ 8.0%

○ 8.7%

○ 12.7%

2.15 SF has 7% bonds in issue with a nominal value of $100 each. The bonds are redeemable at a 10% premium in six years' time. The bonds are currently trading at a market value of $97.

SF pays tax at 30%. SF wishes to calculate the net present value of cash flows using 5% and 10% discount rates for use in the internal rate of return formula.

The net present value of the market value of the bond now, annual interest (post-tax) and the final redemption value is $9.94 at a discount rate of 5%.

What is the net present value of the bond's post-tax cash flows at a discount rate of 10%?

○ -$4.48

○ -$13.62

○ -$16.32

○ -$19.26

2.16 RH has just paid a dividend of 10 cents per share. This was 30% of earnings per share. RH's return on net assets is 20%. The current share price is $3.50.

What is RH's cost of equity? Give your answer to the nearest whole percentage.

[   ] %

2.17 XY has 1 million $1 ordinary shares and has just paid a dividend of $40,000. The current share price of XY is $2.80. XY's return on net assets is 25%.

An extract from XY's statement of changes in equity for the year is shown below:

	Retained earnings $
Balance b/d	340,000
Profit for the year	100,000
Dividend paid	(40,000)
Balance c/d	400,000

Using the current reinvestment levels method to calculate dividend growth, what is the cost of equity of XY?

- ○ 11.6%
- ○ 16.4%
- ○ 16.6%
- ○ 26.8%

2.18 FJ has just paid a dividend of 90c per share. Seven years ago the dividend was 50c per share. FJ wishes to calculate its cost of equity using the dividend valuation model.

When calculating the cost of equity using the dividend valuation model, what percentage would FJ use for dividend growth under the historic growth method? Give your answer as a percentage to one decimal place.

☐ %

2.19 HK is about to pay a dividend of 45c per share. Four years ago the dividend was 35c per share. HK's share price is 845c cum div.

Using the historic growth method to calculate 'g', what is HK's cost of equity?

- ○ 6.0%
- ○ 12.1%
- ○ 12.2%
- ○ 12.5%

2.20 SF has a bank loan of $500,000 on which it pays fixed interest at a rate of 8%. Corporate income tax is payable at 25%.

What is the post-tax cost of debt for SF's bank loan? Give your answer to the nearest whole percentage.

☐ %

2.21 When calculating the cost of debt for convertible bonds, what is the relevant cash flow at the end of the bond's term?

○ The cash payable on redemption

○ The estimated future value of the shares

○ The lower of the cash payable on redemption and the estimated future value of the shares

○ The higher of the cash payable on redemption and the estimated future value of the shares

2.22 RH has the following capital structure:

	Cost of capital %	Market value $m
Ordinary shares	14	100
Bank loan	7 (post-tax)	30
Bonds	5 (post-tax)	20

What is RH's weighted average cost of capital? Give your answer as a percentage to one decimal place.

[ ] %

3 Revenue

3.1 On 1 December 20X5, SF sold and delivered goods for $10,000 including servicing fees for four months from that date. The standalone price of the goods and four months' servicing would be $9,600 and $2,400 respectively.

How much should SF recognise as revenue for the month of December 20X5?

○ $8,500

○ $9,600

○ $10,000

○ $10,200

3.2 On 31 March 20X7, DT received an order from a new customer, XX, for products with a sales value of $900,000. XX paid a deposit of $90,000 at the date of ordering.

On 31 March 20X7, DT had not completed its credit check of XX and had not despatched any goods.

Which of the following would be the correct accounting entry to record the transaction with XX for the year ended 31 March 20X7?

○ Dr Cash $90,000, Dr Trade receivables $810,000; Cr Revenue $900,000

○ Dr Trade receivables $900,000; Cr Revenue $900,000

○ Dr Cash $90,000; Cr Revenue $90,000

○ Dr Cash $90,000; Cr Contract liability $90,000

3.3 On 1 July 20X5, AX, a construction company, entered into a two-year contract to build a property for a customer on the customer's land. The contract specifies that control of the property is transferred to the customer as it is constructed.

The position of the contract at 30 June 20X6 is as follows.

	$
Contract price	900,000
At 30 June 20X6	
Costs to date	600,000
Estimated costs to completion	200,000
Progress payments invoiced and received	500,000
Work certified	540,000

AX wishes to use an input method to assess progress towards complete satisfaction of its performance obligation.

How much revenue should AX recognise in relation to this contract for the year ended 30 June 20X6?

- ○ $540,000
- ○ $600,000
- ○ $675,000
- ○ $900,000

3.4 On 1 December 20X5, FC received a non-refundable upfront fee of $80,000 for services. The services will be provided from February to March 20X6.

What is the correct accounting treatment for this fee in the year ended 31 December 20X5?

- ○ Recognise revenue of $80,000
- ○ Recognise revenue of $20,000 and a contract liability of $60,000
- ○ Recognise a contract liability of $80,000
- ○ Recognise a contract asset of $80,000

3.5 On 31 December 20X2, SL sold goods to a customer for $100,000 on a sale or return basis. Historically, 40% of goods sold to this customer have been returned.

How much revenue should SL recognise in relation to this sale for the year ended 31 December 20X2?

- ○ $0
- ○ $40,000
- ○ $60,000
- ○ $100,000

3.6 On 1 November 20X8, AB, an online travel agent, received $4,000 from a customer for a holiday in C-land. It will pass 95% of this amount to the company providing the holiday, with payment due on 31 January 20X9. In the event of any problems, the customer will deal directly with the company providing the holiday.

How much revenue should AB recognise in relation to this transaction in its financial statements for the year ended 31 December 20X8?

○ $0
○ $200
○ $3,800
○ $4,000

3.7 LP sold goods to a customer and delivered the goods to the customer's premises on 31 December 20X5. The contract requires the customer to pay for the goods in three equal instalments of $10,000 on 1 January 20X6, 1 January 20X7 and 1 January 20X8.

The appropriate discount rate is 5%.

How should LP account for the contract in the year ended 31 December 20X5?

○ Dr Trade receivables $30,000; Cr Revenue $30,000
○ Dr Contract asset $27,230; Cr Revenue $27,230
○ Dr Trade receivables $28,590; Cr Revenue $28,590
○ Dr Trade receivables $30,000; Cr Contract liability $30,000

3.8 KL enters into a contract with a customer to build a customised asset. The promised consideration is $5 million but this amount will be increased by $20,000 for each day before 30 June 20X7 that the asset is complete. At the year end of 31 March 20X7, KL expects that there is a 5% chance of the construction being completed on time, a 15% chance of it being completed one day early, a 20% chance of it being completed two days early and a 60% chance of it being completed three days early.

What is the estimated transaction price at the year end of 31 March 20X7?

○ $4,953,000
○ $5,000,000
○ $5,047,000
○ $5,060,000

3.9 On 1 November 20X5, MN entered into a contract with a customer to bore a river tunnel at a fixed price of $100 million. MN commenced construction on that date. Control is transferred to the customer over the period of the contract as the tunnel is built. However, as this is the first river tunnel that MN has built, it is not possible to reliably estimate future costs or a completion date. The costs to date are $5 million. MN has invoiced the customer for $7 million, all of which had been received by 31 December 20X5.

How much revenue should MN recognise in respect of this contract for the year ended 31 December 20X5?

○ $0
○ $5 million
○ $7 million
○ $100 million

3.10 Where a performance obligation is satisfied over time, IFRS 15 *Revenue from Contracts with Customers* requires revenue to be recognised over time by measuring progress towards complete satisfaction. Appropriate methods of measuring progress include output and input methods.

Which TWO of the following would qualify as output methods?

☐ A survey of performance completed to date
☐ Costs incurred to date as a proportion of total expected costs
☐ Units delivered to the customer
☐ Labour hours expended as a proportion of total expected labour hours
☐ Machine hours used as a proportion of total expected machine hours

3.11 In March 20X6, PL enters into a contract to extend a retail unit for an agreed fee of $30 million. The contract terms state that if the extension is completed by 30 November 20X6, an additional bonus equivalent to 10% of the agreed fee becomes payable. PL expects that there is a 70% chance of the project being completed by 30 November 20X6 and a 30% chance of the project being completed after that date.

PL decides that the expected value method is not appropriate in determining the transaction price.

What is the transaction price of this contract?

○ $27,000,000
○ $30,000,000
○ $32,100,000
○ $33,000,000

3.12 CD is a plumbing company. It sells boilers to customers with a free one-year standard warranty, which provides assurance that the boiler will function as intended for 12 months from the date of purchase. It also offers customers the option to purchase an additional warranty to cover repair costs from the end of the first year when the standard warranty expires until five years after the date of the boiler purchase.

What is the correct accounting treatment for the standard warranty and additional warranty?

- ○ Account for the standard warranty and additional warranty as separate performance obligations under IFRS 15 *Revenue from Contracts with Customers*
- ○ Recognise a provision under IAS 37 *Provisions, Contingent Liabilities and Contingent Assets* for the standard warranty and treat the additional warranty as a separate performance obligation under IFRS 15
- ○ Recognise a provision under IAS 37 for both the standard warranty and additional warranty
- ○ Treat the delivery of the boiler, the standard warranty and the additional warranty as a single performance obligation under IFRS 15

3.13 HS, a contractor, signed a two-year fixed price contract on 31 March 20X8 for $300,000 to build a bridge. Control is transferred to the customer as the bridge is built. Total costs were originally estimated at $240,000.

At 31 March 20X9, HS extracted the following figures from its financial records:

	$'000
Contract value	300
Costs incurred to date	120
Estimated costs to complete	80
Progress payments received	130
Value of work completed	165

HS wishes to use an output method to calculate progress towards satisfaction of its performance obligation.

How much revenue should HS recognise in relation to this contract for the year ended 31 March 20X9?

- ○ $120,000
- ○ $130,000
- ○ $165,000
- ○ $180,000

3.14 On 30 September 20X8, NM enters into a contract to transfer Products A and B to a customer in exchange for $100,000. The contract requires Product A to be delivered first and states that the payment for Product A is conditional on the delivery of Product B. Therefore, the consideration of $100,000 is only due after NM has transferred both Products A and B to the customer.

NM identifies the promises to transfer Products A and B as separate performance obligations. On the basis of their relative standalone selling prices, NM allocates $40,000 to the performance obligation to transfer Product A and $60,000 to the performance obligation to transfer Product B.

On 31 December 20X8, NM transfers Product A to the customer. NM intends to transfer Product B to the customer on 31 March 20X9.

What accounting entry should NM make to record the transfer of Product A to its customer on 31 December 20X8?

- ○ Dr Contract asset $40,000; Cr Revenue $40,000
- ○ Dr Trade receivables $40,000; Cr Revenue $40,000
- ○ Dr Contract asset $100,000; Cr Revenue $100,000
- ○ Dr Trade receivables $100,000; Cr Revenue $40,000, Cr Contract liability $60,000

3.15 RL operates a number of fashion outlets. On 31 December 20X8, it sells 50 identical coats to different customers for $300 each. The coats cost $120 each. The customers have 28 days in which they can return purchases for a full refund. Based on past experience, RL expects returns level of 10%. RL's January sale starts on 1 January 20X9 and the selling price of the coats will be reduced to 50% of the original price from that date.

Which TWO of the following statements are correct in relation to RL's accounting entries for the year ended 31 December 20X8?

- ☐ Recognise an asset of $600 for the right to recover returned coats from customers on settling the refund
- ☐ Recognise $6,000 in cost of sales in relation to the 50 coats sold
- ☐ Recognise revenue of $13,500 and a refund liability of $1,500
- ☐ Recognise revenue of $15,000
- ☐ Recognise $750 as inventory in respect of coats expected to be returned

3.16 OM sells a machine to a customer for $390,000 cash on 31 December 20X5. The sales contract provides a standard warranty giving the customer assurance that the machine complies with agreed-upon specifications and will function for 12 months. The sales contract also provides access to four days of training services on the machine within the first six months of ownership at no additional cost to the customer. Such training is usually charged out to other customers at $2,500 day; however, in this case, access to the training services is not reflected in the $390,000 transaction price, which is the standalone selling price of the machine.

Which TWO of the following reflect the correct accounting treatment by OM for this sales contract in the year ended 31 December 20X5?

- ☐ Provide for expected costs to be incurred as a result of the warranty offered
- ☐ Recognise revenue of $400,000
- ☐ Recognise revenue of $380,250 and a contract liability of $9,750
- ☐ Recognise a contract asset of $10,000
- ☐ Recognise a trade receivable for $390,000

3.17 UJ provides a 'shopfront' website, linking customers to sellers of unusual gifts. The individual seller sets the price that is to be charged for an item on the website. Payment is made by the customer to UJ who forwards the receipt, net of 8% commission, to the seller. UJ does not usually hold goods in inventory. When an order is placed, UJ advises the seller of the order and delivery address. UJ retains control of the website and reserves the right to 'display' goods as it sees fit. In the year ended 31 December 20X8, UJ sells goods for a total of $2,000,000.

Which TWO of the following statements are correct?

- ☐ UJ is the agent.
- ☐ UJ is the principal.
- ☐ UJ should recognise revenue of $2,000,000 for the year ended 31 December 20X8.
- ☐ UJ should recognise revenue of $160,000 for the year ended 31 December 20X8.
- ☐ UJ bears the inventory risk.

3.18 On 31 December 20X8, GF received $100,000 from a customer in relation to some goods. The goods were delivered to the customer on 2 February 20X9.

How should GF account for the delivery of the goods to its customer on 2 February 20X9?

- ○ Dr Cash $100,000; Cr Contract liability $100,000
- ○ Dr Contract liability $100,000; Cr Revenue $100,000
- ○ Dr Revenue $100,000; Cr Contract asset $100,000
- ○ Dr Revenue $100,000; Cr Trade receivables $100,000

3.19 Under IFRS 15 *Revenue from Contracts with Customers*, which of the following is an indicator that a performance obligation has been satisfied at a point in time?

- ○ The entity's performance does not create an asset with an alternative use to the entity and the entity has an enforceable right to payment for performance completed to date.
- ○ The customer has the significant risks and rewards of ownership of the asset.
- ○ The entity's performance creates or enhances an asset that the customer controls as the asset is created or enhanced.
- ○ The customer simultaneously receives and consumes the benefits provided by the entity's performance as the entity performs.

3.20 On 31 December 20X4, ZY's year end, ZY received $50,000 from a customer for goods. However, ZY did not deliver the goods to the customer until 10 January 20X5.

What accounting entry is required by ZY on 10 January 20X5?

- ○ Dr Contract asset $50,000; Cr Revenue $50,000
- ○ Dr Contract liability $50,000; Cr Cash $50,000
- ○ Dr Cash $50,000; Cr Contract liability $50,000
- ○ Dr Contract liability $50,000; Cr Revenue $50,000

4 Leases: Lessor accounting

4.1 **Complete the following sentence by selecting the correct option to fill each space.**

IFRS 16 *Leases* defines a lease as 'a contract, or part of a contract, that conveys [____←1] to [____←2] for [____←3] in exchange for [____←4].'

Pull down list 1:

an obligation
the right

Pull down list 2:

transfer economic benefits
use an asset

Pull down list 3:

a period of time
the asset's useful life
the lease term

Pull down list 4:

cash
consideration
lease payments

4.2 RH enters into a contract with a freight carrier, LM. The contract specifies the following:

- LM provides RH with the use of 12 specific railcars of a particular type for four years.
- The railcars are owned by LM.
- When the railcars are not in use to transport goods as determined by RH, they are kept at RH's premises.
- RH can use the railcars for another purpose (eg storage) if it chooses to.
- If a particular railcar needs to be serviced or repaired, LM is required to substitute a railcar of the same type.
- Otherwise, LM cannot retrieve the railcars during the four-year period.

Which TWO following statements are true in relation to this contract?

☐ This is not a lease because LM can substitute the railcars with alternative railcars.

☐ RH has the right to control the use of the 12 railcars for the four-year period specified in the contract.

☐ The 12 railcars qualify as identified assets under IFRS 16 *Leases* for the four-year contract period.

☐ LM has the right to direct the use of the 12 railcars during the four-year contract period.

☐ LM is the lessee and RH is the lessor.

4.3 On 1 January 20X0, TY entered into a contract to lease an asset from UV for ten years. For the first seven years, neither TY nor UV has the right to terminate the lease. However, during the remaining three years, TY may terminate the lease at any point but it would incur a significant termination penalty. The asset is a bespoke asset manufactured specifically by UV for TY and is considered to be key to TY's operations.

What is the lease term for this contract?

☐ years

4.4 JK has leased an item of plant to GH. Under the terms of the lease GH will pay $280,000 a year for the next five years. The plant has a fair value of $1,000,000 at the inception of the lease and is expected to have an economic life of ten years from that date. The plant has been modified to suit the specific manufacturing needs of GH. At the inception of the lease GH had no intention of using the asset beyond the five-year term, although there is an option to purchase the asset at the end of the term at a value significantly less than fair value.

Which THREE of the following factors indicates that the lease could be a finance lease in the financial statements of JK, the lessor?

☐ The lease term is not for the majority of the plant's economic life.

☐ The present value of lease payments is likely to cover the fair value of the plant at the inception of the lease.

☐ GH has no intention of keeping the plant for its estimated economic life.

☐ The plant would need to be modified to be used by another entity.

☐ There is an option to purchase the plant at significantly less than fair value in five years' time.

4.5 BG has constructed a bespoke asset for its customer DF. BG leases the asset to DF under a six-year lease term. At the end of the lease term, legal title passes to DF. The present value of the lease payments is $87,000 and the fair value of the asset is $85,000.

Which TWO of the following statements are correct in relation to recording the above lease in the financial statements of BG?

☐ Derecognise the asset, record a lease receivable and then recognise finance income at a constant rate over the lease term.

☐ Continue to recognise the asset and record lease rental income on a straight-line basis over the lease term.

☐ Record a right-of-use asset and a lease liability, then recognise a finance cost at a constant rate over the lease term.

☐ This is a finance lease because the risks and rewards of ownership are transferred to the lessee.

☐ This is an operating lease because the lessor retains the risks and rewards of ownership.

4.6 On 1 January 20X1, JK enters into an arrangement to lease a building from LM for ten years. The expected economic life of the building is 50 years. Annual rental payments of $250,000 are to be paid on 31 December each year. However, as an incentive to JK, the first 12 months are rent free. The present value of lease payments is $1,536,350.

What is the correct accounting entry in relation to this lease in the financial statements of LM for the year ended 31 December 20X1?

○ Dr Accrued income $225,000; Cr Operating lease income $225,000

○ Dr Lease receivable $1,536,350; Cr Property, plant and equipment $1,536,250

○ No accounting entry is required as no cash is received

○ Dr Right-of-use asset $1,536,350; Cr Lease liability $1,536,350

4.7 **Complete the following sentence by selecting the correct options from the relevant pull down list.**

Under a finance lease, in the statement of financial position the lessor should [_____←1] and record a [_____←2]. In the statement of profit or loss, the lessor should record [_____←3] allocated to each period of the lease [_____←4].

Pull down list 1:

continue to recognise the asset
derecognise the underlying asset

Pull down list 2:

lease liability
lease receivable

Pull down list 3:

lease rental income
lease rental expense
finance costs
finance income

Pull down list 4:

on a straight-line basis
at a constant rate on the lease liability
at a constant rate on the lease receivable

4.8 UV leases an asset to XY under a five-year finance lease on 1 January 20X1. The annual instalments are $100,000 payable in arrears on 31 December. The residual value of the asset guaranteed by XY is $10,000 and the expected total residual value of the asset at the end of the lease is $15,000. The present values at the start of the lease discounted at the interest rate of 6% implicit in the lease are as follows:

- Present value of instalments = $421,200
- Present value of guaranteed residual value = $7,470
- Present value of unguaranteed residual value = $3,735

What is the amount of the lease receivable in UV's statement of financial position as at 31 December 20X1?

○ $432,405
○ $358,349
○ $354,390
○ $346,472

4.9 AB is a transatlantic airline with a 31 December year end. On 31 December 20X8, AB leased a surplus aircraft to a rival company under an operating lease with a non-refundable deposit of $15 million due on 31 December 20X8 followed by five annual lease rentals of $10 million commencing on 31 December 20X9.

The present value of the lease payments (including the $15 million deposit) of $56 million has been recognised as income in AB's statement of profit or loss for the year ended 31 December 20X8. The fair value of the aircraft is $80 million at 31 December 20X8. The $15 million deposit was received on its due date of 31 December 20X8.

Which TWO of the following statements are correct in relation to the above accounting treatment in AB's financial statements for the year ended 31 December 20X8?

☐ The above accounting treatment is correct – no adjustment is required.

☐ Lease rental income should have been spread on a straight-line basis over the lease term – only $13 million should have been recognised in profit or loss for the year ended 31 December 20X8.

☐ No lease rental income should have been recognised in profit or loss for the year ended 31 December 20X8 as the lease was entered into on the last day of the accounting period.

☐ A lease receivable of $56 million should have been recorded in AB's statement of financial position as at 31 December 20X8.

☐ The $15 million deposit should have been recognised as deferred income in the statement of financial position as at 31 December 20X8.

4.10 **Which TWO of the following statements regarding the calculation of finance income on the lessor's net investment in the lease are correct?**

☐ The interest rate implicit in the lease is not required.

☐ A greater proportion of finance income will be recognised in the later years of the lease.

☐ A greater proportion of finance income will be recognised in the earlier years of the lease.

☐ Finance income for the period is calculated at a constant periodic rate on the outstanding balance.

☐ The finance income will be spread evenly over the lease term.

4.11 **Which of the following statements is correct in relation to an operating lease?**

○ The lessee has substantially all the risks and rewards of ownership of the underlying asset.

○ The lessor has substantially all the risks and rewards of ownership of the underlying asset.

○ The risks and rewards of ownership of the underlying asset are shared equally between the lessee and the lessor.

○ Neither the lessor nor the lessee has any risks or rewards of ownership of the underlying asset.

4.12 **Which TWO of the following are indicators of a finance lease?**

☐ The underlying asset is of a generic nature such that any entity could use it.

☐ The lessee has the option to purchase the underlying asset at fair value.

☐ The lease term is for the major part of the underlying asset's economic life.

☐ The lease transfers ownership of the underlying asset to the lessee by the end of the lease term.

☐ The present value of lease payments at the inception of the lease is significantly less than the fair value of the underlying asset.

4.13 DE leases an asset to FG on 1 January 20X9 under a finance lease. At that date, the asset has a carrying amount of $450,000. On 1 January 20X9, the present value of lease payments not yet received and the present value of the unguaranteed residual value come to a combined total of $470,000.

What is the accounting entry that DE should make in relation to this lease on 1 January 20X9?

○ Dr Property, plant and equipment $450,000, Dr Profit or loss $20,000; Cr Net investment in the lease $470,000

○ Dr Net investment in the lease $470,000; Cr Property, plant and equipment $450,000, Cr Profit or loss $20,000

○ Dr Net investment in the lease $450,000; Cr Property, plant and equipment $450,000

○ Dr Property, plant and equipment $450,000; Cr Net investment in the lease $450,000

4.14 JK leases an asset to LM on 1 January 20X1 under a five-year finance lease. Lease instalments of $100,000 are payable annually in advance commencing on 1 January 20X1. The total expected residual value at the end of the lease term is $30,000, of which $25,000 is guaranteed by the lessee.

The interest rate implicit in the lease is 8%.

What is the amount of the initial net investment in the lease that the lessor should recognise at 1 January 20X1?

- ○ $348,225
- ○ $351,630
- ○ $419,730
- ○ $451,630

4.15 On 1 July 20X4, PQ leases an asset to TU under a four-year finance lease. PQ paid a lawyer $6,000 to draft the lease contract between PQ and TU.

At 1 July 20X4, the present value of lease payments not received (including the present value of the guaranteed residual value) is $150,000 and the present value of the unguaranteed residual value is $26,000.

What is the net investment in this lease at 1 July 20X4?

- ○ $150,000
- ○ $170,000
- ○ $176,000
- ○ $182,000

4.16 On 1 October 20X3, WX leases an asset to YZ under an eight-year finance lease. Under the terms of the lease, YZ pays WX an initial non-refundable deposit of $5,000 followed by annual instalments of $60,000 due annually in arrears. The asset is estimated to have nil residual value at the end of the lease term and there is no residual value guarantee under the lease contract.

There are no initial direct costs associated with this lease.

The interest rate implicit in the lease is 9%.

What is the amount of finance income that WX should recognise in relation to this lease for the year ended 30 September 20X4?

- ○ $24,489
- ○ $24,939
- ○ $29,889
- ○ $30,339

4.17   On 1 January 20X2, AG leases an asset to ES under a six-year finance lease. Annual instalments of $200,000 are payable in advance, commencing on 1 January 20X2. The total estimated residual value of the asset is $40,000, of which $30,000 is guaranteed by the lessee.

The interest rate implicit in the lease is 10%.

What is the amount of finance income that AG should recognise in relation to this lease for the year ended 31 December 20X2? Give your answer in $ to the nearest whole number.

$ 78,074

4.18   BG leases an item of equipment to LS under a finance lease. In the year ended 31 December 20X4, BG earns $85,000 of finance income on this lease.

What is the accounting entry required by BG to record the finance income on the lease in the year ended 31 December 20X4?

- ○ Dr Finance income $85,000; Cr Net investment in the lease $85,000
- ○ Dr Net investment in the lease $85,000; Cr Finance income $85,000
- ○ Dr Cash $85,000; Cr Finance income $85,000
- ○ Dr Finance income $85,000; Cr Cash $85,000

4.19   On 1 January 20X0, RB leases some equipment to KW under a two-year lease. The economic life of the equipment is ten years. On 1 January 20X0, the present value of lease payments is $86,800 and the fair value of the equipment is $600,000. Annual instalments of $50,000 are payable by KW in arrears. The interest rate implicit in the lease is 10%.

What is the correct accounting treatment for this lease in RB's financial statements for the year ended 31 December 20X0?

- ○ Recognise a lease receivable of $45,480 and finance income of $8,680
- ○ Recognise operating lease income of $50,000
- ○ Recognise operating lease income of $100,000
- ○ Recognise a lease receivable of $86,800

4.20   On 1 January 20X9, KH leases an asset to PT under a five-year operating lease. On 1 January 20X9, KH pays PT a lease incentive of $2,000. Under the terms of the contract, PT then has to pay annual rentals of $9,600 to KH, commencing on 31 December 20X9.

What is the amount of income that KH should recognise in relation to this lease for the year ended 31 December 20X9? Give your answer in $ to the nearest whole number.

$ 9,200

5 Provisions, contingent liabilities and contingent assets

5.1 Which of the following transactions results in the recognition of a provision in the financial statements for the year ended 31 December 20X1 under the terms of IAS 37 *Provisions, Contingent Liabilities and Contingent Assets*?

- ○ XY decided to reorganise a manufacturing facility during November 20X1 and commissioned a consulting engineer to undertake a feasibility study. A provision of $2 million for the reorganisation was created at 31 December 20X1.
- ○ In January 20X2, AB contracted with a training company to provide essential training for its workforce to be carried out in January and February 20X2. A provision for the necessary expenditure was created in its accounts at 31 December 20X1.
- ○ CD was notified in October 20X1 that it was required by environmental law to carry out an environmental cleanup in 20X2 following pollution from one of its factories.
- ○ FG acquired RS and provided for likely future operating losses at the date of acquisition amounting to $250,000.

5.2 ML, a publishing company, is being sued for $1 million in a libel action in respect of a book published in January 20X0.

On 31 October 20X0, the end of the reporting period, the directors believed that the claim had a 10% chance of success. On 30 November 20X0, the date the accounts were approved, the directors believed that the claim had a 30% chance of success.

What is the amount that ML should recognise as a provision in its statement of financial position as at 31 October 20X0?

- ○ $0
- ○ $100,000
- ○ $300,000
- ○ $1,000,000

5.3 FX sells mobile phones with a 12-month warranty. Any defects arising during that period are repaired free of charge. It has been estimated that in any given year 5% of phones sold will require minor repairs and 3% will require major repairs. If all the phones sold in 20X3 required minor repairs the total cost would be $3 million. If all the phones sold in 20X3 required major repairs the cost would be $7 million.

What amount of warranty provision should be included in the statement of financial position of FX as at the end of 20X3?

- ○ $360,000
- ○ $440,000
- ○ $800,000
- ○ $400,000

5.4 Which TWO of the following statements are correct per IAS 37 *Provisions, Contingent Liabilities and Contingent Assets*?

☐ An entity should not recognise a contingent liability in the statement of financial position.

☐ A provision must be recognised when an entity has a present obligation (which must be a legal obligation) as a result of a past event. It is probable that a transfer of economic benefits will be required to settle the obligation and a reliable estimate can be made of the amount of the obligation.

☐ An entity should only recognise a contingent asset if it is more likely than not that a present obligation exists at the balance sheet date.

☐ An entity may choose whether or not to discount a provision, but the decision must be applied consistently.

☐ If discounting is used, the unwinding of the liability over time should be recognised as an interest expense.

☐ IAS 37 allows entities to prudently 'build up' provisions to replace machinery in future over a number of years, where this is the management's intention.

5.5 DE prepares its accounts to 30 September each year. During the year to 30 September 20X2 DE's engineering division was being sued for damages relating to a faulty product it manufactured. Independent consultants have prepared a report that confirms that the product was faulty but this was partly due to the failure of a component that was manufactured by CL. The damages are estimated at $1 million and the level of contributory negligence of CL is considered to be 40%.

How should the above be shown in the financial statements of DE for the year ended 30 September 20X2?

○ Provision of $1 million liability and an asset of $400,000 (40%) shown separately on the statement of financial position

○ Disclosure of a contingent liability and no disclosure of the contingent asset as it is not virtually certain

○ Disclosure of a contingent liability and disclosure of the contingent asset as it is probable that they will have to pay out and reclaim 40%

○ A provision of $1 million and disclosure of the contingent asset

5.6 On 1 January 20X0, UV entered into a five-year lease for 100 telephones at $10 per telephone a month. UV elected to apply the IFRS 16 *Leases* recognition exemption for leases of low value assets.

On 31 December 20X1, UV introduced a new company policy to communicate via an internet-based communication system rather than telephone. Therefore, UV no longer has a use for the telephones. UV has identified another business which would be prepared to sublease the telephones from UV at $6 per telephone per month. Alternatively, UV could cancel the contract but would incur a penalty of $15,000.

What is the amount of the provision that UV should recognise in relation to this contract as at 31 December 20X1?

○ $0
○ $14,400
○ $21,600
○ $36,000

5.7 Which **THREE** of the following statements about IAS 37 *Provisions, Contingent Liabilities and Contingent Assets* are correct?

☐ Provisions should be made for constructive obligations (those arising from a company's pattern of past practice) as well as for obligations enforceable by law.

☐ Discounting must be used when estimating the amount of a provision if the effect is material.

☐ A restructuring provision must include the estimated costs of retraining or relocating continuing staff.

☐ A restructuring provision may only be made when a company has a detailed plan for the restructuring and a firm intention to carry it out.

☐ For onerous contracts, a provision should be made at the higher of the cost of fulfilling the contract and penalties from failure to fulfil the contract.

☐ Contingent assets should be recognised in the statement of financial position when an inflow of economic benefits is probable.

5.8 DH has the following two legal claims outstanding:

- A legal action against DH claiming compensation of $700,000, filed in February 20X7. DH has been advised that it is probable that the liability will materialise.

- A legal action taken by DH against another entity, claiming damages of $300,000, started in March 20X4. DH has been advised that it is probable that it will win the case.

How should DH report these legal actions in its financial statements for the year ended 30 April 20X7?

○ *Legal action against DH* *Legal action taken by DH*
  Disclose as a note No disclosure

○ *Legal action against DH* *Legal action taken by DH*
  Make a provision No disclosure

○ *Legal action against DH* *Legal action taken by DH*
  Make a provision Disclose as a note

○ *Legal action against DH* *Legal action taken by DH*
  Make a provision Accrue the income

5.9 **In which of the following circumstances would a provision be recognised under IAS 37 *Provisions, Contingent Liabilities and Contingent Assets* in the financial statements for the year ending 31 March 20X6?**

1 A board decision was made on 15 March to close down a division with potential costs of $100,000. At 31 March the decision had not been communicated to managers, employees or customers.

2 There are anticipated costs from returns of a defective product in the next few months of $60,000. In the past all returns of defective products have always been refunded to customers.

3 It is anticipated that a major refurbishment of the company head office will take place from June onwards costing $85,000.

○ 1 and 2 only

○ 2 and 3 only

○ 2 only

○ 3 only

5.10 **In accordance with IAS 37 *Provisions, Contingent Liabilities and Contingent Assets*, provisions for restructuring a business are to be recognised only when an entity has an obligation to carry out the restructuring.**

An obligation arises when an entity:

○ Makes the decision to restructure

○ Announces the main features of the restructuring plan to those who will be affected by it

○ Completes the restructuring

○ Is first invoiced for restructuring costs

5.11 **Which of the following would be valid grounds for recognising a provision?**

○ A company has decided to close down a division and has estimated the restructuring costs.

○ A law comes into force which means that by the end of the following year a company will have to install safety guards on its machinery. The cost involved has been reliably estimated.

○ A company enters into a contract to construct an asset on the customer's premises for a fixed price in the hope of winning further work. Total estimated costs of fulfilling the contract exceed the contract price.

○ An ex-employee is suing the company for wrongful dismissal. It is almost certain that damages will have to be paid but the amount cannot be estimated reliably.

5.12 CT is facing a legal claim from a customer regarding a faulty product. The total amount being claimed is $3.6 million and it is estimated by lawyers that the customer has a 75% chance of being successful.

What amount, if any, should CT provide in respect of this claim in accordance with IAS 37 Provisions, Contingent Liabilities and Contingent Assets?

○ $3.6 million

○ $2.7 million

○ $0.9 million

○ No amount should be provided

5.13 ER organises music festivals throughout Europe. In September 20X3 there was accident at a concert and one of the main performers was injured. This performer is pursuing a lawsuit, claiming that the safety equipment provided by ER was faulty and that ER was responsible for the accident. The lawsuit was filed in November 20X3 and at the year end ER's legal advisers advised that ER was likely to lose the case although at that time no reliable estimate of the likely payout could be made.

Which of the following statements is true in respect of this scenario?

☐ The lawsuit has not concluded at the reporting date and so no disclosures about the accident are required to be included in ER's financial statements at 31 December 20X3.

☐ A probable future outflow of economic benefit will result from this lawsuit and so a provision should be recorded in ER's statement of financial position at 31 December 20X3.

☐ There is a probable outflow of economic benefit but the timing and amount is uncertain and so a contingent liability should be included in ER's financial statements at 31 December 20X3.

☐ There is a probable outflow of economic benefit but the timing and amount is uncertain and so no disclosure is necessary as at 31 December 20X3.

5.14 GT incurs a present obligation on 31 December 20X5 in relation to the restoration of a piece of machinery which expects to settle in five years' time for $400,000. The appropriate discount rate is 8%.

The 8% five-year simple discount factor is 0.681.

What accounting entry should GT make to record this obligation on 31 December 20X5? Use the pull down lists to select the correct account references and amount.

	Account reference	Amount in $
Debit	←1	←2
Credit	←1	←2

Pull down list 1:

Cash
Expense
Machinery
Provision

Pull down list 2:

0
272,400
400,000

5.15 UH manufactures and supplies large printing presses. During 20X8 it supplied an item of equipment to TT which subsequently failed to function correctly and TT filed a claim for damages against UH. At the end of 20X8 the claim had not been resolved. However, UH's solicitors believe that there is a 40% chance of UH winning the case and a 60% chance of UH losing the case which would result in damages payable of approximately $1 million.

What is the amount of the provision that should be recognised in the statement of financial position as at the end of 20X8?

- ○ $1,000,000
- ○ $600,000
- ○ $400,000
- ○ $0

5.16 On 1 January 20X5, AB leased an asset from CD under a 12-month lease at a rental of $1,000 a month. Under the contract, if AB cancels the lease, it will have to pay CD compensation of $300 per month remaining on the lease. As this qualifies as a short-term lease, AB elected to account for the lease in accordance with the IFRS 16 *Leases* recognition exemption.

On 30 September 20X5, AB ceased the operations of the division which had been using the asset as they had become loss-making. This resulted in the leased asset becoming surplus to requirements. AB could sublease the asset to another company for the remaining three months of the lease at a monthly rental of $600.

What is the amount of the provision that should be recognised in AB's accounting records as at 30 September 20X5?

- ○ $0
- ○ $900
- ○ $1,200
- ○ $3,000

5.17 **Why is there a need for disclosure in relation to contingent liabilities?**

- ○ To maximise the amount of information available in the notes to the financial statements
- ○ To make the users of financial statements aware of the potential adverse impact on cash flows and profit
- ○ To prevent the auditors from asking too many questions
- ○ To alert the organisation's stakeholders to the probable future inflow on settlement of the liability

5.18 According to IAS 37 *Provisions, Contingent Liabilities and Contingent Assets*, which THREE of the following should be disclosed in relation to a contingent liability where practicable?

☐ A brief description of its nature and an estimate of its financial effect
☐ Comparative information for the previous year
☐ An indication of the uncertainties relating to the amount or timing of any outflow
☐ The possibility of any reimbursements
☐ The names of the parties involved in the transaction

5.19 CD is a publishing company. CD is suing a third party for copyright infringement. CD's lawyers believe that CD has a 90% chance of winning the case and, if successful, is likely to be awarded damages of $150,000.

Which TWO of the following should CD disclose in relation to this contingent asset if practicable?

☐ The contingent asset relates to a court case regarding copyright infringement
☐ If CD wins the court case, lawyers estimate that damages of $150,000 will be awarded
☐ There is a 90% chance of CD winning the court case
☐ An indicator of the uncertainties relating to the amount and timing of the inflow
☐ A detailed description of how the third party breached CD's copyright

5.20 At 31 December 20X4, EF had a provision of $100,000 in relation to a court case. On 10 February 20X5, EF settled this provision for $120,000.

What is the accounting entry required by EF on 10 February 20X5 in relation to this provision?

○ Dr Provision $100,000, Dr Profit or loss $20,000; Cr Cash $120,000
○ Dr Cash $120,000; Cr Provision $100,000, Cr Profit or loss $20,000
○ Dr Expense $120,000; Cr Provision $120,000
○ Dr Provision $120,000: Cr Expense $120,000

6 Financial instruments

6.1 Which of the following statements correctly describes the appropriate accounting treatment, as required by IFRS 9 *Financial Instruments*, for gains and losses on financial assets held both to collect contractual cash flows (of interest and principal only) and to sell.

○ These assets are held at cost and gains and losses will only be recognised on disposal of the assets.
○ These assets are held at amortised cost and the effective interest on the assets will be recognised in profit or loss over the term of the asset.
○ These assets are remeasured to fair value and gains and losses are recognised in other comprehensive income.
○ These assets are remeasured to fair value and gains and losses are recognised in profit or loss.

6.2 ZX issues 6% redeemable preference shares on 31 December 20X3.

Which of the following statements is true?

○ The issue is classified as equity because shares certificates are issued.

○ The dividend payable on these shares will be included in the statement of changes in equity.

○ The issue will be recorded by debiting investment and crediting bank.

○ The dividend payable will be included in ZX's finance cost as a period expense.

6.3 On 1 January 20X1 PP issued 290,000 $100 zero-coupon bonds for $66 each. Issue costs amount to $22,200 in total. The redemption value of the zero-coupon bonds is slightly higher than the net issue proceeds, which gives rise to an implicit annual rate of interest of 5%.

What will be the carrying amount of the bonds as at 31 December 20X1? Give your answer to the nearest $.

$ [   ]

6.4 W Co issued 1,500 convertible bonds on 1 January 20X7. The bonds have a two-year term and are issued at par with a face value of $500 per bond. Interest is payable annually in arrears at a nominal annual interest rate of 5%. Each bond is convertible at any time up to maturity into 200 ordinary shares.

When the bonds were issued the prevailing market interest rate for similar debt without conversion options was 7%.

The two-year 7% simple and cumulative discount factors are 0.873 and 1.808 respectively.

What is the value of the equity component of the bond on 1 January 20X7? Give your answer to the nearest $.

$ [   ]

6.5 UH issued a $4 million 6% convertible bond on 1 January 20X4 at its nominal value. In five years' time the bond is redeemable at par or can be converted into equity shares. The prevailing market rate at 1 January 20X4 for a similar bond without conversion rights is 9% per annum. It has been established that the present value of the principal and interest cash flows associated with the bond is $3,689,000 using 9% as a discount rate.

What is the value that will be credited to equity on the issue of this instrument? Give your answer to the nearest $.

$ [   ]

6.6 On 1 January 20X3, an entity issued a debt instrument with a coupon rate of 3.5% at a par value of $6,000,000. The directly attributable costs of issue were $120,000. The debt instrument is repayable on 31 December 20X9 at a premium of $1,100,000. The effective interest rate is 6%.

The entity accounted for the proceeds and issue costs correctly on 1 January 20X3 and recorded the interest paid in profit or loss on 31 December 20X3.

What is the accounting entry to correct the amount recognised as a finance cost in profit or loss in relation to this debt for the year ended 31 December 20X3?

○ Dr Finance costs $150,000; Cr Financial liability $150,000

○ Dr Finance costs $352,800; Cr Bank $352,800

○ Dr Bank $210,000; Cr Finance costs $210,000

○ Dr Finance costs $142,800; Cr Financial liability $142,800

6.7 PS issued 1,000,000 $1 cumulative, redeemable preference shares on 1 April 20X8. The shares were issued at a premium of 25% and pay a dividend of 4% per year.

The issue costs incurred were $60,000. The shares are redeemable for cash of $1.50 on 31 March 20Y8 (ten years after the issue date). The effective interest rate is 5.18%. Ignore all tax implications.

The management accountant of PS has extracted the following amounts from the preference shares ledger account for the year ended 31 March 20X9:

Account: Preference shares	$
Net amount received on issue	1,190,000
Finance cost @ 5.18%	61,642
Less dividend paid	(40,000)
Balance at 31 March 20X9	1,211,642

Complete the proforma below by selecting the correct amounts from Pull down list 1 and the correct headings from Pull down list 2 to be recorded in the financial statements of PS for the year ended 31 March 20X9 in relation to these preference shares.

	Statement of financial position	Statement of profit or loss and other comprehensive income	Statement of changes in equity
Heading	←1	←1	←1
Amount (in $)	←2	←2	←2

Pull down list 1:

Equity
Non-current liability
Current liability
Finance cost
Dividends paid
N/A

Pull down list 2:

1,250,000
1,211,642
1,190,000
61,642
60,000
40,000
N/A

6.8 AP acquired 10% of BQ by purchasing 40,000 ordinary shares on 1 January 20X2 for $2.12 per share. Transaction costs of 3% were paid to a broker on the acquisition date. On initial recognition, AP made the irrevocable election to measure the investment at fair value through other comprehensive income. At the year end 31 March 20X2 the shares were trading at $2.43.

What amounts should be included in AP's statement of profit or loss and other comprehensive income for the year ended 31 March 20X2?

○ Expense to profit or loss $2,544; Gain to OCI $9,856

○ Gain to OCI $9,856

○ Expense to profit or loss $2,544; Gain to OCI $12,400

○ Gain to profit or loss $9,856

6.9 PZ purchased a 2% holding in equity shares in a listed company, FJ. PZ's intention is to hold this investment for the long term. PZ's policy is to take gains and losses on investments to other comprehensive income wherever there is the option to do so under IFRS.

How should this financial asset be measured in accordance with IFRS 9 *Financial Instruments*?

	Initial measurement	Subsequent measurement
○	Fair value	Fair value through other comprehensive income
○	Fair value	Amortised cost
○	Fair value plus transaction costs	Fair value through profit or loss
○	Fair value plus transaction costs	Fair value through other comprehensive income

6.10 BX purchased a small holding in shares in a listed company, NM. BX's intention is to realise this investment within a few months when seasonal fluctuations in its business make a cash shortfall probable.

How should this financial asset be measured in accordance with IFRS 9 *Financial Instruments*?

	Initial measurement	Subsequent measurement
○	Fair value	Fair value through other comprehensive income
○	Fair value	Fair value through profit or loss
○	Fair value plus transaction costs	Fair value through profit or loss
○	Fair value less transaction costs	Amortised cost

6.11 LU issued a debt instrument on 1 January 20X4 at its nominal value of $4,000,000. The instrument carries a fixed coupon interest rate of 6%, which is payable annually in arrears. Transaction costs associated with the issue were $200,000. The effective interest rate applicable to this instrument has been calculated at approximately 8.4%.

Select the correct options from the pull down list for the opening balance and the finance cost in the calculation of LU's liability for this debt instrument at 31 December 20X4.

Liability	$
Opening balance	⬜
Plus: finance cost	⬜
Less: interest paid	(X)
Closing balance	X

Pull down list:

4,000,000
4,200,000
3,800,000
319,200
336,000
352,800

6.12 CS issued 3,000 6% convertible bonds on 1 April 20X4. The bonds have a three-year life and were issued at their face value of $100 per bond. Interest is paid annually in arrears and each bond is convertible any time up to maturity into 50 ordinary shares.

At 1 April 20X4 the market interest rate for similar debt without the conversion option was 9%. The 9% three-year simple and compound discount factors are 0.772 and 2.531 respectively.

What was the value of the equity component in the bond on issue? Give your answer to the nearest $.

- ○ $300,000
- ○ $231,600
- ○ $45,558
- ○ $22,842

6.13 EM acquired a debt instrument on 1 January 20X3 at its nominal value of $2,000,000. The instrument carries a fixed coupon interest rate of 7%, which is receivable annually in arrears. Transaction costs associated with the acquisition were $20,000. EM intends to hold the debt instrument until maturity to collect the associated contractual cash flows of principal and interest.

What accounting entry is required by EM to record the purchase of the debt instrument and the associated transaction costs on 1 January 20X3?

- ○ Dr Investment $1,980,000; Cr Bank $1,980,000
- ○ Dr Investment $2,000,000, Dr Profit or loss $20,000; Cr Bank $2,020,000
- ○ Dr Investment $2,020,000; Cr Bank $2,020,000
- ○ Dr Investment $1,980,000, Dr Profit or loss $20,000; Cr Bank $2,000,000

6.14 **Complete the sentence below by selecting the correct option from each of the pull down lists.**

A financial liability is any liability that is a contractual [____←1] to deliver [____←2], or a financial asset to another entity, or to exchange financial assets or liabilities under potentially [____←3] conditions.

Pull down list 1:

obligation
right
option

Pull down list 2:

cash
credit
non-cumulative redeemable preference shares

Pull down list 3:

favourable
unfavourable
contractual

6.15 On 30 September 20X6 MC entered into a speculative futures contract to buy 100 ounces of gold on 31 March 20X7 at a price of $1,300 per ounce. MC intends to settle the contract net and will not take delivery of gold. At 31 December 20X6, MC's year end, the price under a futures contract for purchasing gold with a settlement date of 31 March 20X7 was $1,370 per ounce.

How would the futures contract be recorded in MC's financial statements for the year ended 31 December 20X6?

○ Dr Other comprehensive income $137,000; Cr Financial liability $137,000

○ Dr Financial asset $7,000; Cr Profit or loss $7,000

○ Dr Profit or loss $137,000; Cr Financial liability $137,000

○ Dr Financial asset $7,000; Cr Other comprehensive income $7,000

6.16 On 1 November 20X3, GH entered into a speculative option contract to buy shares in another entity (JK) at a price of $2.50 a share on 28 February 20X4. At the 31 December 20X3 year end, the share price of JK has increased to $2.90.

As the contract is standing at a gain at the 31 December 20X3 year end, it should be recorded as a financial asset in GH's books.

How should the financial asset be measured at 31 December 20X3?

○ At amortised cost

○ At cost

○ At fair value through profit or loss

○ At fair value through other comprehensive income

6.17 QR, which has a functional currency A$, entered into a speculative forward contract on 30 June 20X1 to purchase B$900,000 on 31 December 20X1 at a contracted rate of A$/B$4. The contract cost was nil. QR prepares its financial statements to 30 September 20X1. At 30 September 20X1, an equivalent contract for the purchase of B$900,000 could be acquired at a rate of A$/B$4.50.

Complete the following sentence by selecting the correct option from the relevant pull down list.

In relation to this forward contract, QR should record ⬚ ←1 at 30 September 20X1 at the amount of ⬚ ←2.

Pull down list 1:

cash
a financial asset
a financial liability
a provision

Pull down list 2:

A$0
A$25,000
A$200,000
A$225,000

6.18 **Which THREE of the following are characteristics of a derivative in accordance with the definition of a derivative in IFRS 9 *Financial Instruments*?**

☐ It is settled at a future date.

☐ It only includes forwards, futures, options and swap contracts.

☐ Its value changes in response to an underlying variable.

☐ It is acquired or incurred principally for the purpose of selling or repurchasing it in the near term.

☐ It requires no or little initial net investment.

☐ It is a contractual obligation to deliver cash or another financial asset to another entity.

6.19 **According to IFRS 9 *Financial Instruments*, when should an entity recognise a financial asset in its statement of financial position?**

○ When the financial asset is purchased

○ When the entity becomes party to the contractual provisions of the financial asset

○ When the financial asset meets the *Conceptual Framework*'s definition of an asset

○ When cash is paid in relation to the financial asset

6.20 Which THREE of the following should be classified as financial assets?

- ☐ A trade receivable
- ☐ An issue of redeemable preference shares
- ☐ A purchase of bonds
- ☐ A loan from the bank
- ☐ An acquisition of ordinary shares in another entity
- ☐ An issue of ordinary shares

7 Intangible assets

7.1 Which of the following should be recognised as an expense rather than being capitalised as an intangible asset?

- ○ GK purchased another entity, BN. Goodwill arising on the acquisition was $15,000.
- ○ GK purchased a brand name from a competitor for $65,000.
- ○ GK spent $21,000 during the year on the development of a new product. The product is being launched on the market in four months' time and is expected to be profitable.
- ○ GK spent $12,000 researching a new type of product. The research is expected to lead to a new product line in three years' time.

7.2 Which of the following statements is correct?

- ○ Negative goodwill should be shown in the statement of financial position as a deduction from positive goodwill.
- ○ Purchased goodwill should be amortised on a systematic basis over its useful life.
- ○ As a business grows, internally generated goodwill may be revalued upwards to reflect that growth.
- ○ Internally developed brands must not be capitalised.

7.3 Which TWO of the following conditions would prevent any part of the development expenditure to which it relates from being capitalised?

- ☐ The development is incomplete.
- ☐ The costing system is not sufficiently detailed to reliably measure the expenditure.
- ☐ Funds are unlikely to be available to complete the development.
- ☐ The development is expected to give rise to more than one product.
- ☐ The intention is to use rather than sell the intangible asset on completion.

7.4 In its first year of trading to 31 July 20X6, CD incurred the following expenditure on research and development, none of which related to the cost of non-current assets: $12,000 on successfully devising processes for converting seaweed into chemicals X, Y and Z and $60,000 on developing a headache pill based on chemical Z. No commercial uses have yet been discovered for chemicals X and Y. Commercial production and sales of the headache pill commenced on 1 April 20X6 and are expected to produce steady profitable income during a five-year period before being replaced. Adequate resources exist to achieve this.

What is the carrying amount of the intangible asset relating to development costs that should be recognised in the statement of financial position of CD at 31 July 20X6?

○ $48,000
○ $56,000
○ $60,000
○ $72,000

7.5 A whisky distiller incurs the following costs in the year ended 31 December 20X0:

- $38,000 developing new distilling techniques that will be put in place shortly to cut the production cost of making malt whisky
- $27,000 researching a new process to improve the quality of standard whisky
- $8,000 on market research into the commercial viability of a new type of malt whisky

How much should be charged as research and development expenditure in profit or loss for the year ended 31 December 20X0 (ignore amortisation)?

○ $73,000
○ $35,000
○ $27,000
○ $38,000

7.6 EF has recently been developing a new product. Costs incurred to the year ended 31 December 20X1 have been $570,000, and it is anticipated that a further $80,000 will be required to bring the product to a position where it can be sold. Market research has indicated that the product will be popular, and that it will be five years before a rival product will significantly cut its profitability, and it should therefore be amortised over five years. Unfortunately EF is currently experiencing severe funding difficulties, and the future of the project is in serious doubt.

What is the carrying amount that should be recognised in EF's statement of financial position as at 31 December 20X1 in respect of this intangible asset?

○ $570,000
○ $650,000
○ $0
○ $456,000

7.7 Which of the following could be classified as an intangible asset in MN's statement of financial position as at 31 March 20X9 according to IAS 38 *Intangible Assets*?

- ○ $120,000 spent on developing a prototype and testing a new type of propulsion system for trains; the project needs further work as the propulsion system is currently not viable.

- ○ A payment of $50,000 to a local university's engineering faculty to research new environmentally friendly building techniques.

- ○ $35,000 spent on consumer testing a new type of electric bicycle; the project is near completion but initial results reveal customer dissatisfaction with performance levels of the bicycle.

- ○ $65,000 spent on developing a special type of new packaging for a new energy efficient light bulb; the packaging is expected to be used by MN for many years and is expected to reduce MN's distribution costs by $35,000 a year.

7.8 Which of the following events would result in an intangible asset being recognised in KJ's statement of financial position at 31 January 20X2?

- ○ KJ spent $50,000 on an advertising campaign in January 20X2. KJ expects the advertising to generate additional sales of $100,000 over the period February to April 20X2.

- ○ KJ is taking legal action against a contractor for faulty work. Advice from its legal team is that it is possible that KJ will receive $250,000 in settlement of its claim within the next 12 months.

- ○ KJ purchased the copyright and film rights to the next book to be written by a famous author for $75,000 on 1 March 20X1.

- ○ KJ has developed a new brand name internally. The directors value the brand name at $150,000.

7.9 CD is a manufacturing entity that runs a number of operations including a bottling plant that bottles carbonated soft drinks. CD has been developing a new bottling process that will allow the bottles to be filled and sealed more efficiently.

The new process took a year to develop. At the start of development, CD estimated that the new process would increase output by 15% with no additional cost (other than the extra bottles and their contents).

Development work commenced on 1 May 20X5 and was completed on 20 April 20X6. Testing at the end of the development confirmed CD's original estimates.

CD incurred expenditure of $180,000 on the above development in 20X5/X6.

CD plans to install the new process in its bottling plant and start operating the new process from 1 May 20X6.

CD's year end is 30 April.

Which of the following options describe the appropriate accounting treatment for the development costs?

- ○ Capitalise development costs of $180,000, start to amortise on 30 April 20X6
- ○ Capitalise development costs of $180,000, start to amortise on 1 May 20X6
- ○ Capitalise development costs of $27,000, start to amortise on 30 April 20X6
- ○ Capitalise development costs of $27,000, start to amortise on 1 May 20X6

7.10 Which THREE of the following, if purchased by an entity, are examples of intangible assets?

☐ Patents
☐ Bonds
☐ Properties
☐ Copyrights
☐ Licences
☐ Inventories

7.11 Which THREE of the following should be recognised as intangible assets?

☐ A franchise purchased by an entity
☐ A customer list compiled by an entity
☐ A publishing title acquired as part of a business combination
☐ Computer software bought by an entity
☐ Expenditure to gain new scientific knowledge
☐ The costs of training staff on a new process

7.12 JK purchases computer software for $100,000. The supplier offers JK a 10% prompt payment discount if it settles the amount owed within 30 days. JK settles the invoice within this 30-day period.

JK paid members of its IT department a total of $20,000 in overtime to adapt the computer software to the specific needs of JK. An external IT consultant was contracted at a fixed fee of $4,000 to assist the members of JK's IT department with this task.

$5,000 was then spent on testing the software to ensure that it was functioning properly.

Administration and general overhead costs incurred during the adaptation and testing period amounted to $7,000.

What is the amount that should be capitalised as an intangible asset in relation to this computer software? Give your answer to the nearest whole $.

$ ☐

7.13 On 31 December 20X0, AB acquired 100% of CD. At that date, CD had a customer list. This customer list had not been recognised as an intangible asset in CD's statement of financial position. However, the directors of CD estimate that a total of $500,000 had been spent building up this customer list.

At the acquisition date, as part of the due diligence exercise, external specialists valued CD's customer list at a fair value of $800,000 although the directors of AB believe that it was really worth closer to $1,000,000.

At what amount should AB include this customer list in its consolidated statement of financial position as at 31 December 20X0?

○ $0
○ $500,000
○ $800,000
○ $1,000,000

7.14 GF has been working on a project to design a new tool. On 30 June 20X8, the IAS 38 *Intangible Assets* capitalisation criteria for development costs were met. Prior to that date, GF incurred $490,000 of costs. Between 30 June 20X8 and the year end of 30 September 20X8, GF incurred the following additional costs in relation to this project:

	$
Materials used in developing the tool	80,000
Staff costs on developing the tool	65,000
Costs of training staff to operate the tool	30,000
	175,000

The intention is to start selling the new tool to customers on 1 November 20X8.

What is the amount of the intangible asset that GF should recognise in relation to the development of this new tool in its statement of financial position as at 30 September 20X8?

○ $80,000
○ $145,000
○ $175,000
○ $665,000

7.15 LM is a taxi company. On 1 July 20X4, LM acquired a five-year taxi licence for $200,000 to operate in a new city. There is an active market for taxi licences and the fair value of this taxi licence was $230,000 at 31 December 20X4.

LM wishes to hold intangible assets under the revaluation model where possible.

What is the carrying amount that LM should include in its statement of financial position in relation to this taxi licence as at 31 December 20X4?

○ $180,000
○ $200,000
○ $207,000
○ $230,000

7.16 MB has an intangible asset relating to a production quota. An active market exists for the production quota.

At 31 December 20X9, the carrying amount of the production quota is $75,000 and the balance on the revaluation surplus is $5,000. The fair value of the production quota is found to have fallen to $60,000.

MB elects to account for the production quota under the revaluation model.

Which of the following statements regarding the accounting treatment of the revaluation loss on the production quota at 31 December 20X9 is correct?

○ Recognise $15,000 in profit or loss
○ Recognise $15,000 in other comprehensive income
○ Recognise $5,000 in profit or loss and $10,000 in other comprehensive income
○ Recognise $5,000 in other comprehensive income and $10,000 in profit or loss

7.17 **Which THREE of the following types of intangible assets may NOT be revalued under IAS 38 *Intangible Assets*?**

☐ Licences

☐ Production quota

☐ Brands

☐ Franchises

☐ Patents

☐ Music publishing rights

7.18 On 1 January 20X0, DR acquired computer software. On 31 December 20X1, DR determined that the economic benefits generated by the software in 20X1 had decreased. By 30 June 20X2, DR estimated that the software would only continue to generate economic benefits for another three months. On 30 September 20X2, DR stopped using the software as no further future economic benefits were expected. DR did not sell the software as it believed it to be worthless.

At what date should DR derecognise the intangible asset relating to the computer software?

○ 1 January 20X0

○ 31 December 20X1

○ 30 June 20X2

○ 30 September 20X2

7.19 On 1 January 20X5, DR purchased a ten-year franchise for $800,000. On 31 December 20X6, DR sold this franchise for $975,000. It incurred selling costs of $15,000.

What is the amount of the gain on derecognition of this franchise that DR should recognise in its statement of profit or loss for the year ended 31 December 20X6?

○ $160,000

○ $175,000

○ $320,000

○ $335,000

7.20 NV has an intangible asset of $675,000 relating to development expenditure. On 31 December 20X9, this asset ceased to meet the IAS 38 capitalisation criteria.

What accounting entry is required by NV at 31 December 20X9 in relation to this intangible asset?

○ Dr Intangible asset $675,000; Cr Profit or loss $675,000

○ Dr Profit or loss $675,000; Cr Intangible asset $675,000

○ Dr Intangible asset $675,000; Cr Other comprehensive income $675,000

○ Dr Other comprehensive income $675,000; Cr Intangible asset $675,000

8 Income taxes

8.1 A company purchased some land on 1 January 20X1 for $300,000. On 31 December 20X8 the land was revalued to $500,000. The corporate income tax rate is 30%.

No tax allowances have been granted on this land.

Complete this statement of financial position extract as at 31 December 20X8. Give your answers to the nearest $.

	$
Property	500,000
Deferred tax liability	
Revaluation surplus	

8.2 TX bought a machine on 1 October 20X2 for $600,000. The machine attracted writing down tax allowances at 25% on a reducing balance basis. Depreciation was 10% on a straight-line basis.

Assuming a corporate income tax rate of 30%, calculate the deferred tax liability as at 30 September 20X4. Give your answer to the nearest $.

$ [   ]

8.3 In accounting for deferred tax, could the following items give rise to temporary differences? Select yes or no.

		Yes	No
(a)	Differences between accounting depreciation and tax allowances for capital expenditure	☐	☐
(b)	Expenses charged in the statement of profit or loss and other comprehensive income but disallowed for tax	☐	☐
(c)	Revaluation of a non-current asset	☐	☐
(d)	Unrelieved tax losses	☐	☐

8.4 Which THREE of the following are examples of assets or liabilities whose carrying amount is always equal to their tax base?

☐ Accrued expenses that will never be deductible for tax purposes

☐ Accrued income that will be taxed on a receipts basis

☐ Accrued expenses that have already been deducted in determining the current tax liability for current or earlier periods

☐ Accrued income that will never be taxable

☐ A property that is revalued but the revaluation has no effect on taxable profit

☐ Fixtures and fittings on which the accounting and tax depreciation rates differ

8.5 An item of equipment cost $60,000 on 1 April 20X6. The equipment is depreciated at 20% per annum on a reducing balance basis.

Tax allowances of 50% are awarded in the first year and 25% reducing balance thereafter.

The relevant corporate income tax rate is 30%.

Complete the journal entry below in relation to deferred tax for the year ended 31 March 20X8 by selecting the correct account references and amounts from the pull down lists.

	Account reference	Amount in $
Debit	Deferred tax liability	630
Credit	Deferred tax expense (P/L)	630

Pull down list for account reference:

Deferred tax expense (P/L)
Deferred tax expense (OCI)
Deferred tax asset
Deferred tax liability
Cash

Pull down list for amount:

630
1,350
2,100
4,770
5,400

8.6 The following information relates to ZY.

- At 1 January 20X8, ZY had taxable temporary differences of $850,000 relating to property, plant and equipment.

- For the year ended 31 December 20X8, ZY claimed depreciation for tax purposes of $500,000 and charged depreciation of $450,000 in the financial statements.

- During the year ended 31 December 20X8, ZY revalued a freehold property. The revaluation surplus was $250,000. ZY has no plans to sell the property and realise the gain in the foreseeable future.

Assume a corporate income tax rate of 25%.

What is the deferred tax liability in respect of property, plant and equipment required by IAS 12 Income Taxes as at 31 December 20X8? Give your answer to the nearest $.

$ 287,500

8.7 Current liabilities include accrued expenses with a carrying amount of $1,500. The related expense will be deducted for tax purposes on a cash basis.

Interest receivable has a carrying amount of $700. The interest revenue will be taxed on a cash basis.

What are the tax bases of these items?

- ○ Accrued expenses nil, interest receivable nil
- ○ Accrued expenses $1,500, interest receivable nil
- ○ Accrued expenses nil, interest receivable $700
- ○ Accrued expenses $1,500, interest receivable $700

8.8 QW prepares its financial statements to 31 December each year. On 31 December 20X6 QW had unused tax losses. At that time it was budgeted that QW would not generate sufficient taxable profits in the future against which all of these losses could be recovered.

At 31 December 20X7 the unused tax losses create a deferred tax:

- ○ Liability, which will be provided for in full to ensure that liabilities are complete in the statement of financial position
- ○ Asset, which as long as it can be measured reliably will be included in the financial statements at a value equal to the unused tax losses multiplied by the tax rate
- ○ Liability, which will be treated as a contingent liability because not all of the losses are recoverable
- ○ Asset, which will be included in the statement of financial position at the amount that is expected to be able to be recovered from future expected profits

---

8.9 A property was bought for $600,000 and was revalued to $800,000 in the current financial year. Accumulated depreciation on the property to date is $220,000. The appropriate rate of corporate income tax is 30%.

Which of the following options is correct if the company was not planning to sell the property in the future?

- ○ A deferred tax liability would still be necessary on the revaluation gain as the property will generate taxable income in excess of the depreciation allowed for tax purposes.
- ○ No deferred tax liability would be necessary in relation to the revaluation gain as there will be no future taxable gain; however, the amount would need to be disclosed as unprovided in the accounts.
- ○ No deferred tax liability would be necessary in respect of the revaluation gain as there will be no future taxable gain, nor would the amount need to be disclosed in a notes to the accounts.
- ○ Deferred tax would be recognised in respect of the difference between cumulative depreciation and cumulative tax allowances but not in respect of the revaluation gain.

8.10 HJ buys machinery costing $200,000 and depreciates it over its useful life of ten years on a straight-line basis. For tax purposes the machinery is depreciated at 25% per annum (straight line). The corporate income tax rate is 20%.

What will be the deferred tax expense or income in the fifth year of the life of the machinery? (Give your answer to the nearest whole $ and put a minus sign before any income, eg –1,000.)

$ [   ]

8.11 F has made losses of $5 million to the year ended 31 December 20X7. The tax regime allows F to carry forward losses for one accounting period before they expire. It is expected that F will make taxable profits of $4 million in the year ended 31 December 20X8. F pays tax at 28%.

Complete the following sentence by selecting the correct options from the relevant pull down list.

As F is expected to make [   ]⇐1 in the future, a deferred tax [   ]⇐2 of $ [   ]⇐3 can be recorded in the financial statements for the year ended 31 December 20X7.

Pull down list 1:

profits
losses

Pull down list 2:

asset
liability

Pull down list 3:

1.12 million
1.4 million

8.12 BC had a deferred tax liability of $450,000 in the statement of financial position as at 31 December 20X6. This deferred tax liability was solely due to accelerated tax depreciation on non-current assets. At 31 December 20X7, the carrying amount of these non-current assets was $1,900,000 and the tax base was $1,300,000. There were no other temporary differences at 31 December 20X7.

BC pays corporate income tax at 30%.

Complete the journal entry below in relation to BC's deferred tax for the year ended 31 December 20X7 by selecting the correct account references and amounts from the relevant pull down list.

	Account reference	Amount in $
Debit	[ ]	[ ]
Credit	[ ]	[ ]

Pull down list for account reference:

Deferred tax asset
Deferred tax liability
Deferred tax expense (P/L)
Deferred tax expense (OCI)

Pull down list for amount:

150,000
180,000
270,000
450,000

8.13 At the year end of 31 December 20X0, MJ has accrued expenses of $50,000. The tax authorities will not grant tax relief on these expenses until they are paid.

Assume a corporate income tax rate of 20%.

Which of the following is correct in relation to accounting for the tax on the accrued expenses in MJ's financial statements for the year ended 31 December 20X0?

○ Do not recognise any tax
○ Recognise current tax in profit or loss of $10,000
○ Recognise a deferred tax asset of $10,000
○ Recognise a deferred tax liability of $10,000

8.14 At the year end of 30 June 20X7, KW has accrued income of $95,000. This income will be taxed when it is received.

Assume a corporate income tax rate of 30%.

What is the accounting entry to record the deferred tax on this accrued income in KW's financial statements for the year ended 30 June 20X7?

○ Dr Deferred tax asset $28,500; Cr Deferred tax expense $28,500
○ Dr Deferred tax expense $28,500; Cr Deferred tax asset $28,500
○ Dr Deferred tax liability $28,500; Cr Deferred tax expense $28,500
○ Dr Deferred tax expense $28,500; Cr Deferred tax liability $28,500

8.15 BX is preparing its financial statements for the year ended 31 December 20X5. The tax computation shows tax due for the year ended 31 December 20X5 of $150,000. This is payable nine months and one day after the end of the reporting period.

In the year ended 31 December 20X4, BX reported a current tax expense and a current tax liability of $135,000. However, on 1 October 20X5, BX settled this liability in full for $130,000.

What is the amount that BX should report in relation to current tax in its statement of profit or loss for the year ended 31 December 20X5?

○ $145,000
○ $150,000
○ $155,000
○ $280,000

8.16   YX is based in A-land where corporate income tax is payable in advance based on estimated taxable profit for the year.

In 20X2, YX paid the tax authorities $460,000 in relation to estimated taxable profits for the year. However, at the year end of 31 December 20X2, the tax authorities confirmed that YX should only have paid $440,000.

What should YX recognise in its statement of financial position as at 31 December 20X2 in relation to current tax?

○   A current tax liability of $20,000

○   A current tax asset of $20,000

○   A current tax liability of $440,000

○   A current tax asset of $440,000

8.17   QP's tax computation shows tax due of $290,000 on taxable profits for the year ended 30 June 20X4. The tax due is payable in four equal instalments, two before the year end of 30 June 20X4 and two after the year end.

As at 30 June 20X4, QP has paid the first two instalments.

What should QP recognise in its statement of financial position as at 30 June 20X4 in relation to current tax?

○   A current tax asset of $145,000

○   A current tax liability of $145,000

○   A current tax asset of $290,000

○   A current tax liability of $290,000

8.18   At 31 December 20X0, FB recognised a current tax liability of $50,000. This was settled in full on 1 October 20X1 for $59,000.

What is the accounting entry required by FB on 1 October 20X1?

○   Dr Cash $59,000; Cr Current tax liability $50,000, Cr Profit or loss $9,000

○   Dr Current tax liability $50,000, Dr Profit or loss $9,000; Cr Cash $59,000

○   Dr Current tax expense $59,000; Cr Cash $59,000

○   Dr Cash $59,000; Cr Current tax expense $59,000

8.19 GL is preparing its financial statements for the year ended 31 December 20X3. The tax computation for the current year shows tax due of $750,000. This is payable nine months and one day after the end of the accounting period.

In the year ended 31 December 20X2, GL reported a current tax expense and a current tax liability of $640,000. However, on 1 October 20X3, GL settled this liability in full for $600,000.

What are the amounts that GL should report in relation to current tax in its financial statements for the year ended 31 December 20X3?

	Statement of profit or loss	Statement of financial position
○	Current tax expense of $710,000	Current tax liability of $750,000
○	Current tax expense of $790,000	Current tax liability of $750,000
○	Current tax expense of $710,000	Current tax asset of $750,000
○	Current tax expense of $790,000	Current tax asset of $750,000

8.20 The following figures related to EK's current tax for the year ended 30 September 20X1:

- Current tax expense of $380,000
- Over-provision of $20,000 in relation to the prior year

EK recognised a deferred tax liability of $37,000 at 30 September 20X0 and a deferred tax liability of $50,000 at 30 September 20X1. This deferred tax solely relates to tax depreciation in excess on accounting depreciation on non-current assets.

What is the total tax expense that EK should recognise in its statement of profit or loss for the year ended 30 September 20X1? Give your answer to the nearest whole $.

$ [   ]

9 Consolidated statement of financial position I

9.1 On 31 May 20X8, DN purchased 175,000 of BL's 250,000 $1 ordinary shares for $700,000. At 1 September 20X7, BL's retained earnings were $650,000 (there were no other reserves). During the year ended 31 August 20X8, BL made a profit for the year of $40,000. It can be assumed that BL's revenue and expenses accrue evenly throughout the year.

DN elected to measure non-controlling interests in BL at fair value at the date of acquisition. The fair value of the non-controlling interests in BL at 31 May 20X8 was $300,000.

What is the amount of non-controlling interests in BL that should be included in the consolidated statement of financial position of the DN group as at 31 August 20X8? Give your answer to the nearest $.

$ [   ]

9.2 On 31 May 20X8, DN purchased 175,000 of BL's 250,000 $1 ordinary shares for $700,000. At 1 September 20X7, BL's retained earnings were $650,000 (there were no other reserves). During the year ended 31 August 20X8, BL made a profit for the year of $40,000. It can be assumed that BL's revenue and expenses accrue evenly throughout the year.

DN elected to measure non-controlling interests in BL at fair value at the date of acquisition. The fair value of the non-controlling interests in BL at 31 May 20X8 was $300,000.

What is the goodwill that arose on the acquisition of BL? Give your answer to the nearest $.

$ [ ]

9.3 SD acquired 60% of the 1 million $1 ordinary shares of KL on 1 July 20X0 for $3,250,000 when KL's retained earnings were $2,760,000. SD elected to measure non-controlling interests in KL at fair value at acquisition. The fair value of non-controlling interests in KL on 1 July 20X0 was $1,960,000.

An impairment review was conducted at the year end of 30 June 20X1 and concluded that goodwill had suffered an impairment of $120,000.

What is the goodwill in KL for inclusion in the consolidated statement financial position of the SD group as at 30 June 20X1? Give your answer to the nearest $.

$ [ ]

9.4 AB acquired 4,000 of the 10,000 equity voting shares and 8,000 of the 10,000 non-voting preference shares in CD. AB has no other rights in respect of CD and another investor holds the remaining 6,000 equity voting shares and 2,000 non-voting preference shares.

AB acquired 4,000 of the 10,000 equity voting shares in EF and had a signed agreement giving it the power to appoint or remove all of the directors of EF.

Which investment(s) would be classified as a subsidiary (or subsidiaries) of AB?

○ Both CD and EF
○ CD only
○ EF only
○ Neither CD nor EF

9.5 VZ acquired 75% of KY on 1 July 20X2 when KY's retained earnings were $65,000.

Goodwill of $48,000 arose on acquisition. An impairment review was undertaken at 30 June 20X3 and the goodwill was found to be impaired by $10,000.

VZ elected to measure non-controlling interests in KY at fair value at acquisition. This amounted to $14,800.

KY's retained earnings on 30 June 20X3 had risen to $115,000.

What is the amount of the non-controlling interests in KY that should be included in the consolidated statement of financial position of the VZ group as at 30 June 20X3? Give your answer to the nearest $.

$ [ ]

9.6 QZ acquired 75% of PL on 1 July 20X2 when PL's share capital and retained earnings were $310,000 and $165,000 respectively.

Goodwill of $148,000 arose on acquisition. An impairment review was undertaken at 30 June 20X3 and the goodwill was found to be impaired by $100,000.

QZ elected to measure non-controlling interests in PL at the proportionate share of net assets at acquisition.

PL's retained earnings on 30 June 20X3 had risen to $215,000.

What is the amount of the non-controlling interests in PL that should be included in the consolidated statement of financial position of the QZ group as at 30 June 20X3?

- ○ $131,250
- ○ $106,250
- ○ $172,500
- ○ $156,250

9.7 PA acquired 75% of the equity shares of SD for $280,800. The remaining 25% interest had a fair value of $64,800.

The net assets of SD at acquisition were $306,000.

PA elected to measure non-controlling interests in SD at fair value at acquisition.

What is the goodwill that arose on the acquisition of SD?

- ○ $51,300
- ○ $39,600
- ○ $116,100
- ○ $(46,800)

9.8 CD acquired 60% of the share capital of MB on 1 April 20X3 for $42 million when its retained earnings were $7 million.

The equity sections of the statement of financial position of both companies at 31 March 20X4 are:

	CD $m	MB $m
Share capital – $1 shares	86	22
Retained earnings	26	12
	112	34

Goodwill of $28 million arose on acquisition. An impairment loss of $4 million had arisen at the year ending 31 March 20X4. CD elected to measure non-controlling interests in MB at the proportionate share of the net assets at acquisition.

What is the amount of retained earnings that should be included in the consolidated statement of financial position of the CD group as at 31 March 20X4?

- ○ $27.0 million
- ○ $29.2 million
- ○ $25.0 million
- ○ $26.6 million

9.9 Goodwill arising on acquisition is accounted for according to IFRS 3 *Business Combinations*.

Which statement is correct concerning the accounting treatment of positive goodwill arising on acquisition?

- ○ Carried at cost, with an annual impairment review
- ○ Written off against reserves on acquisition
- ○ Amortised over its useful life
- ○ Revalued to fair value at each year end

9.10 LM acquired 60% of VB on 1 April 20X7 for $6.4 million when VB's retained earnings were $2.3 million.

An extract from the statement of financial position for both entities for the year ended 31 March 20X9 is shown below.

	LM $m	VB $m
Share capital	5.5	4.4
Retained earnings	8.5	3.2
	14.0	7.6

LM elected to measure non-controlling interests in VB at acquisition at the proportionate share of net assets. No impairment of goodwill has arisen since the acquisition date.

What is the amount of the non-controlling interests in VB that should be included in the consolidated statement of financial position of the LM group as at 31 March 20X9?

- ○ $2.68 million
- ○ $3.04 million
- ○ $8.10 million
- ○ $3.96 million

9.11 DS acquired 90% of LO on 1 January 20X1 for $22.8 million when LO's retained earnings were $6.3 million.

Extracts from the statement of financial position of both entities at 31 December 20X1 are shown below.

	DS $m	LO $m
Share capital	55.8	12.6
Retained earnings	42.6	7.9
	98.4	20.5

DS elected to measure non-controlling interests in LO at fair value at the date of acquisition which was $2.3 million.

There has been no impairment of the goodwill arising at acquisition.

What is the amount of the non-controlling interests in LO for inclusion in the consolidated statement of financial position of the DS group as at 31 December 20X1? Give your answer in $ million, rounded to two decimal places.

$ ☐ million

9.12 TR acquired 70% of SD on 1 September 20X5. At this date the equity of SD comprised:

	$m
$1 equity shares	90
Retained earnings	63
Revaluation surplus	32

The equity sections of the statement of financial position for both TR and SD at the 31 August 20X9 are:

	TR $m	SD $m
$1 equity shares	216	90
Retained earnings	142	63
Revaluation surplus	81	54

What is the amount of the revaluation surplus that should be included in the consolidated statement of financial position of the TR group as at 31 August 20X9?

○ $15.4 million
○ $96.4 million
○ $118.8 million
○ $238.4 million

9.13 QZ acquired 80% of the share capital of FT on 1 January 20X9 for $350,000.

The equity sections of the statement of financial position of both companies at 31 December 20X9 are:

	QZ $	FT $
Issued share capital – $1 shares	400,000	140,000
Share premium	320,000	50,000
Retained earnings at 1 January 20X9	140,000	60,000
Profit for the year ended 31 December 20X9	80,000	40,000
	940,000	290,000

Goodwill of $240,000 arose on acquisition. An impairment loss of $36,000 had arisen at the year ending 31 December 20X9.

QZ elected to measure non-controlling interests in FT at fair value at acquisition.

What figure for consolidated retained earnings should appear in the consolidated statement of financial position at 31 December 20X9?

○ $143,200

○ $216,000

○ $223,200

○ $271,200

9.14 PG bought 60% of the share capital of SC for $6,000,000 on 1 October 20X5, when its share capital was $1,000,000, and its retained earnings were $4,500,000.

PG elected to measure non-controlling interests in SC at fair value at the date of acquisition, which was $4,000,000.

An impairment review was carried out at 30 September 20X6, and it was determined that the goodwill on the acquisition of SC had been impaired by 20%.

What is the amount of the goodwill impairment suffered by the shareholders of PG? Give your answer to the nearest $.

$ [   ]

9.15 The summarised statement of financial position of FL and KT at 31 December 20X8 was as follows:

	FL $m	KT $m
Net assets	68	25
Share capital	10	10
Retained earnings	58	15
	68	25

On 1 January 20X8 FL purchased 80% of the equity share capital of KT for $24 million. Goodwill of $10 million arose on acquisition. The goodwill arising on consolidation was impaired by 100% at 31 December 20X8.

KT's retained earnings on 1 January 20X8 were $20 million.

FL elected to measure non-controlling interests in KT at fair value at the date of acquisition.

What is the figure for retained earnings to be included in the consolidated statement of financial position at 31 December 20X8?

- ○ $46 million
- ○ $52 million
- ○ $62 million
- ○ $70 million

9.16 HW acquired 270,000 $1 ordinary shares in SG on 1 January 20X9 at a cost of $400,000. At that date, SG had 300,000 $1 ordinary shares in issue and its retained earnings were $50,000.

HW elected to measure non-controlling interests in SG at the proportionate share of the fair value of the net assets at acquisition.

What is the amount of goodwill arising on the acquisition of SG? Give your answer to the nearest $.

$ [   ]

9.17 **Where the purchase price of an acquisition is less than the aggregate fair value of the net assets acquired, which one of the following accounting treatments of the difference is required by IFRS 3 *Business Combinations*?**

- ○ Deduction from goodwill in the consolidated statement of financial position
- ○ Immediate recognition as a gain in the statement of changes in equity
- ○ Recognition in the statement of profit or loss over its estimated useful life
- ○ Immediate recognition as a gain in the statement of profit or loss

9.18 **Which TWO of the following would be classified as subsidiaries of AB?**

☐ CD – AB has a management contract under which it directs the activities of CD in return for 95% of the profits and 100% of the losses of CD.

☐ EF – AB owns 80% of the ordinary shares in EF but chooses not to exercise its voting rights.

☐ GH – AB owns 50% of the ordinary shares in GH but has no representation on the board of directors.

☐ JK – AB owns 50% of the ordinary shares in JK; the remaining ordinary shares are owned by YZ and unanimous consent is required by AB and YZ for operating and financial decisions.

☐ LM – AB owns 100% of the cumulative irredeemable preference shares in LM.

9.19 **Which THREE of the following are permissible methods of measuring an investment in a subsidiary in the parent's separate financial statements?**

☐ At present value

☐ At cost

☐ At fair value

☐ At the lower of cost and net realisable value

☐ Using the equity method

☐ At amortised cost

9.20 PQ purchased 90% of the equity shares in SV for $500,000 on 1 January 20X1 when SV had retained earnings of $360,000 and no other reserves. On 31 December 20X4, SV had retained earnings of $440,000.

No impairment has arisen since acquisition.

The 90% shareholding in SV had a fair value of $580,000 on 31 December 20X4. The directors estimate the present value of future cash flows from the investment in SV to be $535,000.

PQ wishes to measure its investment in SV as a financial asset under IFRS 9 *Financial Instruments* in its separate financial statements.

What is the carrying amount of the investment in SV in PQ's separate financial statements as at 31 December 20X4?

○ $500,000

○ $535,000

○ $572,000

○ $580,000

10 Consolidated statement of financial position II

10.1 MN acquired 80% of the equity shares in LK on 1 January 20X6. The consideration for the acquisition consisted of the following:

- Cash of $1,200,000 paid on 1 January 20X6
- Cash of $500,000 paid on 1 January 20X8 (a discount rate of 7% was applied to value the liability in the financial statements of MN)
- The transfer of 750,000 shares in MN with a nominal value of $1 each and an agreed value on the date of acquisition of $2 each

What is the best estimate of the fair value of the consideration to be included in the calculation of goodwill arising on the acquisition of LK?

- ○ $2,386,500
- ○ $3,136,500
- ○ $3,167,500
- ○ $3,200,000

10.2 **Which of the following options would affect the calculation of the fair values of the subsidiary's net assets at the date of acquisition?**

- ○ Changes to the assets and liabilities as a result of the post-acquisition intentions or actions of the acquirer
- ○ The existence of contingent liabilities in the books of the subsidiary at the acquisition date
- ○ Provisions for post-acquisition reorganisation costs anticipated by the acquirer at the acquisition date
- ○ Post-acquisition losses anticipated by the acquirer at the acquisition date

10.3 On 1 July 20X1, ML acquired 80,000 of RT's 100,000 $1 ordinary shares for $450,000. At that date RT's shares were trading at $3.75.

At the acquisition date, RT had retained earnings of $165,000 and the carrying amounts of the net assets were approximately equal to their fair values, with the exception of one building which had a fair value of $80,000 in excess of its carrying amount.

ML elected to measure non-controlling interests in ML at fair value at acquisition.

What is the goodwill arising on the acquisition of RT? Give your answer to the nearest whole $.

$ [   ]

10.4 On 1 March 20X5, PB, a listed entity, acquired 80% of 3,000,000 issued ordinary shares of SV. The consideration for each share acquired comprised a cash payment of $1.20, plus two ordinary shares in PB. The market value of a $1 ordinary share in PB on 1 March 20X5 was $1.50, rising to $1.60 by the entity's year end on 31 March 20X5. Professional fees paid to PB's external accountants and legal advisers in respect of the acquisition were $400,000.

What is the fair value of the consideration transferred in respect of the acquisition of SV for inclusion in the goodwill calculation in PB's consolidated financial statements for the year ended 31 March 20X5?

○ $10,080,000

○ $10,480,000

○ $10,560,000

○ $10,960,000

10.5 ZA acquired 75% of the 2 million issued $1 ordinary shares of PJ on 1 January 20X2 for $3,700,000 when PJ's retained earnings were $1,770,000. ZA has no other subsidiaries.

The carrying amount of PJ's net assets was considered to be the same as the fair value at the date of acquisition with the exception of PJ's non-depreciable property. The carrying amount of non-depreciable property at acquisition was $1,890,000 and its fair value was $2,200,000.

Property, plant and equipment of ZA and PJ was included in the individual financial statements at 31 December 20X3 at a carrying amount of $16,000,000 and $1,750,000 respectively.

What is the amount of property, plant and equipment to be included in the consolidated statement of financial position of the ZA group at 31 December 20X3? Give your answer to the nearest whole $.

$ _____

10.6 ZA acquired 75% of the 2 million issued $1 ordinary shares of PJ on 1 January 20X2 for $3,700,000 when PJ's retained earnings were $1,770,000. ZA has no other subsidiaries.

The carrying amount of PJ's net assets was considered to be the same as the fair value at the date of acquisition with the exception of PJ's non-depreciable property. The carrying amount of non-depreciable property at acquisition was $1,890,000 and its fair value was $2,200,000.

Property, plant and equipment of ZA and PJ was included in the individual financial statements at 31 December 20X3 at a carrying amount of $16,000,000 and $1,750,000 respectively.

ZA elected to measure non-controlling interests in PJ at fair value at the acquisition date. The fair value of the non-controlling interest in PJ was $1,140,000 on 1 January 20X2.

An impairment review performed on 31 December 20X3 indicated that goodwill on the acquisition of PJ had been impaired by $100,000. No impairment was recognised in the year ended 31 December 20X2. The retained earnings of PJ at 31 December 20X3 were $2,400,000.

What is the amount of goodwill that in PJ that will be recorded in non-current assets of the ZA group as at 31 December 20X3?

- ○ $540,000
- ○ $660,000
- ○ $760,000
- ○ $970,000

10.7 ZA acquired 75% of the 2 million issued $1 ordinary shares of PJ on 1 January 20X2 for $3,700,000 when PJ's retained earnings were $1,770,000. ZA has no other subsidiaries.

The carrying amount of PJ's net assets was considered to be the same as the fair value at the date of acquisition with the exception of PJ's non-depreciable property. The carrying amount of non-depreciable property at acquisition was $1,890,000 and its fair value was $2,200,000.

Property, plant and equipment of ZA and PJ was included in the individual financial statements at 31 December 20X3 at a carrying amount of $16,000,000 and $1,750,000 respectively.

ZA elected to measure non-controlling interests in PJ at fair value at the acquisition date. The fair value of the non-controlling interest in PJ was $1,140,000 on 1 January 20X2.

An impairment review performed on 31 December 20X3 indicated that goodwill on the acquisition of PJ had been impaired by $100,000. No impairment was recognised in the year ended 31 December 20X2. The retained earnings of PJ at 31 December 20X3 were $2,400,000.

What is the retained earnings of PJ to be included in the consolidated retained earnings of the ZA group at 31 December 20X3?

- ○ $397,500
- ○ $473,000
- ○ $530,000
- ○ $630,000

10.8 ZA acquired 75% of the 2 million issued $1 ordinary shares of PJ on 1 January 20X2 for $3,700,000 when PJ's retained earnings were $1,770,000. ZA has no other subsidiaries.

The carrying amount of PJ's net assets was considered to be the same as the fair value at the date of acquisition with the exception of PJ's non-depreciable property. The carrying amount of non-depreciable property at acquisition was $1,890,000 and its fair value was $2,200,000.

Property, plant and equipment of ZA and PJ was included in the individual financial statements at 31 December 20X3 at a carrying amount of $16,000,000 and $1,750,000 respectively.

ZA elected to measure non-controlling interests in PJ at fair value at the acquisition date. The fair value of the non-controlling interest in PJ was $1,140,000 on 1 January 20X2.

An impairment review performed on 31 December 20X3 indicated that goodwill on the acquisition of PJ had been impaired by $100,000. No impairment was recognised in the year ended 31 December 20X2. The retained earnings of PJ at 31 December 20X3 were $2,400,000.

Which THREE of the following statements are true in respect of the non-controlling interest to be included in the consolidated statement of financial position of the ZA group for the year ended 31 December 20X3?

☐ 25% of PJ's post-acquisition earnings will be debited to it.

☐ It will be included at its fair value on acquisition plus share of post-acquisition earnings of PJ.

☐ It will be included as a separate component of equity.

☐ 25% of the impairment in the goodwill arising on acquisition will be debited to it.

☐ It will be included in the non-current liabilities of the ZA group.

10.9 On 1 January 20X2 CD purchased 60% of the equity share capital of EF for a total cash price of $50 million. The total net assets of EF were $60 million. However, the net assets of EF were believed to have a fair value to the CD group of $65 million in total. The directors of CD considered that a group re-organisation would be necessary because of the acquisition of EF and that the cost of this would be $5 million. This reorganisation was completed by 31 August 20X2.

CD elected to measure non-controlling interests in EF at fair value at acquisition. The fair value of the non-controlling interest in EF on 1 January 20X2 was $30 million.

What is the amount of goodwill arising on acquisition of EF? Give your answer to the nearest $ million.

$ [   ] million

10.10 AJ purchased 4 million of BK's 5,000,000 $1 ordinary shares on 1 April 20X3 for $7.5 million when BK's retained earnings were $1.6 million. During the year ended 31 March 20X4, BK sold goods to AJ for $100,000 at a mark up 25%. At 31 March 20X4, a quarter of these goods had been sold on to third parties.

AJ elected to measure non-controlling interests in BK at the proportionate share of net assets. An impairment review at 31 March 20X4 revealed an impairment loss on the goodwill of BK of $90,000.

The retained earnings of AJ and BK respectively at 31 March 20X4 were $11 million and $2 million.

What is the amount of retained earnings that should be included in the consolidated statement of financial position of the AJ group as at 31 March 20X4? Give your answer to the nearest $.

$ [   ]

10.11 On 1 July 20X1, KH purchased a 60% stake in RP's 1,000,000 $1 equity shares for $1,800,000. At that date the book value of RP's net assets was $1,500,000. The book value of RP's net assets was the same as the fair value with the following exceptions:

- Property, plant and equipment with a book value of $370,000 had a fair value of $430,000.
- RP had an internally generated brand which was not recognised in their financial statements but was attributed a fair value of $80,000.
- RP had disclosed a contingent liability in the note to its financial statements – the fair value of this was considered to be $40,000 at acquisition.

KH anticipated that $100,000 of reorganisation costs would be incurred as a result of the acquisition in RP.

KH elected to non-controlling interests in RP at the proportionate share of the fair value of net assets at acquisition.

What is the amount of goodwill arising on the acquisition of RP? Give your answer to the nearest $.

$ [   ]

10.12 DA owns 60% of CB's ordinary share capital. At the group's year end, 31 December 20X5, CB included $6,000 in its receivables in respect of goods supplied to DA. However, the payables of DA included only $4,000 in respect of amounts due to CB. The difference arose because, on 31 December 20X5, DA sent a cheque for $2,000, which was not received by CB until 3 January 20X6.

Which of the following sets of consolidation adjustments to current assets and current liabilities is correct?

- ○ Deduct $6,000 from both consolidated receivables and consolidated payables
- ○ Deduct $3,600 from both consolidated receivables and consolidated payables
- ○ Deduct $6,000 from consolidated receivables and $4,000 from consolidated payables, and include cash in transit of $2,000
- ○ Deduct $6,000 from consolidated receivables and $4,000 from consolidated payables, and include inventory in transit of $2,000

10.13 YZ acquired 80% of WX on 1 October 20X2.

YZ and WX trade with each other. During the year ended 30 September 20X3 YZ sold WX inventory at a sales price of $28,000. YZ applied a mark up on cost of 33⅓%.

At 30 September 20X3 WX still had remaining in inventory $6,000 of goods purchased from YZ.

Which of the following is the correct journal entry to be made to adjust YZ's consolidated statement of financial position for the year ended 30 September 20X3?

- ○ Dr Retained earnings of YZ $1,500; Cr Consolidated inventory $1,500
- ○ Dr Retained earnings of WX $1,500; Cr Consolidated inventory $1,500
- ○ Dr Retained earnings of YZ $2,000; Cr Consolidated inventory $2,000
- ○ Dr Retained earnings of WX $2,000; Cr Consolidated inventory $2,000

10.14 LP buys goods with a sales value of $100,000 from its 75% owned subsidiary QR. QR earns a mark-up of 25% on such transactions. At the year end of 30 June 20X7, LP had not yet taken delivery of goods, which were despatched by QR on 29 June 20X7.

At what amount would the goods in transit appear in the consolidated statement of financial position of the LP group at 30 June 20X7?

- ○ $60,000
- ○ $75,000
- ○ $80,000
- ○ $100,000

10.15 SV owns 75% of the ordinary share capital of its subsidiary TU. At the group's year end, 28 February 20X7, SV's payables include $3,600 in respect of inventories sold to it by TU.

TU's receivables include $6,700 in respect of inventories sold to SV. Two days before the year end SV sent a payment of $3,100 to TU that was not recorded by the latter until two days after the year end.

How should the cash in transit be dealt with in the consolidated statement of financial position at 28 February 20X7?

- ○ $3,100 added to consolidated cash
- ○ $3,100 deducted from consolidated cash
- ○ $2,325 added to consolidated cash
- ○ $2,325 deducted from consolidated cash

10.16 A parent company sells inventory costing $100,000 at a mark up of 20% to a 90% subsidiary. At the end of the reporting period, half of this inventory remains unsold.

Which of the following is the required consolidation adjustment?

- ○ Reduce group inventory by $100,000 as the sale was not made to a third party
- ○ No adjustment is needed because intra-group trading cancels on consolidation
- ○ Reduce group inventory by $10,000 and reduce parent's profits by $10,000 to eliminate the unrealised profit in inventory
- ○ Reduce group inventory by $10,000 and subsidiary's profits by $10,000 to eliminate the unrealised profit in inventory

10.17 MX acquired 80% of FZ on 1 January 20X9 when FZ's retained earnings were $920,000.

FZ sold goods to MX at a sales value of $300,000. All of these goods remain in MX's inventories at the year end. FZ makes 20% profit margin on all sales.

The retained earnings of MX and FZ as at 31 December 20X9 are $3.2 million and $1.1 million respectively. There has been no impairment to goodwill since the date of acquisition.

What amount will appear in the consolidated statement of financial position of the MX group for retained earnings as at 31 December 20X9?

○ $3,284,000

○ $3,296,000

○ $3,304,000

○ $4,032,000

10.18 PL bought 70% of the share capital of SH on 1 January 20X4 for $6,650,000 when the retained earnings of SH were $4,650,000.

PL elected to measure non-controlling interests in SH at fair value at the date of acquisition, which was $2,844,000.

In the last month of the year, SH sold goods to PL for $600,000. SH applied a mark-up of 20% on the cost of these goods, half of which were still in inventory at the year end.

The balance on SH's retained earnings at 31 December 20X4 was $5,700,000.

What is the amount of non-controlling interests in SH for inclusion in the consolidated statement of financial position of the PL group as at 31 December 20X4?

○ $3,159,000

○ $3,129,000

○ $3,141,000

○ $3,144,000

10.19 XY owns 75% of the issued equity share capital of PQ. At the year end, XY held inventory valued at $160,000 and PQ held inventories valued at $90,000. The inventories held by XY included $20,000 of goods purchased from PQ at a profit margin of 30%. There were also inventories in transit between the two entities; this amounted to a further $10,000 at selling price.

At what amount should inventories appear in the consolidated statement of financial position?

○ $244,000

○ $251,000

○ $253,000

○ $254,000

10.20 AB has a 90% subsidiary, CD. Extracts from their statements of financial position as at 31 December 20X8 are shown below:

	AB $	CD $
Current assets		
Inventories	87,000	49,000
Trade receivables	105,000	62,000
Cash	200,000	94,000
Current liabilities		
Trade payables	77,000	43,000

AB's trade receivables include $22,000 owing from CD. CD's trade payables include $14,000 owing to AB.

At 31 December 20X8, there was cash in transit paid by CD to AB $5,000 and goods in transit from AB to CD of $3,000.

What is the amount of trade receivables that should be included in the consolidated statement of financial position of the AB group as at 31 December 20X8?

- ○ $167,000
- ○ $153,000
- ○ $148,000
- ○ $145,000

---

11 Consolidated statement of profit or loss and other comprehensive income

11.1 AB owns 80% of the ordinary share capital of CD, its only subsidiary.

In the year ended 31 December 20X3, CD has total comprehensive income of $238,000. A fair value adjustment at acquisition results in additional depreciation of $8,000 in the year ending 31 December 20X3. Goodwill on the acquisition of CD was impaired by $10,000 in the year to 31 December 20X3 and $12,000 in the previous year.

AB elected to measure non-controlling interests in CD at fair value at acquisition.

What is the share of total comprehensive income attributable to the non-controlling interests in CD for the year ended 31 December 20X3?

- ○ $41,600
- ○ $43,200
- ○ $44,000
- ○ $47,600

11.2 In the year ended 31 December 20X1, S, an 80% owned subsidiary of P, sold P some goods for $1,000,000 at a mark-up of 25%.

P had sold half of these goods by the year end.

Which FOUR of the following statements are true about that year's consolidated statement of profit or loss?

☐ Revenue will need to be reduced by $1,000,000 to reflect the intra-group trading.

☐ Revenue will not need to be adjusted to reflect the intra-group trading.

☐ Cost of sales will need to be reduced by $1,000,000 to eliminate the intra-group purchase.

☐ Cost of sales will not need to be reduced to reflect the intra-group purchase.

☐ Cost of sales will need to be increased by $100,000 to remove the unrealised profit from closing inventory.

☐ Cost of sales will need to be reduced by $125,000 to remove the unrealised profit in closing inventory.

☐ Non-controlling interest will need to be adjusted to reflect the unrealised profit in closing inventory.

☐ Non-controlling interest will not need to be adjusted to reflect the unrealised profit in closing inventory.

11.3 JF holds an 80% interest in the ordinary share capital of PR.

During the year PR sold goods to JF for $30,000, including a mark-up of 25%. Half of the goods remain in inventory at the year end.

Extracts from the statement of profit or loss are as follows:

	JF $	PR $
Revenue	250,000	180,000

What is the amount to be included in the consolidated statement of profit or loss for revenue?

○ $400,000

○ $415,000

○ $406,000

○ $418,000

11.4 XY owns 80% of the issued share capital of PQ.

During the current accounting period XY sells goods to PQ for $7.8 million. The goods cost $6.5 million. XY achieved a mark-up on cost of 20%. Half of the goods remain in PQ's inventory at the year end.

Which of the following is the correct treatment of this transaction when preparing the consolidated financial statements?

- ○ Remove $7.8 million from revenue and cost of sales. Increase cost of sales and reduce inventory by the profit on the goods remaining in inventory at the year end.
- ○ Increase cost of sales and reduce inventory by the profit on the goods remaining in inventory at the year end.
- ○ Remove $7.8 million from revenue and $6.5 million from cost of sales. Increase cost of sales and reduce inventory by the profit on the goods remaining in inventory at the year end.
- ○ Remove $6.5 million from revenue and cost of sales. Increase cost of sales and reduce inventory by the profit on the goods remaining in inventory at the year end.

11.5 GT regularly sells goods to its subsidiary in which it owns 60% of the ordinary share capital. During the group's financial year ended 31 August 20X7, GT sold goods to its subsidiary valued at $100,000 (selling price) upon which it makes a margin of 20%. By the group's year end all of the goods had been sold to parties outside the group.

What is the correct consolidation adjustment in respect of these sales for the year ended 31 August 20X7?

- ○ No adjustment required
- ○ Dr Revenue $60,000; Cr Cost of sales $60,000
- ○ Dr Revenue $80,000; Cr Cost of sales $80,000
- ○ Dr Revenue $100,000; Cr Cost of sales $100,000

11.6 AB acquired a 60% holding in CD many years ago. At 31 December 20X3 AB held inventory with a carrying amount of $30,000 purchased from CD at cost plus 20%.

What are the effects of adjusting for this intra-group trading on the consolidated statement of profit or loss for the year ended 31 December 20X3?

- ○ Profit attributable to the owners of the parent — Reduced by $3,000
  Non-controlling interest — Reduced by $2,000

- ○ Profit attributable to the owners of the parent — Reduced by $3,600
  Non-controlling interest — Reduced by $2,400

- ○ Profit attributable to the owners of the parent — Reduced by $5,000
  Non-controlling interest — No effect

- ○ Profit attributable to the owners of the parent — Reduced by $6,000
  Non-controlling interest — No effect

11.7 DS acquired 80% of AQ on 1 October 20X7.

The statement of profit or loss for both companies for the year ended 30 September 20X8 is as follows:

	DS	AQ
	$	$
Revenue	8,700	3,600
Cost of sales and expenses	(2,400)	(1,700)
Profit before tax	6,300	1,900
Income tax expense	(1,700)	(800)
Profit for the year	4,600	1,100

DS elected to measure non-controlling interests in AZ at fair value at acquisition. The goodwill arising at acquisition was $4,200 and an impairment loss for the year ended 30 September 20X8 of $600 arose.

What is the profit attributable to the non-controlling interests in AQ for the year ended 30 September 20X8?

○ $100
○ $220
○ $380
○ $5,000

11.8 ZA acquired 70% of MB on 1 January 20X7.

An extract from their respective statements of profit or loss for the year ended 31 December 20X7 is as follows:

	ZA	MB
	$'000	$'000
Profit for the year	7,020	1,980

ZA elected to measure non-controlling interests in MB at the proportionate share of the net assets at acquisition. Goodwill of $7,560,000 arose at acquisition and the impairment loss for the current year is $756,000.

What is the profit attributable to the owners of the parent for inclusion in the consolidated statement of profit or loss for the year ended 31 December 20X7?

○ $846,000
○ $7,650,000
○ $7,877,000
○ $9,162,000

11.9 PR owns 80% of the share capital of SY.

At the year ended 31 December 20X6, an extract from the companies' statements of profit or loss shows the following results:

	PR	SY
	$'000	$'000
Revenue	84,000	26,000
Cost of sales	56,000	22,000
Gross profit	28,000	4,000

During the year ended 31 December 20X6, PR sold goods to SY worth $8,000,000. At the year end, $6,000,000 of these goods had been sold to third parties. PR applies a mark-up on cost of 25%.

What is the gross profit that will appear in the consolidated statement of profit or loss for the year ended 31 December 20X6?

○ $31,600,000
○ $26,400,000
○ $31,500,000
○ $32,000,000

11.10 HD has a 90% subsidiary, LW. During the year ended 31 December 20X2, LW sold goods to HD for $25,000, which was cost plus 25%. At 31 December 20X2, $10,000 of these goods remained unsold.

In the consolidated statement for profit or loss for the year ended 31 December 20X2, what are the amounts revenue and gross profit should be reduced by in respect of this intra-group trading?

○ Reduce revenue by $25,000 and gross profit by $5,000
○ Reduce revenue by $10,000 and gross profit by $2,000
○ Reduce revenue by $25,000 and gross profit by $2,000
○ Reduce revenue by $10,000 and gross profit by $5,000

11.11 PA purchased 75% of the equity share capital of DM many years ago. During the year ended 31 December 20X6, DM made a profit for the year of $240,000.

PA sold inventory to DM during the year for $20,000 achieving a mark-up on cost of 5%. Half of this inventory remained in DM's books at the year end.

What is the profit attributable to non-controlling interests in the consolidated statement of profit or loss for the year ended 31 December 20X6?

○ $45,000
○ $60,000
○ $90,000
○ $180,000

11.12 PT owned 80% of the issued equity share capital of SB. For the year ended 31 December 20X6, SB reported a profit for the year of $55 million. During 20X6, SB sold goods to PT for $15 million at cost plus 20%. At the year end half these goods are still held by PT.

What is the profit attributable to the non-controlling interests in SB in the consolidated statement of profit or loss for the year ended 31 December 20X6?

- ○ $8 million
- ○ $10.7 million
- ○ $10.75 million
- ○ $11 million

11.13 FD acquired 60% of TR on 1 April 20X2. The statements of profit or loss for the year ended 31 December 20X2 for both companies are as follows:

	FD	TR
	$'000	$'000
Revenue	25,000	18,000
Cost of sales and expenses	(16,000)	(14,000)
Profit before tax	9,000	4,000
Income tax expense	(1,300)	(800)
Profit for the year	7,700	3,200

On 1 July 20X2 FD sold goods to TR for $7 million which included a profit on transfer of $3 million. All of these inventories are still in inventory at the year end.

What is the profit for the year attributable to the owners of the parent? Give your answer to the nearest $'000.

$'000	

11.14 HJ has owned an 80% subsidiary, KL, for a number of years. The profits for the year ended 31 December 20X9 of HJ and KL are $900,000 and $600,000 respectively. During the year ended 31 December 20X9, KL declared a dividend of $100,000. HJ's profit figure includes its share of KL's dividend.

What is the profit for the year figure for inclusion in the HJ group's consolidated statement of profit or loss for the year ended 31 December 20X9?

- ○ $1,300,000
- ○ $1,380,000
- ○ $1,420,000
- ○ $1,500,000

11.15 PH has owned a 90% subsidiary, GF, for a number of years. Goodwill of $200,000 was recognised on acquisition. This goodwill has been impaired by a total of $75,000 since acquisition, of which $35,000 arose in the year ended 31 December 20X1.

It is group policy to recognise impairment losses in administrative expenses. Administrative expenses of PH and GH for the year ended 31 December 20X1 amounted to $1,300,000 and $860,000 respectively.

PH elected to measure the non-controlling interest in GH at fair value at acquisition.

What is the amount of administrative expenses that should be included in the PH group's consolidated statement of profit or loss for the year ended 31 December 20X1? Give your answer to the nearest $.

$ [   ]

11.16 MN acquired 70% of PQ's equity shares on 1 January 20X0. At that date, the fair value of PQ's net assets was the same as their carrying amount with the following exceptions:

- Inventory was found to have a fair value of $20,000 higher than its carrying amount – this inventory was sold in the year ended 31 December 20X0
- A contingent liability with a fair value of $18,000 was disclosed in PQ's financial statements – this liability was settled in the year ended 31 December 20X0

For the year ended 31 December 20X0, the profit for the year of MN and PQ amounted to $750,000 and $410,000 respectively.

What is the consolidated profit for the year that should be included in the MN group's consolidated statement of profit or loss for the year ended 31 December 20X0?

○ $1,122,000
○ $1,140,000
○ $1,158,000
○ $1,198,000

11.17 On 1 September 20X4, QR acquired 60% of VB's equity shares. At that date, the fair value of VB's net assets were the same as their carrying amount. No intra-group transactions took place in the year.

For the year ended 31 December 20X4, distribution costs of QR and VB amounted to $1,650,000 and $900,000 respectively.

What is the amount of distribution costs that should be included in the consolidated statement of profit or loss of the QR group for the year ended 31 December 20X4?

○ $2,550,000
○ $2,190,000
○ $1,950,000
○ $1,875,000

11.18 On 1 June 20X0, NH acquired 80% of the ordinary shares in WQ. At that date, goodwill in WQ amounted to $120,000. There was no impairment of this goodwill until the year ended 31 December 20X3, when an impairment review revealed an impairment loss equivalent to 10% of the value of goodwill. NH elected to measure non-controlling interests in WQ at fair value at acquisition.

The only fair value adjustment required in relation to WQ's net assets at acquisition was an increase in value of $360,000 to property, which had a remaining useful life of 20 years at 1 June 20X0.

In the year ended 31 December 20X3, WQ sold goods to NH for $50,000 at a margin of 40%. Half of the goods were still in inventory at the year end.

In the year ended 31 December 20X3, WQ's profit for the year amounted to $970,000.

What is the profit for the year attributable to the non-controlling interests in WQ for inclusion in the consolidated statement of profit or loss of the NH group for the year ended 31 December 20X3? Give your answer to the nearest $.

$ [   ]

11.19 On 1 October 20X2, YC acquired 90% of the equity shares in MX. Both entities hold their owner-occupied properties under the revaluation model. In the year ended 31 December 20X2, the revaluation surplus recognised by YC and MX amounted to $30,000 and $20,000 respectively. No deferred tax arose on these revaluations. The revaluation surplus can be assumed to accrue evenly over the year.

What is the amount of other comprehensive income that should be included in the consolidated statement of profit or loss and other comprehensive income of the YC group for the year ended 31 December 20X2?

- ○ $34,500
- ○ $35,000
- ○ $48,000
- ○ $50,000

11.20 HJ has owned 75% of the equity shares in KX for a number of years.

In the year ended 31 December 20X3, the following consolidation adjustments were required:

- Additional depreciation due to a fair value adjustment on property of $16,000
- Impairment of goodwill in KX of $24,000 (non-controlling interests were measured at the proportionate share of net assets at acquisition)
- Unrealised profit of $12,000 on intra-group sales of inventory by HJ to KX.

The total comprehensive income of HJ and KX for the year ended 31 December 20X3 amounted to $640,000 and $400,000 respectively.

What is the total comprehensive income attributable to non-controlling interests for inclusion in the consolidated statement of profit or loss and other comprehensive income of the HJ group for the year ended 31 December 20X3?

- ○ $87,000
- ○ $90,000
- ○ $91,000
- ○ $96,000

12 Associates and joint arrangements

12.1 EF, in addition to its other holdings, acquired a 30% stake in the 100,000 $1 ordinary shares of SR on 1 January 20X1 for $50,000. At acquisition, SR's retained earnings were $22,000.

During the year ended 31 December 20X4, SR sold goods to EF for $10,000 at a margin of 20%. As at 31 December 20X4, a quarter of these goods had been sold on to third parties.

The retained earnings of the EF group (excluding SR) and SR at 31 December 20X4 were $390,000 and $90,000 respectively. The investment in SR was impaired by $2,920 by 31 December 20X4.

What are the consolidated retained earnings of the EF group (incorporating SR) at 31 December 20X4? Give your answer to the nearest $.

$ _____

12.2 MN acquired 30% of the share capital of TG for $75,000 on 1 July 20X8. MN was able to exercise significant influence over TG from that date. During the year to 30 June 20X9 TG made a profit for the year of $270,000 and paid a dividend of $50,000. At 30 June 20X9, the investment in the associate was considered to be impaired by 10%.

What amount will appear in the consolidated statement of financial position of MN at 30 June 20X9 in respect of its investment in TG? Give your answer to the nearest $.

$ _____

12.3 IFRS 11 *Joint Arrangements* classifies joint arrangements as either joint operations or joint ventures.

Which TWO of the following statements are true?

☐ A joint venture is always structured through a separate vehicle.
☐ A joint operation is never structured through a separate vehicle.
☐ A joint operation gives the parties with joint control rights to the net assets of the arrangement.
☐ A joint venture must have a contractual arrangement.
☐ A joint venture gives the parties with joint control rights to the assets and obligations for the liabilities, relating to the arrangement.

12.4 IFRS 11 *Joint Arrangements* sets out the accounting treatment required for joint arrangements.

Which TWO of the following statements are true in respect of this accounting treatment?

☐ In the group accounts of the joint venturer, the equity method must be applied to its interest in the joint venture.
☐ In the group accounts of the joint operator, the equity method must be applied to its interest in the joint operation.
☐ Joint ventures are accounted for by including the investor's share of assets, liabilities, income and expenses as per the contractual arrangement.
☐ Joint operations are accounted for by including the investor's share of assets, liabilities, income and expenses as per the contractual arrangement.
☐ In the investor's separate financial statements, an investment in a joint venture must always be accounted for at cost.

12.5 On 1 January 20X2 AD purchased 40% of the equity share capital of BL for $60,000. At this date the reserves of BL stood at $30,000. During the year ended 31 December 20X4 AD sold goods to BL for $10,000 and these goods were still in inventory at the year end. AD makes a gross profit margin of 25% on intra-group sales.

The statement of financial position of BL at 31 December 20X4 showed the following:

	$'000
Net assets	320
Share capital	100
Reserves	220
	320

At what amount should AD's interest in BL be stated in its consolidated statement of financial position at 31 December 20X4? Give your answer to the nearest $'000.

$'000 [   ]

12.6 LR owns 35% of the equity share capital of GH. During the year to 31 December 20X3 LR purchased goods with a sales value of $500,000 from GH. One-quarter of these goods remained in LR's inventory at the year ended 31 December 20X3. GH includes a mark-up of 25% on all sales.

Which of the following accounting adjustments would LR process in the preparation of its consolidated financial statements in relation to these goods?

○ Dr Share of profit of associate $25,000; Cr Inventories $25,000

○ Dr Cost of sales $25,000; Cr Inventories $25,000

○ Dr Investment in associate $8,750; Cr Cost of sales $8,750

○ Dr Share of profit of associate $8,750; Cr Inventories $8,750

12.7 T has a 25% share in UV, which is a joint operation.

How should T account for its interest in UV in its individual financial statements?

○ Nothing should be included in the individual statements – it is only included on consolidation

○ At the cost of the investment in UV as an investment in non-current assets

○ Include 25% of the assets and liabilities of UV and 25% of the revenue and expenses generated by UV

○ As an investment in equity instrument under IFRS 9 *Financial Instruments*

12.8 On 1 January 20X4 HR, a company with subsidiaries, acquired 25% of KP for $650,000, when KP's retained earnings were $720,000. At 31 December 20X4 KP had retained earnings of $1,600,000 and HR recognised an impairment loss of $300,000 in respect of its investment in KP.

What amount will be shown as investment in the associate in the consolidated statement of financial position of HR as at 31 December 20X4?

- ○ $870,000
- ○ $570,000
- ○ $350,000
- ○ $830,000

12.9 HL owns 35% of CK, its only associate. During the year to 31 December 20X4 CK made a profit for the year of $721,000. This included sales of $240,000 to HL, on which CK made a gross profit margin of 40%. 30% of these goods were still held in inventory by HL at 31 December 20X4.

HL considers its investment in CK to have suffered a $20,000 impairment during the year.

At what amount should the share of profit of associate be stated in the consolidated statement of profit or loss of CK for the year ended 31 December 20X4?

- ○ $235,270
- ○ $225,150
- ○ $222,270
- ○ $218,750

12.10 AB and CD, together with other investors, hold interests in a separate legal entity, XY. AB and CD own 35% of the ordinary shares each, with the remaining 30% being held by multiple other small investors. There is a contractual arrangement between AB and CD to vote together in matters relating to XY. At least a majority of the voting rights are required to make decisions about the relevant activities of XY.

Which of the following statements is correct?

- ○ AB and CD have joint control of XY.
- ○ AB, CD and the remaining investors have joint control of XY.
- ○ XY is an associate of AB and CD.
- ○ XY is a subsidiary of AB and CD.

12.11 On 30 June 20X3, SG entered into an agreement with two other investors to establish a new entity, PC. All three investors subscribed for one-third of the equity shares in PC and each share carries one vote. All three investors appointed two representatives to the six-member board of directors of PC. All key policy decisions require the agreement of five of the six board members. A contractual agreement gives the three investors rights to the net assets of PC.

Which THREE of the following statements are correct in relation to the treatment of the investment in PC in the consolidated financial statements of SG for the year ended 30 September 20X3?

☐ PC will be treated as a joint venture simply because the three investors hold one-third of the shares each.

☐ PC will be treated as a joint venture in this case but only because key policy decisions require the consent of at least five of the directors and each of the investors has rights to the net assets of PC.

☐ SG should account for its share of PC's assets, liabilities, expenses and revenue in its own financial statements.

☐ SG should equity account for PC in its consolidated financial statements.

☐ In SG's own financial statements, the investment in PC should be held at cost in accordance with IFRS 9 *Financial Instruments*, or using the equity method as described in IAS 28 *Investments in Associates and Joint Ventures*.

12.12 CD owns the following equity shareholdings in other entities:

AB 25%

SL 20%

WR 30%

CD has a seat on the board of AB. CD owns the largest shareholding in AB (no other shareholdings are larger than 10%).

Three of CD's senior managers work two days a month at SL.

Another entity holds 70% of WR's equity and is the only shareholder with seats on the board.

Which entity or entities are associates of CD?

○ AB only

○ AB and SL

○ SL and WR

○ AB, SL and WR

12.13 RS owns 30% of EF and has joint control of EF with two other parties. The three parties sharing control have rights to the net assets of EF.

During the year ended 31 December 20X8, EF sold goods to RS for $160,000. EF applies a 25% mark up on cost. RS still had 10% of these goods in inventory at the year end.

What amount should be deducted from consolidated retained earnings in respect of this transaction?

○ $4,000

○ $3,200

○ $1,200

○ $960

12.14 AB acquired 25% of the ordinary share capital of GH on 1 October 20X8. AB has joint control of GH with three other parties. All four parties have rights to the net assets in GH.

GH sold goods to AB on 1 May 20X9 with a sales value of $80,000. Half of these goods remained in AB's inventories at the year end. GH makes 25% profit margin on all sales.

GH's profit for the year ended 30 June 20X9 was $100,000.

What is the share of profit of the joint venture for inclusion in the consolidated statement of profit or loss for the year ended 30 June 20X9?

○ $16,250
○ $16,750
○ $18,750
○ $22,500

12.15 The HC group acquired 30% of the equity share capital of AF on 1 April 20X0, paying $25,000. The remaining shares are owned by two other entities and the three parties have joint control over AF and rights to the net assets of AF.

At 1 April 20X0 the equity of AF comprised:

	$
$1 equity shares	50,000
Share premium	12,500
Retained earnings	10,000

AF made a profit for the year to 31 March 20X1 (prior to dividend distribution) of $6,500 and paid a dividend of $3,500 to its equity shareholders.

What is the value of HC's investment in AF for inclusion in HC's consolidated statement of financial position at 31 March 20X1?

○ $25,000
○ $25,900
○ $26,950
○ $28,000

12.16 On 1 April 20X7 RY acquired 40% of the share capital of HQ for $120,000 when the retained earnings of HQ were $80,000. RY has joint control of HQ with another entity and both entities have rights to the net assets of HQ.

During the year ended 31 March 20X8, RY sold goods to HQ for $30,000 including a profit margin of 25%. These goods were still in inventory at the year end.

At 31 March 20X8 the retained earnings of HQ were $140,000.

At what amount should RY's interest in HQ be shown in the consolidated statement of financial position at 31 March 20X8?

○ $173,000
○ $144,000
○ $141,000
○ $105,000

12.17 AB has several subsidiaries, and exerts joint control over EF, an entity in which it holds 30% of the ordinary share capital. The parties sharing control have rights to the net assets of EF.

During the financial year ended 30 April 20X5, EF sold goods to AB valued at $80,000. The cost of the goods to EF was $60,000. 25% of the goods remained in AB's inventory at 30 April 20X5.

What is the amount of the adjustment required in respect of the inventory? Give your answer to the nearest $.

$ ☐

12.18 **Which THREE of the following are permissible methods of measuring investments in associates and joint ventures in the parent's separate financial statements?**

☐ At value in use
☐ At cost
☐ At fair value
☐ Using the equity method
☐ Using the consolidation method

12.19 QR is one of three shareholders in another entity, LP. The majority shareholder holds 60.1%, the second shareholder holds 20% and QR holds 19.9% of the voting shares. The board of directors comprises six board members from the majority shareholder and two board members from each of QR and the 20% shareholder. A shareholders' agreement states that certain board and shareholder resolutions require unanimous or majority decision. There is no indication that the majority shareholder and the 20% shareholder act together in a common way.

During the year, senior managers of QR were seconded to LP to provide technical advice.

How should QR classify the investment in LP?

○ As a financial asset
○ As an associate
○ As a joint venture
○ As a subsidiary

12.20 **Which THREE of the following statements are true?**

☐ A joint operation is never structured through a separate vehicle.
☐ A joint venture is always structured through a separate vehicle.
☐ To be a joint arrangement, all shareholders must have equal shareholdings.
☐ To be a joint arrangement, all shareholders must have joint control.
☐ A joint venture must be accounted for using the equity method in the consolidated financial statements.
☐ A contractual arrangement and two or more parties sharing control are the key characteristics of a joint arrangement.

13 Foreign transactions and foreign subsidiaries

13.1 VW reports in A$ and has an 80% interest in its subsidiary XY whose functional currency is B$.

It translates the subsidiary's statement of profit or loss and other comprehensive income using the average rate for the period.

The net assets (equity) of XY are B$6,510,000 as at 31 December 20X3 (B$4,557,000 as at 31 December 20X2).

XY made a profit for the year of B$2,325,000 and paid a dividend of B$372,000 on 31 August 20X3. There was no other comprehensive income.

Relevant exchange differences are:

31 December 20X2	A$1:B$1.4
31 August 20X3	A$1:B$1.55
31 December 20X3	A$1:B$1.6
Average for 20X3	A$1:B$1.5

What is the exchange loss on net assets and profit to be reported in other comprehensive income in the consolidated statement of profit or loss and other comprehensive income of the VW group for the year ended 31 December 20X3?

- ○ A$736,250
- ○ A$496,250
- ○ A$488,250
- ○ A$397,000

13.2 Z, an entity based in the US, presents its financial statements in US dollars. On 1 January 20X8, Z purchased 80% of the ordinary share capital of B. B's functional currency is the euro (€) and the 80% investment cost €20 million. The fair value of the net assets of B at the date of acquisition was €19 million. The fair value of the non-controlling interests at 1 January 20X8 was €4.2 million. There has been no impairment in goodwill since acquisition. Z elected to measure non-controlling interests in B at fair value at acquisition.

The relevant exchange rates are as follows:

1 January 20X8	$1: €0.64
31 December 20X8	$1: €0.74
Average for 20X8	$1: €0.68

What is the carrying amount of goodwill (to the nearest $'000) that will appear in the consolidated statement of financial position of Z as at 31 December 20X8?

- ○ $6,486,000
- ○ $7,027,000
- ○ $7,500,000
- ○ $8,125,000

13.3 AB reports in $. On 1 April 20X7, it acquired an 80% interest in EF. EF operates in Country C whose currency is the crown. Net assets of EF as at 1 April 20X7 were 391,680 crowns and 489,600 crowns as at 31 December 20X7, the reporting date. Profit for the period 1 April to 31 December 20X7 is 97,920 crowns and is to be translated at the average rate. There was no other comprehensive income and no dividends were paid. Assume that no goodwill arose on the acquisition. Exchange rates are as follows:

1 April 20X7	$1:crowns 1.8
31 December 20X7	$1:crowns 1.6
Average for the period	$1:crowns 1.7

What is the total effect of this acquisition on group reserves at 31 December 20X7?

- ○ $70,720
- ○ $88,400
- ○ $57,600
- ○ $46,080

13.4 IAS 21 defines two currency concepts:
- The functional currency
- The presentation currency

Which TWO of the following statements about the presentation currency are true?

- ☐ It is the currency of the entity's primary economic environment.
- ☐ It is the currency of the entity's year-end financial statements.
- ☐ It is the currency that mainly influences the entity's sales prices.
- ☐ It is always the same as the entity's functional currency.
- ☐ The entity may choose which presentation currency to use.

13.5 **Complete the sentence below by selecting the correct options from the pull down list.**

When a foreign subsidiary has a different functional currency from the presentation currency of the group financial statements, [_____] assets and liabilities of the subsidiary must be translated at the [_____], income and expenses at the [_____] and exchange differences should be reported in [_____].

Pull down list:

monetary
non-monetary
all
opening rate
closing rate
average rate
profit or loss
other comprehensive income

13.6 RR presents its consolidated financial statements in A$. RR has one subsidiary, NN, which uses B$ as its functional currency. NN was acquired on 1 January 20X1 and goodwill arising on the acquisition was initially measured at B$510,000. There has been no impairment of this goodwill. Relevant exchange rates are:

1 January 20X1	A$1:B$2.10
31 December 20X2	A$1:B$2.50
Average rate for the year ended 31 December 20X2	A$1:B$2.40

What is the carrying amount of goodwill that will be presented in RR's consolidated statement of financial position as at 31 December 20X2? Give your answer to the nearest whole A$.

A$ ☐

13.7 HM acquired 80% of the ordinary share capital of a foreign entity, OS, on 1 January 20X1 for 13,984,000 crowns. At the date of acquisition the net assets of OS had a fair value of 15,800,000 crowns. The only fair value adjustment to OS's net assets related to non-depreciable land.

HM elected to measure non-controlling interests in OS at fair value at the date of acquisition. The fair value of the non-controlling interests at the date of acquisition was 3,496,000 crowns.

Goodwill on the acquisition of OS was 1,680,000 crowns and was impaired by 20% during 20X1. Impairment is translated at the average rate and is charged to group other expenses. OS did not have any other comprehensive income in the year ended 31 December 20X1 nor were any dividends paid.

The condensed statements of profit or loss for HM and OS for the year ended 31 December 20X1 are shown below.

	HM	OS
	$'000	Crowns'000
Revenue	5,200	4,500
Cost of sales	(3,200)	(3,000)
Gross profit	2,000	1,500
Other expenses	(1,420)	(1,050)
Profit for the year	580	450

Exchange rates:

1 January 20X1	$1:Crowns 1.61
31 December 20X1	$1:Crowns 1.52
Average rate for 20X1	$1:Crowns 1.58

What is the consolidated cost of sales of the HM group for the year ended 31 December 20X1?

○ $5,063,000

○ $5,099,000

○ $5,174,000

○ $6,200,000

13.8 HM acquired 80% of the ordinary share capital of a foreign entity, OS, on 1 January 20X1 for 13,984,000 crowns. At the date of acquisition the net assets of OS had a fair value of 15,800,000 crowns. The only fair value adjustment to OS's net assets related to non-depreciable land.

HM elected to measure non-controlling interests in OS at fair value at the date of acquisition. The fair value of the non-controlling interests at the date of acquisition was 3,496,000 crowns.

Goodwill on the acquisition of OS was 1,680,000 crowns and was impaired by 20% during 20X1. Impairment is translated at the average rate and is charged to group other expenses. OS did not have any other comprehensive income in the year ended 31 December 20X1 nor were any dividends paid.

The condensed statements of profit or loss for HM and OS for the year ended 31 December 20X1 are shown below.

	HM	OS
	$'000	Crowns'000
Revenue	5,200	4,500
Cost of sales	(3,200)	(3,000)
Gross profit	2,000	1,500
Other expenses	(1,420)	(1,050)
Profit for the year	580	450

Exchange rates:

1 January 20X1	$1:Crowns 1.61
31 December 20X1	$1:Crowns 1.52
Average rate for 20X1	$1:Crowns 1.58

Complete the calculation of the exchange differences to be charged to other comprehensive income in the year ended 31 December 20X1 by selecting the correct options from the pull down list.

	$'000
On translation of net assets:	
Closing net assets at closing rate	[ ]
Less: opening net assets at opening rate	[ ]
total comprehensive income as translated	[ ]
	X
Translation differences on goodwill	54
	X

Pull down list:

280
285
296
9,814
10,000
10,093
10,284
10,395
10,691

13.9 HM acquired 80% of the ordinary share capital of a foreign entity, OS, on 1 January 20X1 for 13,984,000 crowns. At the date of acquisition the net assets of OS had a fair value of 15,800,000 crowns. The only fair value adjustment to OS's net assets related to non-depreciable land.

HM elected to measure non-controlling interests in OS at fair value at the date of acquisition. The fair value of the non-controlling interests at the date of acquisition was 3,496,000 crowns.

Goodwill on the acquisition of OS was 1,680,000 crowns and was impaired by 20% during 20X1. Impairment is translated at the average rate and is charged to group other expenses. OS did not have any other comprehensive income in the year ended 31 December 20X1 nor were any dividends paid.

The condensed statements of profit or loss for HM and OS for the year ended 31 December 20X1 are shown below.

	HM	OS
	$'000	Crowns'000
Revenue	5,200	4,500
Cost of sales	(3,200)	(3,000)
Gross profit	2,000	1,500
Other expenses	(1,420)	(1,050)
Profit for the year	580	450

Exchange rates:

1 January 20X1 $1:Crowns 1.61

31 December 20X1 $1:Crowns 1.52

Average rate for 20X1 $1:Crowns 1.58

The exchange gains charged to other comprehensive income in the consolidated statement of profit or loss and other comprehensive income for the year ended 31 December 20X1 were $646,000.

What is the total comprehensive income attributable to the owners of HM for the year ended 31 December 20X1?

○ $143,000

○ $985,000

○ $1,155,000

○ $1,039,000

13.10   Parent has three overseas subsidiaries.

- A is 80% owned. A does not normally enter into transactions with Parent, other than to pay dividends. It operates as a fairly autonomous entity on a day-to-day basis although Parent controls its long term strategy.

- B is 100% owned and has been set up in order to assemble machines from materials provided by Parent. These are then sent to the UK where Parent sells them to third parties.

- C is 75% owned and is located in France. It manufactures and sells its own range of products locally. It negotiates its own day-to-day financing needs with French banks.

Which of the subsidiaries are likely to have a different functional currency from Parent?

○   A and B

○   A and C

○   B and C

○   All three subsidiaries

13.11 RA acquired 75% of equity shares of MO, a foreign operation, on 1 January 20X5. The functional currency of MO is the unit. On 1 January 20X5, MO had reserves of 220,000 units. The fair value of MO's net assets was considered to be the same as their carrying amounts at the date of acquisition. Summarised statements of financial position of the two entities at 31 December 20X6 are shown below:

	RA $'000	MO Unit'000
Investment in MO	350	–
Other assets	3,550	1,260
	3,900	1,260
Share capital ($1/Unit1 ordinary shares)	1,000	500
Reserves	1,900	460
	2,900	960
Liabilities	1,000	300
	3,900	1,260

Exchange rates:

1 January 20X5 $1:2.0 units

31 December 20X6 $1:2.5 units

RA elected to measure non-controlling interests in MO at their proportionate share of net assets at acquisition. Total cumulative exchange losses on goodwill as at 31 December 20X6 are $16,000. There has been no impairment of goodwill since acquisition.

What are consolidated reserves at 31 December 20X6? Give your answer to the nearest $.

$ _____

13.12 YH prepares its financial statements in dollars. YH acquired 80% of the equity share capital of OP on 1 January 20X3. OP operates in Country L, which has the ludd as its currency. OP sources the majority of its raw materials locally and is subject to local taxes and corporate regulations. The current workforce is recruited locally, although the majority of its sales are to customers in other countries. During the year OP secured a four-year term loan from a bank in L to fund its own capital investment requirements.

Which TWO of the following statements are true?

☐ OP is a subsidiary of YH and should therefore select the dollar as its functional currency because the entities are part of a group.

☐ The functional currency of OP will be determined by the currency that dominates the primary economic environment in which OP operates.

☐ The functional currency of OP will be the dollar as the majority of the sales revenue is generated outside of L.

☐ OP operates autonomously and raises its own finance which indicates that its functional currency should be ludd.

☐ OP must adopt the ludd as its presentational currency.

13.13 **Which THREE of the following statements regarding functional currency are correct?**

☐ A company can select any functional currency it chooses.

☐ The functional currency of a subsidiary is determined by its parent.

☐ If a subsidiary is autonomous, its functional currency will be its own local currency.

☐ If the level of intra-group transactions with a foreign subsidiary is high, this is an indicator that the functional currency of the subsidiary is the parent's currency.

☐ If the cash flows of a foreign subsidiary are sufficient to service its own debt, the functional currency of the subsidiary is likely to be the subsidiary's local currency.

☐ If the cash flows of a foreign subsidiary directly affect the cash flows of its parent, this implies that the functional currency of the subsidiary is the subsidiary's local currency.

13.14 AB owns 80% of CD. AB's functional currency and the presentation currency of the group accounts is the A$. CD's functional currency is the C$. AB acquired its shareholding in CD on 1 January 20X5 and is currently preparing its consolidated financial statements for the year ended 31 December 20X5.

CD's total comprehensive income for the year ended 31 December 20X5 was C$450,000.

AB elected to measure non-controlling interests in CD at fair value at acquisition. Goodwill was impaired by C$30,000 in the year ended 31 December 20X5. AB translates impairment of goodwill at the closing rate.

Exchange rates were as follows:

1 January 20X5	A$1:C$4
Average for the year ended 31 December 20X5	A$1:C$4.5
31 December 20X5	A$1:C$5

Exchange losses of A$25,000 and A$10,000 arose on translation of CD's net assets and goodwill respectively in the year ended 31 December 20X5.

What is the total comprehensive income attributable to non-controlling interests in CD for inclusion in the consolidated statement of profit or loss and other comprehensive income for the year ended 31 December 20X5? Give your answer to the nearest whole A$.

A$ ☐

13.15 PQ owns 75% of SW. The presentation currency of the group accounts is the A$. The functional currency of SW is the B$. PQ acquired its shareholding in SW on 1 January 20X9. PQ elected to measure the non-controlling interests in SW at their fair value of B$600,000 at acquisition. Goodwill of B$450,000 arose on acquisition of SW.

Translated post-acquisition reserves of SW (including exchange differences on translation of net assets) amount to A$260,000.

No impairment of goodwill has arisen since acquisition.

Exchange rates are as follows:

1 January 20X9	A$1:B$3
Average for the year ended 31 December 20X9	A$1:B$2.5
31 December 20X9	A$1:B$2

At what amount should non-controlling interests in SW be included in the consolidated statement of financial position of the PQ group as at 31 December 20X9? Give your answer to the nearest whole A$.

A$ [   ]

13.16 **Which THREE of the following foreign currency balances would be retranslated at the closing rate at the year end?**

☐ Loan
☐ Inventory
☐ Trade payable
☐ Property (held under the cost model)
☐ Cash
☐ Licence (held under the cost model)

13.17 The functional currency of NM is the A$. On 1 November 20X2, NM sold goods to an overseas customer for B$110,000 when the exchange rate was A$1:B$10. At the year end of 31 December 20X2, the full balance was still outstanding and the exchange rate had moved to A$1:B$11.

Which of the following is correct in respect of the exchange difference on the trade receivable in the financial statements of NM for the year ended 31 December 20X2?

○ Recognise an exchange gain of A$1,000 in profit or loss
○ Recognise an exchange loss of A$1,000 in profit or loss
○ Recognise an exchange gain of A$1,000 in other comprehensive income
○ Recognise an exchange loss of A$1,000 in other comprehensive income

13.18 The functional currency of VK is the A$. On 15 December 20X4, when the exchange rate was A$1:B$4, VK purchased goods from an overseas supplier for B$900,000. At the year end of 31 December 20X4, the full balance was still outstanding and the exchange rate was A$1:B$4.5. On 10 January 20X5, when the exchange rate was A$1:B$5, VK settled the balance in full.

What is the accounting entry required by VK on 10 January 20X5 in relation to the settlement of the trade payable?

○ Dr Trade payable A$200,000; Cr Cash A$180,000, Cr Profit or loss A$20,000

○ Dr Cash A$180,000, Dr Profit or loss A$20,000; Cr Trade payable A$200,000

○ Dr Trade payable A$225,000; Cr Cash A$180,000, Cr Profit or loss A$45,000

○ Dr Cash A$180,000, Cr Profit or loss A$45,000; Cr Trade payable A$225,000

13.19 The functional currency of LJ is the A$. On 1 January 20X0, LJ purchased some land in a foreign country for B$300,000 when the exchange rate was A$1:B$5. LJ holds its land under the revaluation model and revalues it every three years. On 31 December 20X2, the fair value of the land is B$450,000 and the exchange rate is A$:B$6.

What is the correct accounting treatment for the revaluation of the land on 31 December 20X2? Select the correct options from the pull down lists.

Amount of gain in A$:   Recognise gain in:

[   ] ←1   [   ] ←2

Pull down list 1:

15,000
25,000
30,000

Pull down list 2:

Profit or loss
Other comprehensive income

13.20 **Complete the following sentence by selecting the correct option from the relevant pull down list.**

Foreign transactions should initially be translated at the [   ] ←1 at the date of the transaction. At the year end all [   ] ←2 assets and liabilities should be retranslated at the [   ] ←1. Exchange differences must be recognised in [   ] ←3.

Pull down list 1:

spot rate
average rate
opening rate
closing rate

Pull down list 2:

current
non-current
monetary
non-monetary

Pull down list 3:

profit or loss
other comprehensive income

14 Consolidated statement of changes in equity

14.1 SP has a 75% subsidiary, AX, and a 30% associate, CR. In the year to 31 December 20X9 the companies paid the following dividends:

	$
SP	1,000,000
AX	400,000
CR	200,000

What total amount will appear in the consolidated statement of changes in equity of the SP group at 31 December 20X9 in respect of dividends paid?

○ $1,000,000

○ $1,100,000

○ $1,160,000

○ $1,400,000

14.2 P acquired 80% of S on 1 January 20X1. For the year ended 31 December 20X3, the total comprehensive income for P and S respectively was $200,000 and $100,000. During December 20X3, S sold goods to P for $15,000 at a margin of 20%. One-third of these goods had been sold to third parties by the year end.

What figures should be reported in the consolidated statement of changes in equity for total comprehensive income (TCI) attributable to the owners of the parent and to the non-controlling interests?

○ TCI for owners of parent   TCI for non-controlling interests
      $285,000 $20,000

○ TCI for owners of parent   TCI for non-controlling interests
      $277,600 $19,400

○ TCI for owners of parent   TCI for non-controlling interests
      $300,000 $20,000

○ TCI for owners of parent   TCI for non-controlling interests
      $278,400 $19,600

14.3 **Which THREE of the following would be presented as a separate line item in a consolidated statement of changes in equity?**

☐ A gain on revaluation of a property
☐ Profit for the year
☐ Issue of share capital
☐ Other comprehensive income for the year
☐ Total comprehensive income for the year
☐ Dividends

14.4 AA owns 80% of its subsidiary BB. In the year ended 31 December 20X4, AA issued 500,000 shares for $2.00 per share. The nominal value of each share is 50c.

How should this share issue be recorded in the consolidated statement of changes in equity of the AA group for the year ended 31 December 20X4?

○ As an increase to the equity attributable to the owners of the parent of $250,000

○ This is an intra-group transaction which cancels on consolidation so will not appear in the consolidated statement of changes in equity

○ As an increase to the equity attributable to the owners of the parent of $1,000,000

○ As a decrease of $800,000 to the equity attributable to the owners of the parent and of $200,000 to the non-controlling interests

14.5 BC acquired 90% of DE's 100,000 $1 shares on 1 January 20X4 when DE's reserves were $90,000. BC elected to measure non-controlling interests in DE at fair value at acquisition. The fair value of one share in DE on 1 January 20X4 was $2.20.

DE's total comprehensive income for the year ended 31 December 20X4 of the year was $25,000. DE paid dividends of $5,000 during the year.

Enter the figures required to complete the non-controlling interests column in the consolidated statement of changes in equity for the BC group for the year ended 31 December 20X4 (enter all numbers as positive and rounded to the nearest $).

EXTRACT FROM THE CONSOLIDATED STATEMENT OF CHANGES IN EQUITY OF THE BC GROUP FOR THE YEAR ENDED 31 DECEMBER 20X4

	Non-controlling interests $
Balance at 1 January 20X4	
Total comprehensive income for the year	
Less dividends paid	
Balance at 31 December 20X4	

14.6   P acquired 80% of S on 1 January 20X4 for $20 million when its retained earnings were $12.3 million.

P acquired 30% of A on 1 January 20X6 for $1.9 million when its retained earnings were $3 million.

During the year ended 31 December 20X7, S sold goods to P for $1,400,000, which had cost S $1,000,000. Three-quarters of these goods had been sold to third parties by the year end.

Equity at 31 December 20X7 of the three entities comprises:

	P $'000	S $'000	A $'000
Share capital	2,900	1,500	1,000
Retained earnings	78,200	38,500	16,000
	81,100	40,000	17,000

What is the equity attributable to the owners of the parent as at 31 December 20X7 for inclusion in the consolidated statement of changes in equity of the P group (in $'000)?

○ $102,980

○ $105,640

○ $105,860

○ $105,880

14.7   **Which THREE of the following statements about the consolidated statement of changes in equity are true?**

☐ It is only relevant to shareholders of the parent company.

☐ It is a primary statement required by IAS 1 *Presentation of Financial Statements*.

☐ The total comprehensive income for the year row comes from the ownership reconciliation in the consolidated statement of profit or loss and other comprehensive income.

☐ Subsidiaries must be excluded from the consolidated statement of changes in equity.

☐ Associates must have their own column in the consolidated statement of changes in equity.

☐ It reconciles equity from the prior year's consolidated statement of financial position to equity from the current year's consolidated statement of financial position.

14.8   LK acquired a 75% stake in SW several years ago when the reserves of SW were $350,000. The share capital and share premium of LK are $1,000,000 and $200,000 respectively.

Reserves of LK and SW on 1 January 20X5 stood at $4,500,000 and $500,000 respectively.

What is the equity attributable to the owners of the parent at 1 January 20X5 for inclusion in the consolidated statement of changes in equity of the LK group for the year ended 31 December 20X5? Show your answer to the nearest $.

$ ☐

14.9 Which of the following statements is true in relation to the dividends line in the consolidated statement of changes in equity?

- ○ It includes the group share of dividends received from subsidiaries and associates.
- ○ It includes dividends paid by the parent and dividends paid by the subsidiary to its external shareholders.
- ○ It includes dividends paid by the parent and dividends paid by the subsidiary to all of its shareholders.
- ○ It includes dividends paid by the parent and the group share of dividends paid by the subsidiary.

14.10 Which THREE of the following statements are correct in relation to the equity attributable to the owners of the parent year-end figure in the consolidated statement of changes in equity?

- ☐ It should include profit from intra-group trading on items left in inventory at the year end.
- ☐ It should include the share capital and share premium of the parent and the year-end consolidated reserves figure.
- ☐ It should come to the same figure as equity before non-controlling interests in the year-end consolidated statement of financial position.
- ☐ It can be calculated as the broughtdown equity attributable to the owners of the parent, plus total comprehensive income for the year attributable to the owners of the parent, less the parent's dividends paid plus any share issues by the parent in the year.
- ☐ It should include the share capital and share premium of the parent and its subsidiaries plus consolidated reserves at the year end.
- ☐ The non-controlling interests at the year end should be included in the equity attributable to the parent year-end figure.

14.11 Summarised statements of changes in equity for the year ended 31 March 20X8 for AA and its only subsidiary, BB, are shown below:

	AA	BB
	$'000	$'000
Balance at 1 April 20X7	662,300	143,700
Profit for the year	81,700	22,000
Dividends	(18,000)	(6,000)
Balance at 31 March 20X8	726,000	159,700

Notes

1. AA acquired 80% of the issued share capital of BB on 1 April 20X5, when BB's total equity was $107.7 million. The first dividend BB has paid since acquisition is the amount of $6 million shown in the summarised statement above. The profit for the year of $81.7 million of AA includes its share of the dividend paid by BB.

2. AA elected to measure non-controlling interests in BB at acquisition at their fair value of $24 million. There has been no impairment of goodwill since acquisition.

What is the non-controlling interests figure at 31 March 20X8 for inclusion in the consolidated statement of changes in equity of the AA group? Give your answer to the nearest $'000.

$'000 [   ]

14.12 Summarised statements of changes in equity for the year ended 31 December 20X9 for AB and its only subsidiary, CD, are shown below:

	AB Equity $	CD Equity $
Balance at 1 January 20X9	420,000	175,000
Total comprehensive income for the year	125,000	93,000
Dividends	(80,000)	(40,000)
Balance at 31 December 20X9	465,000	228,000

AB acquired 90% of CD's equity shares on 1 January 20X7 when CD had equity of $105,000.

AB has share capital of $200,000 and share premium of $65,000.

What is the equity attributable to the owners of the parent as at 1 January 20X9 for inclusion in the consolidated statement of changes in equity of the AB group for the year ended 31 December 20X9?

- ○ $483,000
- ○ $490,000
- ○ $577,500
- ○ $748,000

14.13 Summarised statements of changes in equity for the year ended 31 December 20X4 for EF and its only subsidiary, GH, are shown below:

	EF Equity $	GH Equity $
Balance at 1 January 20X4	670,000	240,000
Total comprehensive income for the year	200,000	80,000
Dividends	(150,000)	(60,000)
Balance at 31 December 20X4	720,000	260,000

EF acquired 80% of GH's equity shares on 1 January 20X3 when GH had equity of $170,000. EF elected to measure non-controlling interests in GH at fair value at acquisition. Since acquisition, there has been an impairment of $35,000 of the goodwill of GH.

In the year ended 31 December 20X4, GH sold goods to EF for $20,000 at a margin of 40%. Three-quarters of these goods were still in inventory at the year end.

AB has share capital of $1,000,000 and share premium of $300,000.

What is the equity attributable to the owners of the parent as at 31 December 20X4 for inclusion in the consolidated statement of changes in equity of the EF group for the year ended 31 December 20X4? Give your answer to nearest whole $.

$ [   ]

14.14 PQ has three subsidiaries. In the year ended 31 December 20X2, PQ issued 1 million $1 shares for $3.50 each.

What is the amount that should be included in relation to this share issue in the equity attributable to the owners of the parent column in the consolidated statement of changes in equity for the PQ group for the year ended 31 December 20X2?

- ○ $0
- ○ $1,000,000
- ○ $2,500,000
- ○ $3,500,000

14.15 On 1 January 20X2, JM acquired 60% of NV's 1 million $1 ordinary shares. NV is the only subsidiary of JM. On 1 January 20X2, NV had share premium of $200,000, retained earnings of $440,000 and a revaluation surplus of $90,000. JM elected to measure non-controlling interests in NV at the proportionate share of net assets at acquisition. There have been no impairment losses on goodwill.

At 1 January 20X3, there has been no change to NV's share capital and share premium. Its retained earnings and revaluation surplus stand at $510,000 and $100,000 respectively.

What is the equity attributable to non-controlling interests in NV at 1 January 20X3 for inclusion in the consolidated statement of changes in equity of the JM group for the year ended 31 December 20X3? Give your answer to the nearest whole $.

$ [   ]

14.16 On 1 January 20X0, RH acquired a 60% subsidiary, LM. At that date, LM had retained earnings of $880,000 and no other reserves. The fair value of LM's net assets was the same as their carrying amount, with the exception of a property that had a carrying amount of $150,000 and a fair value of $190,000, with a remaining useful life of ten years.

RH elected to measure non-controlling interests in LM at their fair value of $520,000 at acquisition. There has been no impairment of goodwill since acquisition.

In the year ended 31 December 20X4, LM sold goods to RH for $200,000, at a mark up of 25% on cost. A quarter of these goods are still in inventory at the year end.

At 31 December 20X4, LM has retained earnings of $1,760,000.

What is the equity attributable to non-controlling interests in LM at 31 December 20X4 for inclusion in the consolidated statement of changes in equity of the RH group for the year ended 31 December 20X4? Give your answer to the nearest whole $.

$ [   ]

14.17 On 1 January 20X4, PW acquired a 55% subsidiary, XZ. The total comprehensive income of XZ for the year ended 30 September 20X4 amounted to $1,200,000.

The fair value of the net assets of XZ at acquisition was the same as their carrying amount with the exception of inventory which had a fair value of $30,000 in excess of its carrying amount. This inventory was sold in August 20X4.

On 20 September 20X4, PW sold goods to XZ for $45,000 at a margin of 20%. All of these goods were still in inventory at the year end.

What is the total comprehensive income for the year attributable to the non-controlling interests of XZ for inclusion in the consolidated statement of changes in equity of the PW group for the year ended 30 September 20X4?

- ○ $540,000
- ○ $405,000
- ○ $391,500
- ○ $387,450

14.18 HM has owned its 70% subsidiary, BL, for a number of years. HM has no other subsidiaries. The following figures are relevant for the year ended 31 December 20X6:

	HM $	BL $
Profit for the year	650,000	235,000
Other comprehensive income for the year	30,000	15,000

HM elected to measure non-controlling interests at fair value at acquisition. An impairment in the goodwill of BL of $40,000 arose in the year ended 31 December 20X6.

There was no intra-group trading in the year and the fair value of BL's net assets at acquisition was the same as their carrying amount.

What is the total comprehensive income for the year attributable to the owners of the parent for inclusion in the consolidated statement of changes in equity of the HM group for the year ended 31 December 20X6?

- ○ $680,000
- ○ $815,000
- ○ $827,000
- ○ $855,000

14.19 **In a consolidated statement of changes in equity, which THREE of the following would be included in equity attributable to the owners of the parent?**

- ☐ Parent's share capital
- ☐ Parent's share premium
- ☐ Subsidiary's share capital
- ☐ Subsidiary's share premium
- ☐ Consolidated reserves
- ☐ Non-controlling interests

14.20 AV has an 85% subsidiary, CQ, which it has owned for a number of years. In the year ended 31 December 20X7, dividends disclosed in AV and CQ's statements of changes in equity amounted to $750,000 and $380,000 respectively.

What is the total amount that will appear in the dividends row in the consolidated statement of changes in equity of the AV group for the year ended 31 December 20X7?

○ $750,000

○ $807,000

○ $1,073,000

○ $1,130,000

15 Consolidated statement of cash flows

15.1 RN GROUP: CONSOLIDATED STATEMENT OF PROFIT OR LOSS AND OTHER COMPREHENSIVE INCOME (EXTRACT) FOR THE YEAR ENDED 31 DECEMBER 20X5

	$
Profit attributable to:	
Owners of the parent	295,000
Non-controlling interests	55,000
	350,000
Total comprehensive income attributable to:	
Owners of the parent	340,000
Non-controlling interests	60,000
	400,000

RN GROUP: CONSOLIDATED STATEMENT OF FINANCIAL POSITION (EXTRACT) AS AT 31 DECEMBER

	20X5	20X4
	$	$
Non-controlling interests	550,000	525,000

During the year ended 31 December 20X5, RN acquired a 75% interest in the equity shares of PD when the net assets of PD were $400,000. RN elected measure non-controlling interests in PD at the proportionate share of the subsidiary's net assets at acquisition.

What was the dividend paid to non-controlling interests in the year ended 31 December 20X5?

○ $135,000

○ $185,000

○ $35,000

○ $15,000

15.2 AB GROUP: CONSOLIDATED STATEMENT OF FINANCIAL POSITION (EXTRACT) AS AT 31 DECEMBER

	20X8	20X7
	$	$
Inventory	550,000	475,000
Trade receivables	943,000	800,000
Trade payables	620,000	530,000

AB GROUP: CONSOLIDATED STATEMENT OF PROFIT OR LOSS (EXTRACT) FOR THE YEAR ENDED 31 DECEMBER 20X8

	$
Profit before tax	775,000

During the year AB acquired an 80% interest in the equity share capital of CD. Extracts from the statement of financial position of CD at acquisition are as follows:

	$
Inventory	80,000
Trade receivables	110,000
Trade payables	70,000

Assume there is no depreciation, investment income or interest expense.

What is the cash generated from operations figure to appear in the consolidated statement of cash flows of the AB group for the year ended 31 December 20X8?

- ○ $647,000
- ○ $743,000
- ○ $767,000
- ○ $783,000

15.3 CONSOLIDATED STATEMENT OF PROFIT OR LOSS AND OTHER COMPREHENSIVE INCOME (EXTRACT) FOR THE YEAR ENDED 31 DECEMBER 20X2

	$
Profit before interest and tax	50,000
Share of profit of associate	10,000
Profit before tax	60,000
Income tax expense	(25,000)
Profit for the year	35,000
Other comprehensive income	
Gain on property revaluation	20,000
Share of associate's other comprehensive income	5,000
Total comprehensive income for the year	60,000

CONSOLIDATED STATEMENT OF FINANCIAL POSITION (EXTRACT) AS AT 31 DECEMBER

	20X8	20X7
	$	$
Investment in associate	116,600	107,900

What is the dividend received from the associate for inclusion in the consolidated statement of cash flows? Give your answer to the nearest whole $.

$ ☐

15.4 **What is the correct treatment of dividends paid to non-controlling interests in a group statement of cash flows?**

○ Include under the heading 'operating activities' or 'financing activities'

○ Include under the heading 'operating activities' only

○ Include under the heading 'financing activities' only

○ Dividends do not need to be disclosed in a statement of cash flows

15.5 BR acquired a 75% interest in the share capital of ED on 1 July 20X6. The property, plant and equipment of ED at that date was $500,000.

Extracts from the consolidated statement of financial position of BR as at 31 December are as follows:

	20X6	20X5
	$	$
Property, plant and equipment	4,100,000	3,700,000

Depreciation charged for the year ended 31 December 20X6 was $970,000.

What is the amount to be included in the consolidated statement of cash flows for additions to property, plant and equipment?

○ $870,000
○ $1,370,000
○ $995,000
○ $70,000

15.6 The following information appears in the consolidated statement of financial position of the QR group at 31 December 20X8:

	20X8	20X7
	$'000	$'000
Property, plant and equipment	720	515
Revaluation surplus	50	–

The depreciation charge for the year was $60,000. On 1 July 20X8 QR acquired a subsidiary which had property, plant and equipment of $90,000. There were no disposals of property, plant and equipment during the year.

What was the cash paid to acquire property, plant and equipment during the year ended 31 December 20X8?

○ $65,000
○ $125,000
○ $175,000
○ $215,000

15.7 $ 375,000

15.8 $ 120,000

15.9
- [ ] Dividends paid to non-controlling interests
- [ ] Profit on sale of property, plant and equipment
- [x] Cash paid to acquire an interest in an associate
- [x] Acquisition of equipment for cash
- [ ] Interest paid on borrowings
- [x] Dividends received from an associate

15.10 CONSOLIDATED STATEMENT OF PROFIT OR LOSS AND OTHER COMPREHENSIVE INCOME (EXTRACT) FOR THE YEAR ENDED 31 DECEMBER 20X2

	$
Group profit before tax	30,000
Tax	(10,000)
Profit for the year	20,000
Other comprehensive income	5,000
Total comprehensive income	25,000

Profit attributable to:

	$
Owners of the parent	14,000
Non-controlling interests	6,000
	20,000

Total comprehensive income attributable to:

	$
Owners of the parent	18,000
Non-controlling interests	7,000
	25,000

CONSOLIDATED STATEMENTS OF FINANCIAL POSITION (EXTRACTS) AS AT 31 DECEMBER

	20X2 $	20X1 $
Non-controlling interests	111,000	100,000

On 1 October 20X2, a new 75% subsidiary was acquired. The parent company elected to measure non-controlling interests in the new subsidiary at their fair value of $8,000 at acquisition.

What is the amount of dividends paid to non-controlling interests for the year ended 31 December 20X2? Give your answer as a positive number to the nearest whole $.

$ ☐

15.11 EF acquires 100% of the issued share capital of WG or $500,000 in consideration, comprising $150,000 in cash and 100,000 $1 ordinary shares with a market value of $3.50 each.

At the date of acquisition WG has an overdraft of $80,000.

What are the amounts to be disclosed in investing activities in the consolidated statement of cash flows of EF in respect of the acquisition of WG?

○ $230,000 outflow in one line

○ $150,000 outflow and $80,000 outflow in two separate lines

○ $70,000 outflow in one line

○ $580,000 outflow in one line

15.12 SM acquired 75% of the ordinary shares in TR on 1 July 20X1 for $500,000. The net assets of TR on that date included the following:

	$
Cash and bank	15,000
Bank overdraft	(50,000)
Bank loan (repayable 20X9)	(300,000)

What will appear as the net cash outflow in respect of the acquisition of TR in the consolidated statement of cash flows of SM for the year ended 31 December 20X1?

○ $(465,000)

○ $(485,000)

○ $(535,000)

○ $(835,000)

15.13 BH has several subsidiaries and a 25% associate, WN. BH's investment in WN (as shown in its consolidated statement of financial position) was $490,000 at the beginning of the year and $550,000 at the end of the year.

The summarised statement of profit or loss and other comprehensive income of WN for the year is shown below:

	$'000
Profit from operations	510
Finance costs	(120)
Profit before tax	390
Income tax expense	(90)
Profit for the year	300
Other comprehensive income	100
Total comprehensive income	400

What amount should appear under dividends from associate in the consolidated cash flow statement for the year?

○ $15,000
○ $40,000
○ $62,500
○ $160,000

15.14 PY has a number of subsidiaries and joint ventures. Investments in joint ventures in the consolidated statement of financial position of the PY group amounted to $685,000 and $924,000 at 31 December 20X4 and 20X5 respectively.

The group share of joint ventures' profit and other comprehensive income for the year ended 31 December 20X5 were reported as $219,000 and $51,000 respectively.

PY paid $115,000 on 1 September 20X5 to acquire a new joint venture.

What is the amount of dividends received from joint ventures for inclusion in the consolidated statement of cash flows of the PY group for the year ended 31 December 20X5? Give your answer to the nearest whole $.

$ ☐

15.15 What is the correct treatment of dividends received from associates and joint ventures in a group statement of cash flows?

○ Include under the heading 'investing activities' only
○ Include under the heading 'operating activities' or 'investing activities'
○ Include under the heading 'investing activities' or 'financing activities'
○ Include under the heading 'operating activities' or 'financing activities'

15.16 On 10 December 20X4, MN acquired a new 80% subsidiary for $759,000. At that date, MN had a cash balance of $63,000 and an overdraft of $22,000.

What is the net cash flow on acquisition of the new subsidiary to be included in the consolidated statement of cash flows of the MN group for the year ended 31 December 20X4?

○ ($718,000)
○ ($726,200)
○ ($791,800)
○ ($800,000)

15.17 What is the correct treatment for the group share of the associate's profit in the consolidated statement of cash flows prepared under the indirect method?

○ Deduct it from the profit before tax figure in 'operating activities'
○ Add it to the profit before tax figure in 'operating activities'
○ Show it as a cash inflow in 'investing activities'
○ Show it as a cash outflow in 'investing activities'

15.18 The consolidated statements of financial position at 31 December 20X1 and 20X2 of the RP group include the following tax balances:

	20X1	20X2
	$	$
Current tax liability	800,000	1,000,000
Deferred tax liability	150,000	200,000

The consolidated statement of profit or loss and other comprehensive income of the RP group for the year ended 31 December 20X2 include the following items in relation to tax:

	20X2
	$
In profit or loss	
Current tax expense	400,000
Deferred tax expense	60,000
In other comprehensive income	
Deferred tax	30,000

In the year ended 31 December 20X2, RP acquired a new 90% subsidiary, GF. At the acquisition date, GF had a current tax liability of $70,000 and a deferred tax liability of $24,000.

What is the amount of tax paid that should be included in the consolidated statement of cash flows of the RP group for the year ended 31 December 20X2? Give your answer as a positive number to the nearest whole $.

$ ☐

15.19 The consolidated statement of financial position of the AB group includes inventory of $389,000 and $473,000 as at 31 December 20X2 and 20X3 respectively.

On 5 October 20X3, AB acquired a new 65% subsidiary, CD. At the acquisition date, CD had inventory of $56,000.

The AB group prepares its consolidated statement of cash flows under the indirect method.

How should the change in inventory in the year be reported in the consolidated statement of cash flows of the AB group for the year ended 31 December 20X3?

○ An inflow of $28,000
○ An outflow of $28,000
○ An inflow of $47,600
○ An outflow of $47,600

15.20 Goodwill in the consolidated statement of financial position of the EF group was $775,000 at 31 December 20X1 and $900,000 at 31 December 20X2.

On 1 September 20X2, EF acquired 80% of GH's equity shares by issuing 100,000 shares with a market value of $8.20 per share and paying cash of $300,000. At acquisition, the fair value of GH's net assets was $1 million.

EF elected to measure the non-controlling interests in GH at their fair value of $280,000 at acquisition.

The EF group prepares its consolidated statement of cash flows under the indirect method.

What is the impairment of goodwill that should be included as an adjustment to profit before tax in the consolidated statement of cash flows of the EF group for the year ended 31 December 20X2? Give your answer as a positive number to the nearest whole $.

$ ☐

16 Disclosure standards

16.1 Under IAS 24 *Related Party Disclosures* transactions between the reporting entity and certain other types of entities are excluded from the disclosure requirements.

Which of the following transactions would need to be disclosed under IAS 24? (Assume all are material.)

○ A loan from Midwest Bank secured against machinery
○ A collective wages agreement with the main trade union employees belong to
○ Sponsorship for an industrial training programme agreed with the Mid Eastern Training and Enterprise Council
○ Arrangements entered into by the production director of the reporting entity to provide a review of the production facilities of a company controlled by his wife – the service will be provided at a full commercial price

16.2 **Which TWO of the following aspects of a related party transaction must be disclosed under IAS 24 *Related Party Disclosures*?**

☐ The names of the related parties involved in transactions
☐ The details of the transaction and a description of the nature of the relationships between the parties
☐ The amount involved
☐ The date the transaction occurred
☐ Whether the transaction price was equivalent to market value

16.3 **Which THREE of the following would be related parties of WH?**

☐ A person with a controlling shareholding in the parent company of WH
☐ An entity in which the wife of the finance director of WH owns a controlling stake
☐ BK, which has joint control with WH over a joint venture
☐ WH's major customer who accounts for 80% of WH's revenue
☐ A subsidiary of one of WH's associates

16.4 **Which of the following would find related party disclosures the most useful?**

○ Directors
○ Shareholders of a large listed entity
○ Group companies
○ Employees

16.5 **Which THREE of the following would normally be treated as a related party of HJ in accordance with IAS 24 *Related Party Disclosures*?**

☐ KL – an entity in which the controlling shareholder of HJ has a 30% shareholding and significant influence
☐ MN – both HJ and MN are associates of the same parent company
☐ Mr Smith – the domestic partner of Ms Wilson who is a director of HJ
☐ WX – the defined benefit pension plan for the employees of HJ
☐ Ms Green – the secretary to the chief executive officer at HJ
☐ The trade union to which the majority of HJ's employees belong

16.6 **Which of the following would be regarded as a related party transaction of the entity NV?**

○ A close family member of the chief executive of NV purchased an asset from NV.
○ XYZ Bank loaned NV $100,000 on commercial loan terms.
○ The government of Country X awarded NV a grant of $25,000 to help fund a new production facility.
○ YU supplied 60% of NV's raw materials.

16.7 **Which THREE of the following items are related party transactions under IAS 24 *Related Party Disclosures*?**

☐ Purchase of inventory by a parent from an associate
☐ Sale of a company asset to the managing director of the reporting entity, at an externally agreed fair value
☐ Sale of an asset by Company A to an entity in which the wife of the managing director of Company A has a controlling interest
☐ Provision of venture capital by a venture capital company on the condition that the money will be repaid in 36 months
☐ Sale of goods at cost from one associate to another associate
☐ Purchases from a supplier which the entity uses for 75% of its purchases and receives a trade discount

16.8 **Which TWO of the following would be regarded as related parties of BS?**

☐ TX, a major customer of BS
☐ The chief executive officer of the BS board
☐ EF, an entity with which BS shares control of a joint venture
☐ CD, an entity in which the husband of the chief executive officer of the BS board has a controlling shareholding
☐ GH, BS's main banker

16.9 CB is an entity specialising in importing a wide range of non-food items and selling them to retailers. George is CB's chief executive officer and founder and owns 40% of CB's equity shares.

Which TWO of the following transactions should be disclosed in the financial statements of CB in accordance with IAS 24 *Related Party Disclosures*?

☐ CB's largest customer, XC, accounts for 35% of CB's revenue. XC has just completed negotiations with CB for a special 5% discount on all sales.

☐ During the accounting period, George purchased a property from CB for $500,000. CB had previously declared the property as surplus to its requirements and had valued it at $750,000.

☐ George's son, Arnold, is a director and controlling shareholder of a financial institution, FC. During the accounting period, FC advanced $2 million to CB as an unsecured loan at a favourable rate of interest.

☐ FG and CB are associates within the same group. During the current year, the parent, HI, required CB to sell goods to FG at cost.

☐ The finance director of CB is an executive director of LK. LK provided cleaning services to CB during the current accounting period.

16.10 AB has a subsidiary, CD and two associates, EF and GH. During the year ended 31 December 20X1, the following transactions took place:

- AB charged a management fee to each of CD, EF and GH.
- EF sold goods to GH at cost (EF's normal selling price is cost plus 20%).
- CD sold goods to AB at market value.

Which of the following should be disclosed in the financial statements of EF?

○ The management fee payable by EF to AB

○ The sale of goods by EF to GH

○ The sale of goods by CD to AB

○ The management fee payable by CD and GH to AB

16.11 **Which of the following statements about the earnings per share ratio is correct?**

○ All entities must disclose earnings per share in their financial statements.

○ Earnings per share represents the return on the investment for all capital providers.

○ Earnings per share is calculated as profit after tax divided by the total number of ordinary shares at the year end.

○ The denominator of the earnings per share ratio is the weighted average number of ordinary shares outstanding during the period.

16.12 On 1 April 20X7 MK made a bonus issue of 1 for 2 from retained earnings.

MK reported basic earnings per share for the year ended 31 December 20X6 of 26.5c per share.

What is the comparative figure for basic earnings per share for the year ended 31 December 20X6 for disclosure in the financial statements of MK for the year ended 31 December 20X7? Give your answer in cents to one decimal place.

☐ cents

16.13 The weighted average number of ordinary shares in issue for the year to 31 December 20X7 is 5,000,000.

Options to purchase 500,000 $1 ordinary shares at $2.80 per share were issued on 1 January 20X7. These options are exercisable between 1 January 20X9 and 31 December 20Y0. The average market value of each $1 ordinary share during the year ended 31 December 20X7 is $3.50.

What is the weighted average number of shares to be used in the calculation of diluted earnings per share for the year ended 31 December 20X7?

○ 4.9 million
○ 5.1 million
○ 5.4 million
○ 5.5 million

16.14 YZ had 80,000 shares in issue on 1 January 20X6 and made a 1 for 4 rights issue on 1 September 20X6 at $1.00 per share. The fair value before the rights issue was $1.50. Total earnings for 20X6 were $120,000.

What is YZ's basic earnings per share for the year to 31 December 20X6? (Give your answer in $ to two decimal places.)

$ [ ]

16.15 JKL is a listed entity preparing its financial statements to 31 December. The figures correctly used in the basic earnings per share calculation for the year ended 31 December 20X4 were:

- Earnings figure – $2,763,000
- Weighted average number of equity shares – 6,000,000 shares

On 1 January 20X4, JKL issued five-year convertible loan notes of $2,000,000. The liability element of the loan notes on 1 January 20X4 was $1,836,000 and the effective interest is 7%. The terms of conversion (which are at the option of the stockholder) are as follows:

For each $100 of loan notes:

- Conversion at 31 December 20X7: 105 shares
- Conversion at 31 December 20X8: 103 shares

JKL is subject to a corporate income tax rate of 30%.

What is the diluted earnings per share of JKL for the year ended 31 December 20X4?

○ 35.2c
○ 35.4c
○ 35.7c
○ 46.1c

16.16 The following figures relate to GF for the year ended 31 December 20X2:

	$
Profit before tax	1,000,000
Tax	200,000
Non-controlling interests in profit for the year	100,000
Preference dividend on non-cumulative irredeemable preference shares	20,000
Preference dividend on cumulative redeemable preference shares	8,000
Ordinary dividend	55,000

The weighted average number of shares was 1,278,376.

What is the basic earnings per share figure for GF for the year ended 31 December 20X2?

○ 62.5c
○ 54.8c
○ 53.2c
○ 48.9c

16.17 On 1 January 20X3, WB has 500,000 $1 ordinary shares. On 1 March 20X3, WB made a 1 for 5 rights issue at $5 a share. The market price of one ordinary share immediately before the exercise on 1 March 20X3 was $11.

During the year ended 31 December 20X3, WB made a profit for the year of $320,000. Dividends of $20,000 on non-cumulative irredeemable preference shares were paid on 31 December 20X3.

What is the basic earnings per share figure for WB for the year ended 31 December 20X3?

○ 50.7c
○ 54.1c
○ 50.0c
○ 51.1c

16.18 NAT, a listed entity, had 10 million $1 ordinary shares in issue on 1 January 20X3.

On 1 October 20X3, NAT issued 2 million $1 ordinary shares at their full market price of $7.60 per share.

NAT's profit for the year ended 31 December 20X3 was $8,200,000.

What is NAT's basic earnings per share of the year ended 31 December 20X3? Give your answer in cents to one decimal place.

[   ] cents

16.19 Throughout the year ended 31 December 20X9, CSA, a listed entity, had 3,000,000 $1 ordinary shares in issue.

The profit before tax of CSA for the year ended 31 December 20X9 was $1,040,000 and income tax for the year was $270,000.

On 1 January 20X9, CSA issued convertible loan stock. Assuming that the conversion was fully subscribed, there would be an increase of 2,400,000 ordinary shares in issue. The liability element of the loan stock is $4,000,000 and the effective interest is 7%.

CSA is subject to an income tax rate of 30%.

What is the diluted earnings per share for the year ended 31 December 20X9? Give your answer in cents to one decimal place.

[_____] cents

16.20 BN is a listed entity preparing its financial statements for the year ended 31 December 20X1.

Throughout the year, BN has 5,000,000 $1 shares in issue.

BN generated profit for the year of $3.8 million for the year ended 31 December 20X1.

On 1 January 20X1, the ordinary shareholders of BN held options to purchase 1,000,000 $1 ordinary shares at $3.10 per share. The options are exercisable between 31 December 20X2 and 31 December 20X4. No further options were issued in the year. The average market value of one $1 ordinary share of BN during the year ended 31 December 20X1 was $4.00.

What is the diluted earnings per share figure for BN for the year ended 31 December 20X1?

☐ 63.3c
☐ 75.8c
☐ 72.7c
☐ 76.0c

17 Integrated reporting and sustainability reporting

17.1 Which of the following statements best describes the purpose of sustainability reporting?

○ To ensure all companies calculate and report greenhouse gas emissions consistently
○ To enhance financial reporting with additional sustainability disclosures
○ To provide information to stakeholders on environmental, social and governance issues
○ To combine financial and non-financial information with a forward-looking perspective to help users understand the overall value of the business

17.2 Which of the following is a key objective of the International Sustainability Standards Board?

○ To meet the information needs of investors
○ To combine different strands of reporting (financial, management commentary, governance, sustainability reporting) into a coherent whole
○ To explain to providers of financial capital how an organisation creates value over time

○ To establish mandatory sustainability reporting standards

17.3 Which of the following best describes integrated reporting?

○ A combination of the primary financial statements and the accompanying notes to the accounts in a company's annual report

○ A process founded on integrated thinking resulting in a periodic report about value creation, preservation or erosion over time

○ The preparation of a social, environmental and economic report regarding an organisation's sustainability

○ The consideration by an organisation of the relationships between its various operating and functional units

17.4 Which TWO of following are features of integrated thinking?

☐ Considering the relationships between an entity's operational and functional units and its capitals

☐ Taking into account the views and opinions of all of an organisation's stakeholders

☐ Making decisions and taking actions that promote the creation, preservation or erosion of value over the short, medium and long term

☐ Combining the opinions of regulators, investors, companies, standard-setters, the accounting profession and non-government organisations

☐ Ensuring that executive and non-executive directors are consulted on key strategic business decisions

17.5 What is the purpose of the Integrated Reporting Framework?

○ To ensure that organisations follow a rules-based approach to integrated reporting

○ To establish guiding principles and content elements that govern the overall content of an integrated report, and to explain the fundamental concepts that underpin them.

○ To enable all stakeholders to make decisions from the content of an integrated report

○ To prescribe a fixed format for those organisations preparing an integrated report

17.6 Which THREE of the following are the fundamental concepts of the Integrated Reporting Framework?

☐ Connectivity of information
☐ Value creation, preservation or erosion
☐ Conciseness
☐ The capitals
☐ Materiality
☐ The process through which value is created, preserved or eroded

17.7 The **Integrated Reporting** Framework contains seven guiding principles.

Which THREE of the following are among those seven principles?

- ☐ Strategic focus and future orientation
- ☐ Integrated thinking
- ☐ Reliability and completeness
- ☐ Consistency and comparability
- ☐ Governance
- ☐ Transformation of capital

17.8 Under the Integrated Reporting Framework, which TWO of the follow metrics should be used to provide insight into an organisation's impact and influence on its intellectual capital?

- ☐ Return on capital employed (ROCE)
- ☐ Internal quality inspections
- ☐ Research and development spending
- ☐ CO_2 emissions
- ☐ Number of new products developed

17.9 'The active consideration by an organisation of the relationships between its various operating and functional units and the capitals that the organisation uses or affects.'

What is this a definition of?

- ○ Integrated thinking
- ○ Integrated reporting
- ○ The Integrated Reporting Framework
- ○ The International Integrated Reporting Council

17.10 The Integrated Reporting Framework defines six categories of capital.

Debt, equity and grants are examples of which type of capital?

- ○ Intellectual capital
- ○ Social and relationship capital
- ○ Manufactured capital
- ○ Financial capital

17.11 **Which THREE of the following are among the six capitals defined in the Integrated Reporting Framework?**

- ☐ Physical capital
- ☐ Operational capital
- ☐ Intellectual capital
- ☐ Human capital
- ☐ Environmental capital
- ☐ Natural capital

17.12 Which THREE of the following are examples of natural capital per the Integrated Reporting Framework?

- ☐ Air
- ☐ Water
- ☐ Buildings
- ☐ Intellectual property
- ☐ Biodiversity
- ☐ Shared norms

17.13 The Integrated Reporting Framework contains eight content elements.

Which THREE of the following are among those eight elements?

- ☐ Governance
- ☐ Risks and opportunities
- ☐ Availability, quality and affordability of the capitals
- ☐ The value creation process
- ☐ Strategy and resource allocation
- ☐ Connectivity of information

17.14 'To what extent has the organisation achieved its strategic objectives and what are its outcomes in terms of effects on the capitals?'

Which content element of an integrated report should answer this question?

- ○ Governance
- ○ Business mode
- ○ Outlook
- ○ Performance

17.15 What is the objective of IFRS S1 *General Requirements for Disclosure of Sustainability-related Financial Information*?

- ○ To require an entity to disclose information about its sustainability-related risks and opportunities that is useful to the primary users of general purpose financial reporting is making decisions relating to providing resources to the entity
- ○ To provide information about the governance processes, controls and procedures used to monitor and manage sustainability-related risks and opportunities
- ○ To identify, evaluate, prioritise and monitor sustainability-related risks and opportunities
- ○ To measure progress towards targets in relation to sustainability-related risks and opportunities

17.16 'The relationships in place within an entity and between an entity and its external stakeholders such as suppliers, customers, governments and the community in which the entity operates.'

This is the Integrated Reporting Framework definition of which type of capital?

- ○ Intellectual capital
- ○ Social and relationship capital

○ Human capital

○ Manufactured capital

17.17 **Which TWO of the following are examples of a climate-related transition risk?**

☐ A warehouse being damaged in a hurricane

☐ Product obsolescence due to customer preference for a more environmentally friendly product

☐ Closure of a production site to meet carbon emission targets set by national government

☐ Lack of availability of raw materials due to biodiversity loss

17.18 **Which of the following is a benefit of the Integrated Reporting Framework?**

○ The principles-based approach allows the report to be tailored to specific entities.

○ The rules-based approach encourages consistency of preparation between entities.

○ It is mandatory for all listed entities around the world.

○ It provides a prescribed format for entities to follow when preparing an integrated report.

17.19 **Which of the following is a limitation of the Integrated Reporting Framework?**

○ It gives no guidance as to the content of an integrated report.

○ It needs to be adapted for not-for-profit and public sector companies as it is primarily aimed at private sector for-profit companies.

○ It is very inflexible by requiring all entities to classify their capitals into six fixed categories.

○ It only focuses on creation of value over the short and medium term but not the long term.

17.20 **Which THREE of the following are benefits to an organisation of preparing an integrated report?**

☐ Improved co-operation between different departments

☐ A focus on verifiable backward-looking information rather than subjective forward-looking data

☐ A better understanding of the business as a result of improved internal processes

☐ Increased engagement of senior management in the long-term sustainability of the business

☐ An instant increase in profit as a direct result of preparing an integrated report

☐ A guaranteed positive response from all stakeholders

18 Working with financial statements I

18.1 ED has the following current assets and current liabilities:

	$
Receivables	158,000
Inventories	20,000
Short-term investments	18,000
Trade payables	61,000
Bank overdraft	64,000
Corporate income tax payable	10,000
Deposits received in advance	5,000

What is the acid test ratio of ED?

- ○ 1.13:1
- ○ 1.26:1
- ○ 1.35:1
- ○ 1.40:1

18.2 The table shows extracts from the financial statements of CD for the year ended 31 December 20X2.

Statement of financial position	$'000
Issued share capital	2,500
Retained earnings	1,050
	3,550
12% long term loan	1,000
	4,550

Statement of profit or loss	$'000
Profit before interest and tax	600
Less loan interest	(120)
Profit before tax	480

What is the return on capital employed of CD for the year ended 31 December 20X2?

- ○ 11%
- ○ 13%
- ○ 14%
- ○ 17%

18.3 PQ has an operating profit margin of 12% this year as compared to 11% last year.

Which of the following would be a possible reason for the improvement?

○ PQ reclassified some expenses from administrative expenses to cost of sales in the current year.

○ PQ changed its financing structure during the year and as a result had significant interest savings.

○ PQ uses the revaluation model for its property, plant and equipment. During the year, PQ recorded a significant increase in the carrying amount of its head office.

○ PQ moved to an out-of-town location where the rent and employment costs were less than in the previous year.

18.4 DT's quick ratio has fallen from 0.9:1 to 0.6:1.

Which of the following might explain this decline?

○ Credit control has been poor.

○ Inventory levels have fallen.

○ The allowance for receivables has been reduced.

○ The entity has purchased a property for cash.

18.5 Below are extracts from CD's statement of financial position at the end of 20X9:

	$
Current liabilities	50,000
Retained earnings	30,000
Revaluation surplus	20,000
Ordinary share capital	200,000
6% redeemable preference share capital	100,000
Non-current liabilities	475,000

What is CD's gearing ratio (calculated as [debt/(debt + equity)]) at the year end?

○ 71.4%

○ 75.8%

○ 69.7%

○ 74.2%

18.6 **Which TWO of the following are valid reasons why the inventory days of a company might increase from year to year?**

☐ A marketing decision to reduce selling prices

☐ Increased inventory obsolescence

☐ Slowdown in trading

☐ Seasonal fluctuations in sales orders

☐ Changing a key supplier

18.7 The following is an extract from the financial statements of WH for the year ended 31 December 20X7.

	20X7	20X6
	$000	$000
Statement of profit or loss		
Revenue	32,785	31,390
Gross profit	16,880	14,310
Profit for the year	3,300	2,700
Statement of financial position		
Current assets		
Inventory	430	445
Trade receivables	3,860	2,510
Cash	12	37
Current liabilities		
Trade payables	4,660	2,890
Bank overdraft	280	40

WH secured a new contract to supply goods to a large department store across a two year period from 1 August 20X7. WH normally offers wholesale customers 30 days' credit, but the department store would only agree to the contract on 90 days credit. The directors of WH agreed to this as they believed it was worth it to have their products placed with this department store. WH has an average 45 day credit from its suppliers. The bank overdraft is used to fund working capital and currently has a limit of $300,000.

Which TWO of the following are realistic conclusions about WH's liquidity?

☐ WH's liquidity has deteriorated year on year

☐ WH has a net current asset position in 20X7

☐ WH is funding working capital using a bank overdraft nearing its limit

☐ In 20X7, WH can afford to pay its current liabilities out of its current assets

☐ The new department store contract has had a positive impact on WH's liquidity

---

18.8 GH's current ratio was 1.4:1 in 20X9 compared with 1.2:1 in 20X8.

Which TWO of the following might explain the increase?

☐ GH paid its payables earlier than usual by making use of its bank overdraft facility.

☐ GH bought a lot of goods for cash just before the year end, and these remained in inventory.

☐ GH made an unusually large sale just before the year end.

☐ GH paid its payables earlier than usual, because it had a positive cash balance.

☐ GH negotiated longer credit terms with its suppliers in an effort to adhere to its overdraft limit.

18.9 The return of capital employed (ROCE) for JT has reduced from 22.6% to 14.4% in the year to 31 December 20X3.

Which THREE of the following independent options would be a valid reason for this reduction?

☐ Increase in the average interest rate payable on existing borrowings

☐ Increase in payroll costs due to staff bonuses

☐ Major investment in property, plant and equipment shortly before the year end

☐ A large tax bill accrued in the year end accounts

☐ A revaluation of property in the year resulting in a significant uplift in value

☐ Repayment of a long-term bond during the year

18.10 STATEMENT OF PROFIT OR LOSS OF Z (EXTRACT)
FOR THE YEAR ENDED 31 DECEMBER 20X3

	$m
Gross profit	320
Operating expenses	(184)
	136
Finance costs	(42)
Profit before tax	94

STATEMENT OF FINANCIAL POSITION (EXTRACT) OF Z AS AT 31 DECEMBER 20X3

	$m
Non-current liabilities	
Borrowings	310
Deferred tax	30
	340

What is the interest cover for Z for the year to 31 December 20X3? Give your answer to two decimal places.

☐

18.11 **Which THREE of the following statements about EBITDA are correct?**

☐ It is calculated as earnings before interest, tax, depreciation and amortisation.

☐ It is a measure of cash flows.

☐ It is useful in assessing an entity's performance.

☐ It reflects an entity's financial position.

☐ It equates to an entity's gross profit figure.

☐ It is a non-GAAP financial measure.

18.12 An electrical store and a cake shop both have the same mark-up on cost. However, the gross profit margin of the electrical store is significantly higher than that of the cake shop.

Which of the following is a possible reason for this?

○ The electrical store takes advantage of trade discounts for bulk buying.
○ The cake shop has a higher turnover of inventory than the electrical store.
○ The cake shop has a higher level of wastage of inventory than the electrical store.
○ The cake shop's revenue is increasing, while that of the electrical store is decreasing.

18.13 **Which THREE of the following are likely to result from the upwards revaluation of property, plant and equipment?**

☐ Return on capital employed will decrease.
☐ Gearing will increase.
☐ The current ratio will decrease.
☐ Net profit margin will decrease.
☐ Non-current asset turnover will decrease.
☐ Interest cover will increase.

18.14 YT enters into a non-cancellable contract to lease an asset from PK for a period of ten years. The asset has a fair value of $200,000.

What impact will YT's accounting entry at the inception of the lease have on the following ratios?

○ Decrease in return on capital employed; decrease in gearing
○ Decrease in return on capital employed; increase in gearing
○ Increase in return on capital employed; decrease in gearing
○ Increase in return on capital employed; increase in gearing

18.15 The following is an extract from the financial statements of RF for the year to 31 December 20X8:

	20X8 $m	20X7 $m
Equity and liabilities		
Share capital	600	400
Share premium	360	40
Other reserves	16	–
Retained earnings	980	1,320
Total equity	1,956	1,760
Non-current liabilities		
Long-term borrowings	420	400

Which THREE of the following statements about the changes in the capital structure of RF could be realistically concluded from the extract provided above?

☐ Gearing of RF has decreased due to the increase in total equity.

☐ RF must have made a loss in the year as retained earnings have fallen.

☐ RF must have secured additional long-term borrowings of $20 million.

☐ Shares were issued at a premium to nominal value.

☐ The only change in share capital has been a bonus issue on a 1 for 2 basis.

☐ RF may have paid a dividend to shareholders in 20X8.

18.16 The following is an extract from the statement of financial position of WR:

	$m
Equity	
Share capital ($1 shares)	30
Share premium	10
Revaluation surplus	20
Retained earnings	160
	220
Non-controlling interest	24
Total equity	244
Non-current liabilities	
Long-term borrowings	100
Redeemable preference shares	40
Deferred tax	16
Total non-current liabilities	156

What is the gearing ratio of WR (calculated as debt/equity)? Give your answer as a percentage to one decimal place.

☐ %

18.17 XX has the following working capital ratios:

	20X9	20X8
Current ratio	1.2	1.5
Receivables days	75 days	50 days
Payables days	30 days	45 days
Inventory days	42 days	35 days

Which of the following statements is correct?

○ XX's liquidity and working capital has improved in 20X9.

○ XX is receiving cash more quickly from customers in 20X9 than in 20X8.

○ XX is suffering from a worsening liquidity situation in 20X9.

○ XX is taking longer to pay suppliers in 20X9 than in 20X8.

18.18 AB prepares its financial statements in accordance with International Financial Reporting Standards and is listed on its local stock exchange. AB is considering the acquisition of overseas operations. Two geographical areas have been targeted, S-land and Y-land. Entity S operates in S-land and entity Y operates in Y-land. Each entity is listed on its local stock exchange and uses its local accounting standards.

The most recent financial statements of entities S and Y have been converted into AB's currency for ease of comparison. The financial indicators from these financial statements and those of AB are provided below.

	AB	S	Y
Revenue	$500m	$220m	$380m
Gross profit margin	27%	33%	17%
Operating profit margin	15%	11%	12%
Gearing	29%	60%	30%
Average rate of interest available to each entity in the last 12 months	7%	4%	9%

Which of the following statements is a realistic conclusion that could be drawn from the above information?

○ Y's management is less efficient at controlling administrative expenses than S's management.

○ Y's management appears to have secured better supplier discounts than either of the other two entities.

○ S is less likely to be benefiting from economies of scale.

○ S-land has a lower tax rate than Y-land.

18.19 X's asset turnover is very low compared with that of its main competitor.

Which of the following could be the reason for this?

○ X carries its non-current assets at historic cost, while its competitor carries them at current value.

○ X embarked on a major programme of capital investment towards the end of the previous year.

○ X has a smaller proportion of productive assets than its competitor.

○ X has recruited a number of additional production staff during the year.

18.20 UV is a national supermarket chain.

Which of the following would be most likely to result in an increase in UV's EBITDA?

○ Taking longer to pay its suppliers
○ Increasing the useful life of its non-current assets
○ Renegotiating its loans to pay a lower rate of interest
○ Requiring external IT contractors to take an extra two weeks' holiday

19 Working with financial statements II

19.1 The finance director of QR is worried about its current ratio, which she has calculated to be 0.75. She is considering a number of actions that she hopes will improve QR's current ratio.

Which of the following actions would increase QR's current ratio?

○ Offer a settlement discount to customers
○ Make a bonus issue of ordinary shares
○ Make a rights issue of ordinary shares
○ Sell current asset investments for their carrying amount

19.2 AB wishes to increase its return on capital employed.

Which of the following courses of action will help to achieve this in the short term?

○ An increase in revenue
○ A decrease in the level of dividends paid to equity shareholders
○ The issue of ordinary equity shares
○ An upward revaluation of land and buildings

19.3 VQ's working capital cycle has increased from 60 days in 20X1 to 80 days in 20X2. As a result, VQ has become heavily reliant on its overdraft which is shortly up for renewal. The chief executive of VQ would like to reduce its working capital cycle and overdraft to encourage the bank to renew its overdraft facility.

Which THREE of the following actions would be likely to reduce VQ's working capital cycle?

☐ Negotiating a longer credit term with customers
☐ Switching slow paying customers to cash only
☐ Taking advantage of settlement discounts offered by suppliers
☐ Introducing a just-in-time ordering system for inventory
☐ Sending final demands to very overdue customers
☐ Bulk purchasing inventory

19.4 RC has an acid test ratio of 0.4. It is planning two changes:

- Proposal 1: Offering a 2% early settlement discount to credit customers
- Proposal 2: Delaying payment to all trade payables by one extra month

What effect would each of these proposals have on the acid test ratio?

- ○ Proposal 1 increase ratio / Proposal 2 decrease ratio
- ○ Proposal 1 increase ratio / Proposal 2 increase ratio
- ○ Proposal 1 decrease ratio / Proposal 2 decrease ratio
- ○ Proposal 1 decrease ratio / Proposal 2 increase ratio

19.5 **Which THREE of the following are valid limitations of ratio analysis of published financial statements?**

- ☐ Published accounts are frequently unreliable as a result either of fraud or of error on the part of management.
- ☐ Published financial statements contain estimates such as depreciation.
- ☐ There are no prior year figures to compare to current year figures.
- ☐ Accounting policies may vary between companies, making comparisons difficult.
- ☐ The nature and character of a business may change over time, making strictly numerical comparisons misleading.
- ☐ The nature of the industry may be volatile making intercompany comparison within the industry misleading.

19.6 **Which of the following is most likely to increase an entity's working capital?**

- ○ Delaying payment to trade payables
- ○ Reducing the credit period given to customers
- ○ Purchasing inventory on credit
- ○ Paying a supplier and taking an early settlement discount

19.7 The following is an extract from the statement of cash flows of QW for the year ended 31 December 20X1:

	$m
Cash flows from operating activities	600
Cash flows from investing activities	(800)
Cash flows from financing activities	(200)
Net decrease in cash and cash equivalents	(400)
Cash and cash equivalents at the beginning of the period	100
Cash and cash equivalents at the end of the period	(300)

Based on the information provided, which of the following independent statements would be a realistic conclusion about the financial adaptability of QW for the year ended 31 December 20X1?

- ○ The failure of QW to raise long-term finance to fund its investing activities has resulted in a deterioration of QW's financial adaptability and liquidity.
- ○ QW must be in decline as there is a negative cash flow relating to investing activities.
- ○ The management of QW has shown competent stewardship of the entity's resources by relying on an overdraft to fund the excess outflow on investing activities not covered by the inflow from operating activities.
- ○ The working capital management of QW has deteriorated year on year.

19.8 An entity wishes to increase its return on capital employed (ROCE).

Which of the following courses of action will help to achieve this in the short term?

- ○ Increase sales
- ○ Restructure its long-term finance exchanging debt for equity
- ○ Issue ordinary shares
- ○ Revalue land and buildings upwards

19.9 An analyst is comparing the non-current asset turnover ratios of two listed businesses engaged in similar activities. The non-current asset turnover ratio of one entity is almost 50% higher than that of the other entity, and she concludes that the entity with the higher non-current asset turnover ratio is utilising its assets far more effectively.

Which THREE of the following suggest this conclusion might not be valid?

- ☐ One entity revalues its properties and the other entity holds its assets under the cost model.
- ☐ One entity buys its assets for cash and the other entity leases assets for the entirety of their useful life.
- ☐ One entity has assets nearing the end of their useful life whereas the other entity has recently acquired new assets.
- ☐ One entity depreciates its assets over a much shorter useful life than the other entity.
- ☐ One entity pays a higher rate of interest on their borrowings than the other.
- ☐ One entity has significantly higher gearing than the other.

19.10 An individual is considering acquiring a small shareholding in LP, an entity listed on the stock market. He has performed some limited analysis on the financial statements of LP but is concerned that its high gearing (mainly due to a new long-term loan) renders the entity a high risk investment.

Which THREE of the following options would be considered realistic next steps for the individual to take prior to investing?

☐ Request copies of the board minutes for the month that the new long-term loan finance was secured.

☐ Search online for articles on LP, particularly in the financial press, and review these articles to assess the market's view of the future of LP.

☐ Contact the chief financial officer and clarify whether the funds from the loan were invested in the business and likely to bring future increased profits.

☐ Review the narrative reports within the financial statements that give details of recent investment and related financing to assess if the business is undergoing expansion and likely to bring additional future returns.

☐ Review the financial report to establish the dividend per share paid over the last few years and to identify whether increased gearing has negatively impacted on investor returns.

☐ Request copies of forecasts to assess expected future performance.

19.11 GH has changed its accounting policy in the year and now revalues all of its property and depreciable plant.

Which THREE of the following ratios would be directly affected by this change in policy resulting in a lack of comparability of this year's ratio to that calculated last year?

☐ Gearing
☐ Return on capital employed
☐ Receivable days
☐ Current ratio
☐ Interest cover
☐ Quick ratio

19.12 The following is an extract from the statement of cash flows for LM for the year ended 31 December 20X9:

	$m
Cash flows from operating activities	2,150
Cash flows from investing activities	(4,200)
Cash flows from financing activities	2,000
Net cash flow in the year	(50)

Based on the information provided, which of the following independent statements would be a reasonable conclusion about the financial adaptability of LM for the year to 31 December 20X9?

○ The management of LM has failed to exercise competent stewardship of the entities resources since there is a net cash outflow despite generating cash inflow from operating activities.

○ LM must be in decline as there is a negative cash flow relating to investment activities.

○ LM's management has shown competent stewardship of the entity's resources by increasing long-term finance to partly fund investing activities.

○ LM must be insolvent at 31 December 20X9 because it has a net cash outflow for the year.

19.13 PR is a global mobile phone manufacturer which reports to its board by geographical area. An extract from PR's segment report is shown below:

	20X7	20X6	% growth in revenue
Revenue	$'000	$'000	
Europe	25,416	20,236	25.6
Asia	19,062	18,840	11.8
America	14,296	13,258	7.8
Middle East	8,736	5,582	56.5
	67,510	57,916	

	20X7	20X6
Operating profit margin	%	%
Europe	14.4	9.8
Asia	13.9	9.2
America	11.4	8.7
Middle East	10.5	11.5

Which THREE of the following statements would be reasonable conclusions about the performance of PR's segments?

- [ ] PR's largest segment has the best operating profit margin in 20X7.
- [ ] The largest revenue growth has been in the most profitable segment.
- [ ] Operating profit margin has improved year on year in all segments.
- [ ] The smallest revenue growth has been in the least profitable segment.
- [ ] PR's smallest segment has the worst operating profit margin in 20X7.
- [ ] The segment with the best operating profit margin in 20X6 has the worst operating profit margin in 20X7.

19.14 JK is a tuition provider in the professional education sector. When it was founded 30 years ago, it offered accountancy courses. 15 years ago, JK introduced law courses. In the current year, JK opened its School of Health offering new courses in nursing and dentistry.

JK reports to its board on the basis of its business activities (accountancy, law and health). The operating margins of the three segments in the current year were:

Segment	Operating margin
Accountancy	15%
Law	17%
Health	–8%

Which TWO of the following could explain why the health segment has a negative operating margin whereas the other segments have positive operating margins?

- [ ] Health is a new division, requiring start-up costs in its first year which could lead to a loss.
- [ ] The health division is likely to have a lower asset base than the other divisions.
- [ ] There is little competition in the health market.
- [ ] JK has large established clients in the accountancy and law markets but, in order to retain its business, offers these companies a lower price than to smaller firms and individual students.
- [ ] JK is offering heavily discounted prices for its nursing and dentistry courses to win market share.

19.15 **The question 'why did it happen?' refers to which type of analytics from the Gartner data analytics maturity model?**

- ◯ Descriptive
- ◯ Diagnostic
- ◯ Predictive
- ◯ Prescriptive

19.16 Which of the following statements analysing a company's gearing would qualify as 'prescriptive' according to Gartner's data analytics maturity model?

- ○ Gearing (debt/debt + equity) increased from 50% in 20X4 to 70% in 20X5.
- ○ The reason for the increase is gearing was a new bank loan taken out in 20X5.
- ○ Future funds raised should be equity finance rather than debt finance to avoid increasing gearing further.
- ○ A significant decline in profitability in 20X6 could result in the company not being able to service its debt finance.

19.17 'AB's receivable days increased from 70 days in 20X8 to 76 days in 20X9.'

Which type of analytics is this statement according to Gartner's data analytics maturity model?

- ○ Descriptive
- ○ Diagnostic
- ○ Predictive
- ○ Prescriptive

19.18 'CD's non-current asset turnover is likely to increase next year because it has just invested in new machinery which should make its production process more efficient.'

Which type of analytics is this statement according to Gartner's data analytics maturity model?

- ○ Descriptive
- ○ Diagnostic
- ○ Predictive
- ○ Prescriptive

19.19 'The decline in EF's gross margin from 20X0 to 20X1 was caused by introducing a trade discount on the sales price of goods to increase market share.'

Which type of analytics is this statement according to Gartner's data analytics maturity model?

- ○ Descriptive
- ○ Diagnostic
- ○ Predictive
- ○ Prescriptive

19.20 **Which THREE of the following would be valid limitations of comparing AB's and CD's operating profit margin?**

☐ The minimum wage is higher in C-land than B-land.

☐ B-land and C-land operate different tax regimes.

☐ The market rate of interest is much lower in B-land than C-land.

☐ C-land and B-land require the use of different national GAAPs.

☐ Import duties on parts are higher in C-land than B-land.

☐ The stock market in B-land is more liquid than the stock market in C-land.

Answers to objective test questions

1 Types and sources of long-term funds

1.1 The correct answers are:

- Bonds and shares are both securities which can be traded in the capital markets.
- The ability to sell bonds on the capital markets enhances their attractiveness to bondholders.
- Bondholders will normally be paid a fixed return known as the coupon rate.

It is **not correct** to say that either bondholders or shareholders have a right to cash payment. Shareholders receive a dividend only if the company decides to pay a dividend – there is no automatic right to a dividend payment.

It is also **incorrect** to say that bonds and shares will normally be redeemable at **any** point in time – most bonds are redeemable. The redemption date is fixed and is not changeable at the company's discretion.

1.2 The correct answer is: Ordinary shares carry voting rights and **entitlement** to any declared dividend. They are a **flexible** form of finance from the company's perspective.

There is no entitlement to a dividend but if a dividend is declared then ordinary shareholders **do** have an entitlement to receive their share in this dividend. A key attraction of equity finance is that a dividend does not have to be paid – this is risky to the shareholder but is flexible from the **company's perspective**.

1.3 The correct answer is: A negative loan covenant.

This limits the borrower's behaviour.

A positive covenant normally involves achieving something, such as maintaining a key ratio at a certain level. Charges secure a loan against a specific asset (fixed) or the assets in general (floating).

1.4 The correct answers are:

- Underwriters are paid a fee for guaranteeing that the bonds will be purchased.
- The company issuing the bonds reduces its reliance on bank lending.
- Interest costs are often lower than an equivalent bank loan because the bonds can be sold by investors.

The process of producing a prospectus and organising underwriting for a bond issue takes time – a bank loan is quicker to arrange.

Underwriters do not guarantee to the investors that the company can pay the interest on the bond, they simply guarantee to the company that the bonds will be purchased.

1.5 The correct answers are:

- They rank before ordinary shares in the event of liquidation.
- If the issuing entity makes higher profits than expected, the dividend will not rise.
- The issuing entity cannot claim tax relief on the dividends paid.

Preference shares do not have voting rights – only ordinary shares do.

Arrears on non-cumulative preference shares do not have to be paid because if the company is unable to make the dividend payment in a particular year, the dividend never has to be paid. However, if the dividends were cumulative, the missed dividend would have to be paid in future years once sufficient distributable reserves arise.

1.6 The correct answers are:

- Underwriters are paid a fee for guaranteeing that the shares will be purchased.
- There will be lower gearing.

The process of producing a prospectus and organising underwriting for a share issue takes time – a bank loan is quicker to arrange.

Interest cover is profit before interest and tax divided by the interest payable; neither are directly affected by a share issue in a project that will not deliver profits in the short term.

The most common type of share issue is an ordinary share issue and the ordinary shareholders are the owners of a company.

1.7 The correct answer is: Investors in preference shares require a **lower** level of return than ordinary shareholders because they face less **uncertainty** over the level of their return, and therefore face **less** risk.

Preference shareholders face less uncertainty over the level of return than ordinary shareholders because preference shareholders receive a fixed dividend every year whereas ordinary dividends are at the discretion of the directors. Preference shareholders are also paid before ordinary shareholders in the event of a liquidation. Therefore, they face less risk that ordinary shareholder and, as a result, require a lower level of return.

1.8 The correct answer is: A rights issue allows shareholders the right to ensure that their existing shareholding is not diluted.

A rights issue **is** normally at a discount to the existing market price to encourage shareholders to participate in it. **Any** entity, whether listed or not, can initiate a rights issue and it is open to **any** shareholders, whether institutional or not.

1.9 The correct answer is: They normally have a lower coupon rate than redeemable bonds.

As convertible bondholders have the potential additional benefit of the value of shares on conversion being higher than the redemption value of the bond, they typically have a lower coupon rate than redeemable bonds.

It is the bondholder rather than the issuing company who is entitled to choose between redemption and conversion at the end of the bond term.

Security may be offered by the issuing company.

Whilst a discount may be offered on issue, it does not have to be offered on issue. Bonds always issued at a large discount to their nominal value are known as 'deep discount' bonds.

1.10 The correct answer is: 1, 2, 3, 4

In the event of liquidation, the creditor hierarchy dictates the priority of claims. Debt finance is paid off before equity. This makes debt a safer investment than equity. This is why debt investors demand a lower rate of return than equity investors.

Loans with charges are secured on assets and are therefore less risky than trade payables that are unsecured.

1.11 The correct answer is: Higher issue price.

A **placing** involves selling to institutional shareholders who will negotiate a lower price at which they will buy the share.

A **placing** has lower issue costs because they will be no underwriting or advertising.

A placing is likely to be faster than an offer for sale.

Both an initial public offer and a placing will dilute the ownership, and therefore control, of existing shareholders.

1.12 The correct answer is: A rights issue is an offer to **existing** shareholders enabling them to buy more shares, usually at a price **lower than** the current market price, and in proportion to their existing shareholding.

A rights issue provides a way of raising new share capital by means of an offer to existing shareholders, inviting them to subscribe cash for new shares in proportion to their existing holdings.

1.13 The correct answer is: Reporting accountant

In a listing, the reporting accountant reviews a company's listing documents and reports on the company's readiness for listing. The sponsor acts as the lead advisor in an initial public offer (IPO). The bookrunner is the main underwriter for new share and debt issues. The lawyer typically performs legal due diligence, drafts the prospectus and provides legal opinions.

1.14 The correct answer is: Bondholders have the ability to sell the debt on the secondary markets.

Unlike bank loans, investors in conventional bonds have the ability to sell the debt on the secondary markets. They are often referred to as marketable securities.

Bonds may be secured by either a fixed charge on a specific asset or a floating charge on a group of assets. It is certainly not the case that bondholders will never require security.

The bondholders as providers of debt finance are not owners of the business. The ordinary shareholders who have voting rights are the owners of the business.

Investors in bonds face lower risk than investors in ordinary shares as they are first to be paid coupon interest before ordinary dividends. Also, upon liquidation of the issuer bondholders would get their initial investment returned before ordinary shareholder.

1.15 The correct answer is: The interest rate charged by the bank may be fixed, variable or capped.

A bank may charge interest on a loan that may be **fixed** (for the period of the loan), **variable** (set at a fixed percentage above the bank base lending rate) or **capped** (the bank guarantees a maximum rate of interest).

While bonds may be irredeemable, bank loans are always redeemable as banks require their customers to repay amounts borrowed (as well as paying interest on the outstanding balance).

Fixed rate IOUs are conventional bonds that are issued by companies. Interest on bank loans is not necessarily fixed.

Banks face **lower risk** than investors in ordinary shares as they are first to be paid loan interest before ordinary dividends. Also, upon liquidation of the company the bank would get its loan capital returned to it before ordinary shareholders.

1.16 The correct answers are:

- They carry a much lower rate of interest than conventional, fixed rate redeemable bonds.
- They are redeemable at a higher amount than the price at which they are issued.

One of the main attractions of deep discount bonds to investors is that there is a large capital gain offered by the bonds, which is the difference between the issue price and the redemption value. Therefore, deep discount bonds will carry a much lower rate of interest than other types of bond because of this gain offered on redemption.

Deep discount bonds are issued at a large discount to their nominal value but are redeemable at par or above par. Therefore, the redemption value will be higher than the issue price.

Convertible bonds are a different type of bond away from conventional and deep discount bonds because they give the bondholders the right (but not the obligation) to convert their bonds at a specified future date into new equity shares of the company, at a conversion rate that is also specified when the bonds are issued.

All bonds have a par or nominal value attached to them.

1.17 The correct answer is: The **primary** markets enable organisations to raise new finance by issuing new securities whereas **secondary** markets enable existing investors to sell their investments.

The financial markets serve two main purposes.

(a) As **primary markets** they enable organisations to **raise new finance** by issuing new shares or new bonds. In the UK a company must have public company status (be a publicly listed company, or plc) to be allowed to raise finance from the public on a capital market.

(b) As **secondary markets** they enable existing investors to **sell their investments**, should they wish to do so. The marketability of securities is a very important feature of the capital markets, because investors are more willing to buy stocks and shares if they know that they can sell them easily.

'Capital' and 'financial' markets are both more generic terms that cover both types of stock market; ie primary and secondary markets.

1.18 The correct answers are:

- It will improve the marketability of the shares.
- It is appropriate for a large private company whose shares are widely held.

By this method of obtaining a quotation, **no shares** are made available to the market, neither existing nor newly created shares; nevertheless, the stock market grants a quotation.

This will only happen where **shares** in a large private company are **already widely held**, so that a market can be seen to exist.

A company might want an **introduction** to obtain **greater marketability** for the shares because it enables holders of existing shares to trade their shares more easily to a wider pool of potential investors on the new market that the company has been introduced on to.

As no new shares are issued and therefore the company is receiving no new cash, an introduction will not need to be underwritten by an issuing house.

1.19 The correct answer is: Co-ordinates the overall initial public offer (IPO) process and advises the board of directors of the company

Generally it will be a financial institution such as an investment bank or large accountancy firm that will perform the role of sponsor.

The underwriter of the issue is referred to as the bookrunner. The bookrunner undertakes to raise finance for investors on behalf of the company. If the bookrunner is unable to find enough investors, it will hold some of the shares itself.

The reporting accountant will perform financial due diligence and provide tax advice for the issuing company in an IPO.

The role of the lawyer in an IPO is to perform legal due diligence, draft the prospectus and provide legal opinions.

1.20 The correct answer is: It could lead to a higher issue price and therefore could raise more capital for the company.

The other options are advantages of a placing rather than an IPO.

2 Cost of long-term funds

2.1 The correct answer is: 6.0%

An IRR approach should be used to calculate the cost of redeemable debt.

$$IRR = L + \left[\frac{NPV_L}{NPV_L - NPV_H} \times (H - L)\right]$$

$$IRR = 4 + \left[\frac{NPV@4\%}{NPV@4\% - NPV@7\%} \times (7 - 4)\right]$$

$$= 4 + \left[\frac{4.91}{4.91 - -2.54} \times 3\right]$$

$$= 4 + \left[\frac{4.91}{4.91 + 2.54} \times 3\right]$$

$$= 4 + 1.98$$

$$= 5.98\% \text{ to 2 decimal places; and } \mathbf{6.0\%} \text{ to 1 decimal place}$$

2.2 The correct answer is: 8%

The cost of equity is calculated as:

$$k_e = \frac{d_1}{P_0} + g$$

$$= \frac{20(1.04)}{530} + 0.04$$

$$= 0.079 \text{ or } 7.9\% \text{ (rounded to 8\% to the nearest whole percentage)}$$

2.3 The correct answer is: 14.9%

Cost of bonds:

$$k_d = \frac{i(1-t)}{P_0}$$

$$= \frac{11(1-0.40)}{100}$$

$$= 6.6\%$$

$$WACC = k_{eg}\left(\frac{V_E}{V_E + V_D}\right) + k_d(1-t)\left(\frac{V_D}{V_E + V_D}\right)$$

V_E = 80m × $1 = $80m   (Value of shares)

V_D = $30m   (11% bonds)

$$WACC = 18\left(\frac{80}{80+30}\right) + 6.6\left(\frac{30}{80+30}\right)$$

$$= 14.9\%$$

2.4 The correct answers are:

- $2 \times (1 - 0.25)$
- 128.8

The expected share price in five years is $4 \times 1.1^5 = \$6.44$ so 20 shares will be worth \$128.80. So conversion is likely to happen as the value of the shares (\$128.80) is higher than the redemption value (\$110).

The cost to the company will be an IRR calculation using the cost of the interest payments post-tax ($\$2 \times (1 - 0.25)$) and the likely cost of redemption which is \$128.80.

The par value of \$100 is not relevant because the bonds are redeemable at a 10% premium (\$110) not at par. However, the redemption value of \$110 is not relevant either because the value of the shares is higher. The amount of \$80 is an incorrect calculation of the value of shares on redemption (20 shares × \$4) because it has not taken into account the likely increase in share price between now and the redemption date in five years' time.

2.5 The correct answer is: 2.4%

The calculation for the cost of irredeemable debt is:

$$k_d = \frac{i(1-t)}{P_0}$$

$i = 4$

$(1 - t) = 0.75$

$P_0 = 125$

$$k_d = \frac{4 \times 0.75}{125}$$

$= 0.024$ or 2.4%

2.6 The correct answer is: 6.3%

The calculation for the yield to maturity for irredeemable bonds is:

$$\text{YTM} = \frac{i}{P_0} = \frac{6}{95} = 6.3\%$$

Tutorial note. The tax relief on the interest (at 25%) is only relevant to calculating the post-tax cost of debt to the company. The yield to maturity is the return on the bonds to the investor so the tax relief that the company receives on its interest payments is irrelevant to this calculation.

2.7 The correct answer is: 8.0%

$$k_{pref} = \frac{d}{P_0}$$

There is no growth in the dividend (and no tax relief) as preference shares pay a fixed dividend (here 6%).

$k_{pref} = 6/75 = 8.0\%$

If this company issued new preference shares today on these terms then they would cost 8.0%.

The other answers are obtained by using the nominal value as the share price and/or by applying tax relief; ie multiplying by $(1 - t)$.

2.8 The correct answer is: 15.5%

Using the formula:

$$k_e = \frac{d_1}{P_0} + g$$

g = 10% or 0.1

P_0 = 420 cents – 20 cents = 400 cents

d_1 = 20 cents × 1.1 = 22 cents

$$k_e = \frac{d_1}{P_0} + g$$

$$= \frac{22}{400} + 0.1$$

= 0.155 or **15.5%**

2.9 The correct answer is: 5.0%

The cost of debt is calculated using:

$$k_d = \frac{i(1-t)}{P_0}$$

i = 6

$(1 - t)$ = 0.75

P_0 = 90% of 100 = 90

$$k_d = \frac{6 \times 0.75}{90}$$

= 0.05 or 5%

2.10 The correct answer is: The weighted average cost of capital (WACC) is the **average cost** of the company's finance (equity, bonds, bank loans) weighted according to the proportion each element bears to the total pool of capital. The weighting is based on **market valuations**, current yields and costs after **tax**.

This is CIMA's official terminology and definition of WACC.

2.11 The correct answers are:

- LL cannot use its current WACC to appraise the new project because it carries a different business risk profile from the training industry it currently operates in.
- LL cannot use its current WACC to appraise the new project because the capital structure will change as a result of undertaking the new project, meaning the WACC will also change.

The WACC is often used as a discount rate when using net present value or internal rate of return calculations for investment appraisal. However, this is only appropriate if the following conditions are met:

- The capital structure is constant. If the capital structure changes, the weightings in the WACC will also change.
- The new investment does not carry a different business risk profile to the existing entity's operations.

- The new investment is marginal to the entity. If we are only looking at a small investment then we would not expect any of k_e or k_d or the WACC to change materially. If the investment is substantial it will usually cause these values to change.

Because the new project will be financed through a substantial share issue, the capital structure (and therefore the gearing level) will change. This means the current WACC is not appropriate as it does not reflect the new proportions of debt to equity.

LL is expanding into a new line of business which means the business risk of the service that it will offer will change. Therefore the return the investors expect will change in line with this change in risk. That means that the costs of finance will change making the current WACC inappropriate for use in LL.

2.12 The correct answer is: 9%

The conversion value would be $(10 \times \$8)^6 = \$107.10$.

This is greater than the par value of $100 and therefore the bonds would be converted.

Time		$	DF @ 8%	PV	DF@10%	PV
0	MV	(90)	1	(90)	1	(90)
1–5	Interest net of tax	5.60 (8 × (1 – 0.3))	3.993	22.36	3.791	21.23
0	Conversion value	107.10	0.681	72.94	0.621	66.51
				5.30		(2.26)

An IRR approach should be used to calculate the cost of redeemable debt.

$$IRR = L + \left[\frac{NPV_L}{NPV_L - NPV_H} \times (H - L)\right]$$

$$IRR = 8 + \left[\frac{NPV@8\%}{NPV@8\% - NPV@10\%} \times (10 - 8)\right]$$

$$= 8 + \left[\frac{5.3}{5.3 - -2.26} \times 2\right]$$

$$= 8 + 1.40$$

= 9.4% to 2 decimal places; and **9% to the nearest whole percentage.**

2.13 The correct answers are:
- $5(1 – 0.3)
- $95
- $110

$5(1 – 0.3) is the post-tax interest that AB will have to pay on the bond. The interest is of $5 calculated as 5% multiplied by the par value of $100. Interest is a tax-deductible expense so the interest will reduce the taxable profit and the tax paid by AB. Therefore, the 30% tax is deducted from the $5 interest.

$95 is the current market value of the bond. From the investor's perspective, this would be what they would pay for the bond now (remember that the return to the investor is the same as the cost to the company with the exception of the tax relief that the company receives on its interest payments). From the company's perspective, this would be what the investor would be prepared to pay them today.

$110 is the redemption value that the company must pay the bondholders at the end of the term. It is calculated as the $100 par value plus the 10% premium (10% × $100 = $10).

The other figures are incorrect because:

- $5 – this ignores the tax relief the company is granted on its interest payments.
- $100 – this is the par value and not a cash outflow or inflow to the company; if the company were to issue the bond today, they would receive $95 and on redemption, due to the 10% premium, the company must repay $110 not $100.
- $100(1 – 0.3) – as explained above, the par value is not relevant here and no tax relief is granted on the redemption amount, only the interest.

2.14 The correct answer is: 8.7%

$$IRR = L + \left[\frac{NPV_L}{NPV_L - NPV_H} \times (H - L) \right]$$

$$= 5 + \left[\frac{10.70}{10.70 - -3.71} \times (10 - 5) \right]$$

$$= 5 + \left[\frac{10.70}{10.70 + 3.71} \times 5 \right]$$

$$= 5 + \left[\frac{10.70}{14.41} \times 5 \right]$$

$$= 5 + 3.7$$

$$= 8.7\%$$

The other answers are incorrect for the following reasons:

- 5.7% – this would be the cost of irredeemable bonds and has been calculated using the formula:

$$\frac{i(1-t)}{P_0}$$

- 8.0% – this is the coupon which is the annual interest paid by the company but does not take into account the tax relief on interest at 25% nor the amount payable on redemption.
- 12.7% – here there has been an error in calculating $NPV_L - NPV_H$ as 10.70 – 3.71 (remember that two minus signs make a plus).

2.15 The correct answer is: –13.62

This is calculated as follows:

Time	0	1–6	6
Cash flow (in $)	(97)	7(1 – 0.3) = 4.9	110
Discount factor at 10%	1	4.355	0.564
Present value	(97)	21.34	62.04
Net present value	–13.62		

The other answers are incorrect because:

- –4.48 – this incorrectly ignores the tax relief on interest.
- –16.62 – this incorrectly uses par value instead of market value at time 0.
- –19.62 – this incorrectly ignores the $10 premium on redemption.

2.16 The correct answer is: 17%

This is calculated as follows:

$$g = r \times b$$
$$= 20\% \times 70\%$$
$$= 14\%$$

$$K_e = \frac{d_1}{P_0} + g$$

$$= \frac{10(1.14)}{350} + 0.14$$

$$= 17.3\% \text{ (rounded to 17\%)}$$

2.17 The correct answer is: 16.6%

This is calculated as follows:

$g = r \times b$

To calculate b, we can see in the statement of changes in equity that XY has a profit of $100,000. $40,000 (ie 40% of this profit) has been paid out of dividends; therefore $60,000 (ie 60% of this profit) is the balance that has been reinvested. So here, b = 60%.

$g = 25\% \times 60\% = 15\%$

Dividend per share = $\dfrac{\$40,000}{1,000,000 \text{ shares}}$ = 4 cents per share

$$k_e = \frac{d_1}{P_0} + g$$

$$= \frac{4(1.15)}{280} + 0.15$$

$$= 0.166 \text{ or } \mathbf{16.6\%}$$

The other answers are incorrect because:

- 11.6% – this has been calculated by incorrectly using the percentage of profits paid out as dividends (40%) as 'b' instead of the percentage of profits reinvested (60%) when calculating 'g'.
- 16.4% – this is incorrect because d_0 (4) rather than d_1 (4(1.15)) has been used in the dividend valuation model formula.
- 26.8% – this answer has incorrectly used the return on net assets of 25% as the growth rate of dividends in the dividend valuation model formula.

2.18 The correct answer is: 8.8%

$$g = \sqrt[7]{\left(\frac{90}{50}\right)} - 1 = 0.088 \text{ (or 8.8\%)}$$

2.19 The correct answer is: 12.5%

$$g = \sqrt[4]{\left(\frac{45}{35}\right)} - 1 = 0.065 \text{ (or 6.5\%)}$$

$$k_e = \frac{d_1}{P_0} + g = \frac{45(1.065)}{800} + 0.065 = 0.1249 \text{ or } \mathbf{12.5\%}$$

The other answers are incorrect for the following reasons:

6.0% – this answer has forgotten to add on g when calculating k_e.

12.1% – this has used d_0 rather than d_1 in calculating k_e.

12.2% – this answer has forgotten to deduct the dividend from the share price to obtain the ex-div share price (as the cum-div share price was given in the question but P_0 should be ex-div).

2.20 The correct answer is: 6%

Cost of debt for a bank loan:

$k_d = i(1 - t)$

$\quad = 8\% (1 - 0.25)$

$\quad = 6\%$

2.21 The correct answer is: The higher of the cash payable on redemption and the estimated future value of the shares

This is based on the assumption that the investor is likely to choose the most favourable option. If the bonds were redeemable rather than convertible, the final cash flow would simply be the amount of cash payable on redemption.

2.22 The correct answer is: 11.4%

$$\text{WACC} = k_{eg}\left(\frac{V_E}{V_E + V_D}\right) + k_d(1-t)\left(\frac{V_D}{V_E + V_D}\right)$$

$$= 14\left(\frac{100}{100 + 30 + 20}\right) + 7\left(\frac{30}{100 + 30 + 20}\right) + 5\left(\frac{20}{100 + 30 + 20}\right)$$

$= 9.3 + 1.4 + 0.7$

$= 11.4\%$

3 Revenue

3.1 The correct answer is: $8,500

Performance obligation	Standalone selling price	% of total	Transaction price allocated
	$		$
Goods	9,600	80%	8,000
Servicing	2,400	20%	2,000
Total	12,000		10,000

Revenue for December 20X5 = $8,000 + ($2,000 × ¼) = $8,500

Where servicing fees are included in the overall price of a product, the amounts relating to the two performance obligations (the goods and the servicing) must be separated ('unbundled') based on the standalone selling price for each element.

The performance obligation for the goods is satisfied at a point in time – on transfer of the goods on 1 December 20X5. Therefore, the $8,000 relating to the transfer of goods is all recognised as revenue in December 20X5.

The performance obligation for the services is satisfied over time – over the four-month servicing period (December 20X5–March 20X6). Therefore, revenue should be recognised over time with one month's worth of revenue recognised in December 20X5. This amounts to $500 ($2,000 × ¼). The combined revenue from the transfer of goods and services amounts to $8,500 ($8,000 + $500).

The other answers are incorrect because:

$9,600 is the standalone price of selling goods and ignores the fact that the combined services and goods bundle has been sold at a discount to standalone prices. It also fails to take into account revenue earned from services in December 20X5.

It would be incorrect to recognise the full $10,000 because it would imply that the company had earned revenue from four months of servicing when it has only completed one.

$10,200 is more revenue than the company will receive from its customer – it is based on an incorrect calculation on the standalone prices ($9,600 + ($2,400 × ¼)) which fails to take into account the discounted price offered to the customer on the combined services and goods bundle.

3.2 The correct answer is: Dr Cash $90,000; Cr Contract liability $90,000

Under IFRS 15 *Revenue from Contracts with Customers*, the sale of goods is not recorded until the performance obligation is satisfied. A performance obligation is satisfied when the entity transfers the promised goods to the customer. However, here the goods have not yet been despatched as at the 31 March 20X7 year end so no revenue should be recorded. Furthermore, another IFRS 15 criteria for revenue recognition is that it must be probable that the entity will collect the consideration; this has not yet been established at the March 20X7 year end as the credit checking has not yet been completed.

Therefore, the $90,000 cash received should be recorded as a contract liability in the statement of financial position. In the year ended 31 March 20X8, once the goods have been delivered, the amount will be transferred from the contract liability in the statement of financial position to revenue in the statement of profit or loss.

3.3 The correct answer is: $675,000

Under IFRS 15 *Revenue from Contracts with Customers* revenue is recognised as or when a performance obligation is satisfied. Here, the performance obligation is satisfied over time since control of the property is transferred to the customer as it is constructed. Therefore, revenue should be recognised on the basis of progress towards satisfaction of the performance obligation.

Input methods measure progress towards satisfaction on the basis of an entity's efforts or inputs (eg costs incurred). Therefore, the progress towards completion under the input method is calculated as:

$$= \frac{\text{Costs to date}}{\text{Total expected costs}} = \frac{600,000}{600,000 + 200,000} = 75\%$$

Revenue = Contract price of $900,000 × Progress towards satisfaction 75% = $675,000

The other answers are incorrect for the following reasons:

$540,000 – this would be the amount of revenue to recognise if AX had elected to measure progress towards satisfaction using an output method (on the basis of direct measurement of the value to the customer of the goods or services transferred).

$600,000 – this is simply the costs incurred to date rather than the proportion of revenue that represents progress towards satisfaction of the performance obligation.

$900,000 – it would be incorrect to recognise the full contract price as revenue since control has not passed to the customer in its entirety; it is only transferred as the property is constructed and construction is only part complete.

3.4 The correct answer is: Recognise a contract liability of $80,000.

IFRS 15 *Revenue from Contracts with Customers* requires revenue to be recognised as or when the performance obligation is satisfied. This occurs when the entity transfers a promised good or service to the customer. In this question, this occurs when FC performs the service from February to March 20X6 which is in the next accounting period. IFRS 15 Application Guidance specifies that if an advance payment is received for future goods and services and it is non-refundable, revenue should be recognised when future goods and services are provided. Therefore, no revenue should be recognised in the year ended 31 December 20X5. Instead, the cash received is recorded as a contract liability (Dr Cash $80,000; Cr Contract liability $80,000). In the following accounting period, as the service is performed, from February 20X6 to March 20X6, $40,000 ($80,000 × ½) will be transferred out of the contract liability into revenue (Dr Contract liability; Cr Revenue) each month.

3.5 The correct answer is: $60,000

The Application Guidance of IFRS 15 *Revenue from Contracts with Customers* outlines the required accounting treatment when goods are sold with a right of return. Revenue should only be recognised for the transferred products in the amount of consideration to which the entity expects to be entitled (ie revenue is not recognised for products expected to be returned). A refund liability should be recognised for products expected to be returned.

Therefore, SL should only recognise revenue in relation to the 60% of goods sold that are not expected to be returned – this results in revenue of $60,000 ($100,000 × 60%). For the remaining 40% that are expected to be returned, SL should recognise a refund liability of $40,000.

3.6 The correct answer is: $200

AB is the agent as it arranges for the holiday company to provide the holiday to the customer. Therefore, it should recognise revenue for the fee it earns from the transaction. As 95% of the transaction price is passed on to the holiday company, AB's fee is the remaining 5%. Therefore, AB should recognise revenue of $200 (5% × $4,000).

The holiday company is the principal as it is primarily responsible for providing the holiday to the company. It would recognise revenue for the full price of the holiday of $4,000 and record the $200 commission payable to the agent as an expense.

3.7 The correct answer is: Dr Trade receivables $28,590; Cr Revenue $28,590

This contract contains a significant financing component as the customer is paying in annual instalments. Therefore, the instalments must be discounted to their present value using the discount factor of 5% provided in the question. The present value is calculated as follows:

	$
1st instalment (no discounting as payable immediately)	10,000
2nd instalment (10,000 × 0.952)	9,520
3rd instalment (10,000 × 0.907)	9,070
Present value	**28,590**

Regarding the accounting entry, the revenue of $28,590 should be recognised in full in the year ended 31 December 20X5 as the performance obligation has been satisfied by delivering the goods to the customer. The other side of the double entry is to record a trade receivable because LP's right to consideration is unconditional (only the passage of time is required before payment is due). It would be incorrect to record a contract asset as a contract asset is only required when the right to consideration is conditional on something other than the passage of time. It would also be incorrect to record a contract liability rather than revenue as LP has satisfied its performance obligation.

3.8 The correct answer is: $5,047,000

This contract includes variable consideration. As there are more than two possible outcomes, the most appropriate method for measuring the transaction price is the probability-weighted expected value. This is calculated as follows:

	$
$5,000,000 × 5%	250,000
$5,020,000 × 15%	753,000
$5,040,000 × 20%	1,008,000
$5,060,000 × 60%	3,036,000
Probability-weighted expected value	**5,047,000**

The other answers are incorrect for the following reasons:

- $4,953,000 – this is the answer you would have reached if you incorrectly deducted $20,000 for each day the contract is completed early.

- $5,000,000 – this fails to take into account the variable element of the consideration.

- $5,060,000 – this is the most likely amount which is a possible method under IFRS 15 *Revenue from Contracts with Customers* but it would be more appropriate if there were only two possible outcomes rather than four.

3.9 The correct answer is: $5 million

Here MN cannot reasonably measure the outcome of the performance obligation but it expects to recover the costs incurred of $5 million in satisfying the performance obligation (as MN has invoiced the customer for $7 million and received this amount by the year end). IFRS 15 *Revenue from Contracts with Customers* requires revenue to be recognised to the extent of recoverable costs incurred. $5 million of costs have been incurred and as the customer has been invoiced for and paid $7 million, all of these costs can be deemed recoverable. Therefore revenue of $5 million should be recognised.

It is incorrect to recognise no revenue here as that would imply that no work had been done when MN has already spent two months constructing the tunnel. It is also incorrect to recognise the amount invoiced of $7 million as revenue as that would mean recording a profit of $2 million when it is uncertain if a profit will be made on this contract. Finally, recognising revenue of $100 million is incorrect as control is transferred as the performance obligation is satisfied (as the tunnel is constructed) rather than on the first day of the contract.

3.10 The correct answers are:

- A survey of performance completed to date
- Units delivered to the customer

Output methods recognise revenue on the basis of direct measurements of the value to the customer of goods or services transferred to date relative to the remaining goods or services promised under the contract.

The other options are all input methods as they would result in revenue being recognised on the basis of the entity's efforts or inputs to the satisfaction of a performance obligation.

3.11   The correct answer is: $33,000,000

This contract contains an element of variable consideration in the form of a 10% bonus that becomes payable if the extension is completed by 30 November 20X6. IFRS 15 *Revenue from Contracts with Customers* requires entities to use one of two methods depending on which one better predicts the amount of consideration to which the entity will be entitled. These two methods are:

- The expected value – more appropriate where there are a large number of contracts with similar characteristics or more than two possible outcomes (the question says that this method is not appropriate here); or
- The most likely amount – this is the single most likely amount in a range of possible consideration amounts and this may be an appropriate estimate if the contract has only two possible outcomes (for example, an entity either achieves a performance bonus or does not).

In this question, there are two possible outcomes, PL will receive a bonus of $3,000,000 (10% × $30,000,000) if the extension is completed by 30 November 20X6 or no bonus if it is completed after that date. As there is a 70% chance of the bonus being earned, the most likely amount of consideration will be the $30 million contract price plus the $3,000,000 bonus, resulting in a total transaction price of $33,000,000.

The other amounts are incorrect for the following reasons:

- $27,000,000 – this amount is arrived at by incorrectly deducting the bonus from the contract price rather than adding it to the contract price.
- $30,000,000 – this fails to take the bonus into account.
- $32,100,000 – this amount is the expected value [($33,000,000 × 70%) + ($30,000,000 × 30%)] but the question specified not to use this method.

3.12   The correct answer is: Recognise a provision under IAS 37 *Provisions, Contingent Liabilities and Contingent Assets* for the standard warranty and treat the additional warranty as a separate performance obligation under IFRS 15 *Revenue from Contracts with Customers*.

IFRS 15 requires a standard warranty providing assurance that a product will function as intended to be accounted for as a provision in accordance with IAS 37 *Provisions, Contingent Liabilities and Contingent Assets*. A provision and corresponding expense should be recognised for the expected repair costs under the 12-month standard warranty period.

IFRS 15 requires an additional warranty available to the customer at a cost to be treated as a separate performance obligation. Therefore, there are two potential separate performance obligations in these contracts – the sale of the boiler (revenue to be recognised on delivery of the boiler to the customer) and the promise to repair the boiler under the additional warranty period (revenue to be recognised over the period of the additional warranty).

3.13   The correct answer is: $165,000

As control is transferred to the customer as the asset is built, the performance obligation is satisfied over time and revenue should be recognised over time, based on progress towards complete satisfaction of the performance obligation. IFRS 15 *Revenue from Contracts with Customers* mentions input and output methods as appropriate methods of measuring progress towards satisfaction and HS wishes to use an output method. Output methods recognise revenue on the basis of direct measurements of the value to the customer of the goods or services transferred to date. In this contract, the value of work completed is $165,000 and, therefore, this is the most appropriate amount to recognise as revenue using an output method.

The other answers are incorrect for the following reasons:

- $120,000 – this is the amount of costs incurred to date which would be the basis of an input method, but the question states that HS wishes to use an output method.
- $130,000 – this is the amount that the customer has been invoiced and has subsequently paid to HS but it is not indicative of the value of work completed to date in this instance and is not an output method mentioned by IFRS 15.
- $180,000 – this has been calculated using an input method based on costs incurred as a proportion of total costs ($300,000 × $120,000/[$120,000 + $80,000]) but the question asks for progress towards satisfaction to be measured using an output method.

3.14 The correct answer is: Dr Contract asset $40,000; Cr Revenue $40,000

Here, NM has transferred the Product A goods before the customer pays and the right to consideration is conditional on something other than the passage of time; ie the delivery of the Product B goods too. Therefore, under IFRS 15 *Revenue from Contracts with Customers*, NM should recognise a contract asset for the $40,000 transaction price relating to Product A.

A trade receivable should not be recognised until the right to consideration is unconditional which will be once NM has transferred the Product B goods to the customer.

It would be incorrect to recognise revenue in relation to the Product B goods as at 31 December 20X8 because NM has not yet transferred these goods to the customer so the performance obligation has not yet been satisfied.

It would be incorrect to recognise a contract liability in relation to the Product B goods because a contract liability only arises if the customer pays consideration or the entity has a right to an amount of consideration that is unconditional before the entity transfers the goods or services to the customer. Neither is the case here because the customer has not paid and the consideration for the Product B goods is conditional on them being delivered to the customer.

3.15 The correct answers are:

- Recognise an asset of $600 for the right to recover returned coats from customers on settling the refund
- Recognise revenue of $13,500 and a refund liability of $1,500

When goods are sold on a sale or return basis, IFRS 15 *Revenue from Contracts with Customers* requires the entity to recognise revenue for the transferred products at the amount to which the entity expects to be entitled (for goods not expected to be returned), a refund liability and an asset for its right to recover products from customers on settling the refund liability.

Here, a returns level of 10% is anticipated. This equates to 5 coats (10% × 50 coats). Therefore, revenue should be recognised in relation to the 45 coats (90% × 50 coats) not expected to be returned. This amounts to $13,500 (45 coats × $300). A refund liability of $1,500 (5 coats × $300) should be recognised for the 5 coats expected to be returned.

Only $5,400 should be transferred to cost of sales in relation to the 45 coats not expected to be returned (45 coats × $120 cost). An asset of $600 (5 coats × $120) should be recognised for the right to recover from customers the 5 coats expected to be returned with a corresponding adjustment to cost of sales. The 'right to recover' asset is measured at the original cost of the coats expected to be returned because, even in the sale, they are capable of being sold at $150 (50% × $300) which is more than the $120 cost.

To assist your understanding, these are the required entries:

Debit	Cash (50 coats × $300)	$15,000	
Credit	Revenue (45 coats × $300)		$13,500
Credit	Refund liability (5 coats × $300)		$1,500

To recognise the sale of coats and the expectation that 10% will be returned

Debit	Asset (right to recover inventory) (5 coats × $120)	$600	
Debit	Cost of sales (45 coats × $120)	$5,400	
Credit	Inventory		$6,000

3.16 The correct answers are:

- Provide for expected costs to be incurred as a result of the standard warranty offered
- Recognise revenue of $380,250 and a contract liability of $9,750

This contract includes three elements: the machine, a 12-month warranty and access to training services.

The 12-month warranty is a standard warranty providing the customer with the assurance that the product will comply with agreed-upon specifications and will operate as promised for one year from the date of purchase. Therefore, the warranty should be accounted for in accordance with IAS 37 *Provisions, Contingent Liabilities and Contingent Assets* by recognising a provision for the expected costs to be incurred as a result of the warranty offered.

In the contract, the access to the training is not offered as a chargeable extra to the customer but is included within the machine sales contract. It therefore represents an additional promise. The customer can benefit from the machine without the training services, and could benefit from the training services alone if it already possessed the machine. Therefore, the promises to transfer the machine and training services are separately identifiable as they are not interdependent, one does not modify the other and the seller does not provide a service of integrating them. This means that there are two performance obligations – the provision of the machine and the provision of the training services. The transaction price of $390,000 is allocated between these two performance obligations on the basis of their standalone prices:

Performance obligation	Standalone selling price	% of total	Transaction price allocated
	$		$
Machine	390,000	97.5%	380,250
Training	4 days × 2,500 = 10,000	2.5%	9,750
Total	400,000		390,000

The only performance obligation to have been satisfied by the 31 December 20X5 year end is the transfer of the machine to the customer so only $380,250 of revenue should be recognised. The remaining $9,750 received by the customer should be recorded as a contract liability. In the following accounting period, as the training is performed, this contract liability will be transferred to revenue.

The accounting entry required on 31 December 20X5 is:

Debit	Cash	$390,000	
Credit	Revenue		$380,250
Credit	Contract liability		$9,750

No contract asset or trade receivable is required as the cash is received in full.

3.17 The correct answers are:

- UJ is the agent.
- UJ should recognise revenue of $160,000 for the year ended 31 December 20X8.

UJ is the agent for the individual sellers, indicated by the following facts:

- The seller is responsible for shipping and holds the goods so bears the inventory risk.
- The seller sets the price of an item.
- The seller is responsible for providing the goods.
- UJ receives consideration in the form of commission.

Therefore, in the year ended 31 December 20X8, UJ should recognise revenue in relation to its 8% commission on the $2,000,000 sales which amounts to $160,000 ($2,000,000 × 8%).

The entities that supply the unusual gifts (the individual sellers) are the principals and they will recognise the full amount of the sales price as revenue and the commission payable to UJ as an expense.

3.18 The correct answer is: Dr Contract liability $100,000; Cr Revenue $100,000

When GF receives the cash from its customer on 31 December 20X8, it has not yet satisfied its performance obligation as it has not yet transferred the goods to the customer. Therefore, no revenue can be recognised on this date. Instead, a contract liability is recognised:

Debit	Cash	$100,000	
Credit	Contract liability		$100,000

However, on 2 February 20X9, GF satisfies its performance obligation by transferring the goods to its customer so revenue should be recognised. Therefore, $100,000 is transferred out of the contract liability and is recorded as revenue:

Debit	Contract liability	$100,000	
Credit	Revenue		$100,000

3.19 The correct answer is: The customer has the significant risks and rewards of ownership of the asset.

The other three are all indicators that a performance obligation is satisfied over time rather than at a point in time.

Other indicators that a performance obligation is satisfied at a point in time include (but are not limited to):

- The entity has a **present right to payment** for the asset
- The customer has **legal title** to the asset
- The entity has **transferred physical possession** of the asset
- The customer has **accepted** the asset

3.20 The correct answer is: Dr Contract liability $50,000; Cr Revenue $50,000

On 31 December 20X4, when ZY receives $50,000 from its customer, ZY must recognise a contract liability rather than revenue as, given that the goods have not been delivered to the customer, ZY has not satisfied the performance obligation. The accounting entry in the year ended 31 December 20X4 would be Dr Cash $50,000; Cr Contract liability $50,000.

On 10 January 20X5, the performance obligation is now satisfied and revenue should be recognised. Therefore, $50,000 is transferred out of the contract liability account and recognised as revenue: Dr Contract liability $50,000; Cr Revenue $50,000.

4 Leases: Lessor accounting

4.1 The correct answer is: IFRS 16 *Leases* defines a lease as 'a contract, or part of a contract, that conveys **the right** to **use an asset** for **a period of time** in exchange for **consideration**.' (IFRS 16: Appendix A)

4.2 The correct answers are:

- RH has the right to control the use of the 12 railcars for the four-year period specified in the contract.
- The 12 railcars qualify as identified assets under IFRS 16 *Leases* for the four-year contract period.

A lease is defined by IFRS 16 as 'a contract, or part of a contract, that conveys the right to use an asset (the underlying asset) for a period of time in exchange for consideration' (IFRS 16: Appendix A). IFRS 16 specifies that a contract is or contains a lease if the contract conveys the right to control the use of the identified asset. This right to control is present if, throughout the period of use, an entity has the right to obtain substantially all of the economic benefits from the use of the identified asset and the right to direct the use of the asset.

In this scenario, RH has the right to control the 12 railcars for the four-year contract period because:

- RH has exclusive use of the railcars throughout the period of use, even when they are not being used to transport RH's goods which gives RH the right to obtain substantially all of the economic benefits for the four-year period; and
- RH makes the relevant decisions about how and for what purpose the railcars are used, when and where they will be used and which goods are transported by the railcars during the four-year period – this is evidence that RH has the right to direct the use of the railcars throughout the period of use.

The 12 railcars qualify as identified assets under IFRS 16 as they are specified in the contract and LM does not have substantive substitution rights through the period of use because substitution is only permitted when a railcar needs to be serviced or repaired.

The other answers are incorrect because:

- This is a lease as it meets the IFRS 16 definition of a lease as explained above.
- RH not LM has the right to direct the use of the 12 railcars for the four-year contract period.
- RH is the lessee (the entity obtaining the right to use the assets) and LM is the lessor (the entity providing the right to use the assets).

4.3 The correct answer is: ten years

IFRS 16 *Leases* defines the lease term as 'the **non-cancellable period** for which a lessee has the **right to use** an underlying **asset**, together with both:

(a) Periods covered by an **option to extend** the lease if the lessee is **reasonably certain to exercise** that option; and

(b) Periods covered by an **option to terminate** the lease if the lessee is **reasonably certain not to exercise** that option.' (IFRS 16: Appendix A)

Here, the non-cancellable period of the lease is seven years but the remaining three years where TY (the lessee) has the option to terminate the lease should be included because TY is reasonably certain not to exercise the termination option. Factors indicating that TY is unlikely to exercise the termination option include the significant costs that TY would incur on termination and the importance of the asset to TY's operations.

4.4 The correct answers are:

- The present value of lease payments is likely to cover the fair value of the plant at the inception of the lease.
- The plant would need to be modified to be used by another entity.
- There is an option to purchase the plant at significantly less than fair value in five years' time.

The fact that the lease term is not for the whole of the asset's economic life is an indicator of an operating lease, not a finance lease. A lease for substantially all of an asset's economic life would be an indicator that the lease was a finance lease.

The intention of the company not to keep the asset beyond the lease term is another indicator that it is an operating rather than finance lease.

The classification of this lease is not clear-cut as there are three indicators of a finance lease and two indicators of an operating lease.

4.5 The correct answers are:

- Derecognise the asset, record a lease receivable and then recognise finance income at a constant rate over the lease term.
- This is a finance lease because the risks and rewards of ownership are transferred to the lessee.

Indicators that this is a finance lease are:

- The asset is specialised.
- Legal title reverts to the lessee at the end of the lease term.
- The present value of lease payments amounts to at least substantially all of the fair value of the underlying asset.

BG is the lessor. Therefore, since the lessee (DF) has the risks and rewards under a finance lease, BG should derecognise the underlying asset and recognise a lease receivable. Finance income will then be recognised on the lease receivable over the lease term based on a pattern reflecting a constant periodic rate of return.

The other options are incorrect because option 2 is the lessor accounting treatment for an operating lease, option 3 relates to lessee accounting and option 5 wrongly concludes that this is an operating lease.

4.6 The correct answer is: Dr Accrued income $225,000; Cr Operating lease income $225,000

This is an operating lease because the lease term (ten years) is significantly less than the economic life of the asset (50 years) indicating that the risks and rewards remain with the lessor (LM). Therefore, the lessor (LM) should retain the asset in its statement of financial position and record the lease rentals as income in profit or loss on a straight-line basis over the lease term. As the first 12 months are rent free, LM will only receive nine lease instalments totalling $2.25 million (9 × $250,000) and these must be spread over the ten-year lease term at $225,000 ($2.25m/10 years) per annum. In the year ended 31 December 20X1, no cash is received, therefore the debit must go to accrued income in the statement of financial position.

The other answers are incorrect for the following reasons:

- Option 2 is incorrect because this is the accounting treatment for a finance lease in the lessor's books (derecognise the underlying asset and recognise a lease receivable).
- Option 3 is incorrect as regardless of whether cash is received, the lease rentals should be recognised as income on a straight-line basis over the lease term.
- Option 4 is incorrect because it represents the accounting treatment for the lessee (JK) rather than the lessor (LM).

4.7 The correct answer is: Under a finance lease, in the statement of financial position, the lessor should **derecognise the underlying asset** and record a **lease receivable**. In the statement of profit or loss, the lessor should record **finance income** allocated to each period of the lease **at a constant rate on the lease receivable**.

Under a finance lease, the lessee has substantially all the risks and rewards of ownership. Therefore, applying the concept of substance over form, the lessor should derecognise the underlying asset. Instead, the lessor should recognise a lease receivable for lease rentals owed by the lessee (discounted to present value) whilst the lessee records a corresponding lease liability (and right-of-use asset). Subsequently, the lessor recognises finance income on its lease receivable and the lessee recognises finance costs on its lease liability.

It is under an operating lease that a lessor recognises lease rentals as income in profit or loss on a straight-line basis over the lease term.

4.8 The correct answer is: $358,349

UV is the lessor. For a finance lease, when lessor accounting, the initial lease receivable is recorded at the present value of lease payments not received at the commencement date (including all instalments due after the commencement date and the guaranteed residual value) plus the present value of the unguaranteed residual value ($15,000 – $10,000 = $5,000 discounted). Therefore, the initial lease receivable on 1 January 20X1 is $432,405 ($421,200 + $7,470 + $3,735). The lessee's (XY's) initial lease liability, on the other hand, would only be for the present value of lease payments not paid at the commencement date (including all instalments due after the commencement date and the guaranteed residual value) and would exclude the unguaranteed residual value resulting in an amount of $428,670 ($421,200 + $7,470).

Subsequently, finance income is recognised on the lease receivable calculated using the interest rate implicit in the lease:

	$
Lease receivable at 1 January 20X1	432,405
Finance income (6% × 432,405)	25,944
Instalment received	(100,000)
Lease receivable at 31 December 20X1	358,349

The other options are incorrect for the following reasons:

- Option 1 is the lease receivable at 1 January 20X1 rather than 31 December 20X1.
- Option 3 incorrectly excludes the present value of the unguaranteed residual value from the initial lease receivable. This would be correct for the lease liability under lessee accounting but is incorrect for the lease receivable when lessor accounting.
- Option 4 incorrectly excludes the entire residual value from the initial lease receivable.

4.9 The correct answers are:

- No lease rental income should have been recognised in profit or loss for the year ended 31 December 20X8 as the lease was entered into on the last day of the accounting period.
- The $15 million deposit should have been recognised as deferred income in the statement of financial position as at 31 December 20X8.

This is an operating lease; therefore, AB retains the risks and rewards of ownership and the aircraft should remain in AB's statement of financial position. AB should recognise the lease rental on a straight-line basis over the lease term, ie $13 million per annum ([$15m + (5 × $10m)]/5 years). However, this should not be recognised until the next accounting period (year ending 31 December 20X9) as the lease only commenced on the last day of the current accounting period. No lease rental income should be recognised in the current accounting period meaning that AB will need to reverse the $56 million recorded in profit or loss. Instead, the deposit received of $15 million should be recognised as deferred income in the statement of financial position as it has not yet been earned.

Recognising a lease receivable at the present value of lease payments would not be appropriate as this is the accounting treatment for a finance lease.

4.10 The correct answers are:

- A greater proportion of finance income will be recognised in the earlier years of the lease.
- Finance income for the period is calculated at a constant periodic rate on the outstanding balance.

The interest rate implicit in the lease (also known as the internal rate of return) is required to calculate the finance income for the period. This rate is applied to the outstanding net investment in the lease balance each period to calculate the finance income for that period. As the instalments received reduce the net investment in the lease over time, finance income reduces over time so a greater proportion of finance income is charged in the earlier years of the lease.

4.11 The correct answer is: The lessor has substantially all the risks and rewards of ownership of the underlying asset.

An operating lease is defined by IFRS 16 *Leases* as 'a lease that does not transfer substantially all the risks and rewards incidental to ownership of an underlying asset'. This means that the lessor retains the risks and rewards.

4.12 The correct answers are:

- The lease term is for the major part of the underlying asset's economic life.
- The lease transfers ownership of the underlying asset to the lessee by the end of the lease term.

The other options are indicators of an operating lease.

4.13 The correct answer is: Dr Net investment in the lease $470,000; Cr Property, plant and equipment $450,000, Cr Profit or loss $20,000

Under a finance lease, the risks and rewards of ownership are substantially transferred to the lessee so the carrying amount of underlying asset is derecognised and a lease receivable known as 'the net investment in the lease' is recognised. The difference is recorded in profit or loss.

4.14 The correct answer is: $351,630

	$	$
Present value of lease payments not received at the commencement date:		
Annual instalments ($100,000 × 3.312)	331,200	
Residual value guarantee ($25,000 × 0.681)	17,025	
		348,225
Present value of unguaranteed residual value (($30,000 – $25,000) × 0.681)		3,405
Initial net investment in the lease		351,630

The other answers are incorrect for the following reasons:

- $348,225 – this incorrectly excludes the present value of the unguaranteed residual value.
- $419,730 – this incorrectly treats the instalments as if they were received in arrears rather than in advance.
- $451,630 – this incorrectly includes the first instalment received in advance on 1 January 20X1 but the initial net investment in the lease is only meant to include lease instalments not received at the commencement date.

4.15 The correct answer is: $176,000

This is calculated as:

	$
Present value of lease payments not received at the commencement date	150,000
Present value of unguaranteed residual value	26,000
Net investment in the lease at 1 January 20X1	176,000

Note. Initial direct costs incurred by the lessor as a result of entering into the lease are **included** in the initial measurement of the net investment in the lease. However, the interest rate implicit in the lease is defined in such a way that there is **no need** to add them separately. (IFRS 16: para. 68).

The other answers are incorrect for the following reasons:

- $150,000 – this incorrectly excludes the present value of the unguaranteed residual value.
- $170,000 – this incorrectly deducts the initial direct costs of $6,000.
- $182,000 – this incorrectly adds on the initial direct costs of $6,000.

4.16 The correct answer is: $29,889

	$
Net investment in the lease on 1 October 20X3 ($60,000 × 5.535 eight-year cumulative discount factor)	332,100
Finance income for the year ended 30 September 20X4 (9% × $332,100)	29,889

Note. The initial deposit of $5,000 is excluded from the initial net investment in the lease because it has already been received at the lease commencement date and the initial net investment in the lease should be measured at the present value of the lease payments not received at the commencement date.

The other answers are incorrect for the following reasons:

- $24,489 – this incorrectly deducts the first instalment before calculating finance income which is incorrect because the instalments are received in arrears so first interest falls due then an instalment is received.
- $24,939 – this is incorrect because the initial deposit has incorrectly been included in the initial net investment in the lease and the first instalment has been deducted before calculating finance income.
- $30,339 – this is incorrect because the initial deposit has incorrectly been included in the initial net investment in the lease.

4.17 The correct answer is: $78,076

The initial net investment in the lease is calculated as follows:

	$
Present value of lease payments not received at the commencement date (excluding the residual value guarantee) ($200,000 × 3.791 five-year cumulative discount factor) (exclude the first instalment as it is received in advance on the commencement date)	758,200
Present value of residual value ($40,000 × 0.564 six-year simple discount factor)	22,560
Net investment in the lease at 1 January 20X2	780,760

Note. The present value of the guaranteed and unguaranteed residual values could have been calculated separately but as both are included in the initial net investment in the lease, they have been calculated together to save time.

Finance income for the year ended 31 December 20X2 is then calculated as follows:

	$
Net investment in the lease on 1 January 20X2	780,760
Finance income for the year ended 31 December 20X2 (10% × $780,760)	78,076

Note. No instalment is deducted in 20X2 as the initial net investment in the lease already excludes the first instalment.

4.18 The correct answer is: Dr Net investment in the lease $85,000; Cr Finance income $85,000

When a lessor earns finance income, it increases the amount owed by the lessee, ie the lease receivable, which is known as the 'net investment in the lease'. As this is an asset, it is a debit balance which is increased with a debit. The corresponding entry to finance income is a credit because income is always recorded with a credit.

4.19 The correct answer is: Recognise operating lease income of $50,000

This is an operating lease as the lease term is significantly less than the economic life of the asset and the present value of lease payments is much lower than the fair value of the equipment. Therefore, RB should recognise the lease payments as income on a straight-line basis over the lease term; ie $50,000 per annum.

If this had been a finance lease the calculations would have been as follows:

	$
Net investment in the lease on 1 January 20X0 (lease receivable)	86,800
Finance income for the year ended 31 December 20X0 (10% × $86,800)	8,680
Instalment received on 31 December 20X0	(50,000)
Net investment in the lease at 31 December 20X0 (lease receivable)	45,480

4.20 The correct answer is: $9,200

The lease payments should be recognised as income on a straight-line basis in profit or loss:

$$= \frac{(\$9,600 \times 5) - \$2,000}{5 \text{ years}}$$

$= \$9,200$

5 Provisions, contingent liabilities and contingent assets

5.1 The correct answer is: CD was ordered by its local authority in October 20X1 to carry out an environmental cleanup in 20X2 following pollution from one of its factories.

The entity has a legal obligation to carry out the work at 31 December 20X1, imposed by the local authority – therefore it is acceptable to create a provision.

XY: The contract was for a feasibility study – there is no commitment to the reorganisation. Provisions should only be recognised when a legal/constructive obligation to transfer economic benefits as a result of past events exists. There is as yet no detailed plan for the reorganisation.

AB: The commitment was entered into after the year end therefore no provision should be established at 31 December 20X1.

FG: Provisions for future operating losses must not be set up at acquisition.

5.2 The correct answer is: $0

Under IAS 37, a provision should only be recognised when it is **probable** that an outflow embodying economic benefits will be required to settle the obligation. An outflow is only regarded as probable if the event is **more likely than not** to occur; ie it has **more than a 50%** chance of occurring. Here, as the percentage is less than 50%, the outflow is not probable so no provision should be made.

5.3 The correct answer is: $360,000

	$'000
Minor repairs (3m × 5%)	150
Major repairs (7m × 3%)	210
	360

5.4 The correct answers are:

- An entity should not recognise a contingent liability in the statement of financial position.
- If discounting is used the unwinding of the liability over time should be recognised as an interest expense.

A provision must be recognised when an entity has a present obligation (ie a legal or constructive obligation) as a result of a past event, it is probable that a transfer of economic benefits will be required to settle the obligation and a reliable estimate can be made of the amount of the obligation.

Note. A constructive obligation is where the event (which may be an action of the entity) creates valid expectations in other parties that the entity will discharge the obligation.

An entity should **not** recognise a contingent asset.

Note. Reimbursements should be recognised only when they are virtually certain.

An entity **must** discount a provision where it is material.

Entities are never allowed to 'build up' provisions. Either an obligating event exists and the provision is recognised in full, or no obligating event exists, meaning no provision can be recognised.

5.5 The correct answer is: A provision of $1 million and disclosure of the contingent asset.

IAS 37 states that a provision can be recognised if there is an obligation based on a past event, a probable outflow which can be reliably estimated, which is the case for the $1 million damages.

The contingent asset regarding the counterclaim should not be recognised in the financial statements unless the claim is virtually certain. This would not seem to be the case, as DE does not yet appear to even have started proceedings against CL. This should be disclosed in the notes to the financial statements as a contingent asset.

5.6 The correct answer is: $14,400

This contract has become onerous as the unavoidable costs of meeting the obligations under the contract exceed the economic benefits expected to be received under it. This is because the remaining lease rentals and the penalty for cancelling the contract both exceed potential lease rental income from subleasing the assets. Therefore, IAS 37 *Provisions, Contingent Liabilities and Contingent Assets* requires a provision to be recognised at the lower of the net cost of fulfilling the contract and any compensation or penalties arising from failure to fulfil it. The net cost of fulfilling the contract is calculated as follows:

	$
Remaining lease rentals payable (100 × $10 × 36 months)	36,000
Potential income from subleasing (100 × $6 × 36 months)	(21,600)
Net cost of fulfilling contract	14,400

As the amount of $14,400 is less than the penalty of $15,000 arising from failure to fulfil the contract, a provision must be made for $14,400.

Note. Only leases for which the underlying asset is of low value (as is the case for UV's telephone lease) or short-term leases which have been accounted for per the IFRS 16 *Leases* recognition exemptions and have become onerous fall within the scope of IAS 37. In other situations, IFRS 16 requires a lease liability to be recognised so no provision is required to reflect amounts that the lessee has an obligation to pay.

5.7 The correct answers are:

- Provisions should be made for constructive obligations (those arising from a company's pattern of past practice) as well as for obligations enforceable by law.
- Discounting must be used when estimating the amount of a provision if the effect is material.
- A restructuring provision may only be made when a company has a detailed plan for the restructuring and a firm intention to carry it out.

IAS 37 specifically excludes retraining and relocation of continuing staff from restructuring provisions. The provision for an onerous contract should be calculated at the lower of the cost of fulfilling the contract and penalties from failure to fulfil it. Contingent assets where an inflow of economic benefits is probable should be disclosed not recognised.

5.8 The correct answer is:

Legal action against DH	Legal action taken by DH
Make a provision	Disclose as a note

The legal action against DH is a potential provision. The filing of the action prior to the year end is the past event and as the legal advisers believe the liability will materialise, it can be concluded that there is a legal obligation and a probable outflow. The amount given of $700,000 implies a reliable estimate; therefore, all three criteria for a provision have been met.

The legal action taken by DH is a potential contingent asset. As the inflow is probable, it should be disclosed in a note to the accounts.

5.9 The correct answer is: 2 only

1. As the board decision had not been communicated to customers and employees there is assumed to be no legal or constructive obligation; therefore, no provision should be made.

2. As refunds have been made in the past to all customers, there is a valid expectation from customers that the refunds will be made; therefore, the amount should be provided for.

3. There is no present obligation to carry out the refurbishment; therefore, no provision should be made under IAS 37.

5.10 The correct answer is: Announces the main features of the restructuring plan to those who will be affected by it.

By announcing its plan to the affected parties, the entity has raised a valid expectation and an obligation is said to exist.

5.11 The correct answer is: A company enters into a contract to construct an asset on the customer's premises for a fixed price in the hope of winning further work. Total estimated costs of fulfilling the contract exceed the contract price.

This is an onerous contract as the costs of meeting the obligations under the contract exceed the economic benefits expected to be received under it. IAS 37 *Provisions, Contingent Liabilities and Contingent Assets* requires a provision to be made for the lower of the net cost of fulfilling the contract (expected costs of fulfilling the contract less the fixed contract price) and any compensation or penalties arising from failure to fulfil it (if, under the terms of the contract the company would be liable to pay a penalty for cancelling the contract).

The company is not obliged to incur the restructuring costs because it has not yet communicated the closure decision to those affected by it.

No provision should be made for the cost of installing the safety guards because no obligating event has yet occurred; ie the installation of safety guards. Furthermore, the company could avoid installing the safety guards by selling the machinery.

No provision can be made for the damages as the amount cannot be estimated reliably.

5.12 The correct answer is: $3.6 million

A provision should definitely be made as there is a probable outflow; ie it is more likely that not that CT will have to pay the claim (greater than a 50% chance).

Where there is a single outcome, as in this scenario, IAS 37 requires a provision to be made for the individual most likely outcome. Expected values are only used where the provision being measured involves a large population of items which is not the case here.

The answer of $2.7 million is reached by incorrectly multiplying the most likely outcome of $3.6 million by 75%. The answer of $0.9 million is reached by incorrectly multiplying $3.6 million by 25%.

5.13 The correct answer is: There is a probable outflow of economic benefit but the timing and amount is uncertain and so a contingent liability should be included in ER's financial statements at 31 December 20X3.

At the year end an assessment should be made regarding whether the company has any obligations. If these obligations are probable and can be reliably estimated, a provision is calculated; if they are probable but cannot be reliably estimated, a contingent liability is disclosed.

5.14 The correct answers are:

	Account reference	Amount in $
Debit	Machinery	272,400
Credit	Provision	272,400

As the costs will be incurred in five years' time, the time value of money is material and the provision must therefore be discounted: $400,000 × 0.681 = $272,400.

Instead of debiting expenses, the provision should be added to the asset which will then be depreciated through profit or loss ensuring that the costs match the revenue generated through use of the asset.

It would be incorrect to credit cash as GT has not yet made any payments to restore the machine.

5.15 The correct answer is: $1,000,000

The solicitors have indicated there is a 40% chance of UH winning the case and a 60% chance that it will lose. Therefore, there is a probable outflow because the event (paying damages) is more likely than not to occur (ie a greater than 50% chance). Where a single obligation is being measured (the damages payable as a result of the court case), IAS 37 *Provisions, Contingent Liabilities and Contingent Assets* requires a provision to be made for the most likely outcome. Therefore, here a provision should be made for $1 million.

A calculation using expected values [(40% × 0) + (60% × $1m)] would not be appropriate here as IAS 37 only requires this measurement approach to be applied where there is a large population of items (for example, goods sold under warranty).

5.16 The correct answer is: $900

This contract has become onerous as the unavoidable costs of meeting the obligations under the contract exceed the economic benefits expected to be received under it. This is because AB has no use for the asset and the remaining lease rentals and the penalty for cancelling the contract both exceed potential lease rental income from subleasing the asset. Therefore, IAS 37 *Provisions, Contingent Liabilities and Contingent Assets* requires a provision to be recognised at the lower of the net cost of fulfilling the contract and any compensation or penalties arising from failure to fulfil it. The net cost of fulfilling the contract is calculated as:

	$
Remaining lease rentals payable ($1,000 × 3 months)	3,000
Potential income from sub-letting ($600 × 3 months)	(1,800)
Net cost of fulfilling contract	1,200

As the compensation arising from failure to fulfil the contract of $900 ($300 × 3 months) is less than the net costs of fulfilling the contract of $1,200, a provision should be made for $900.

Note. Only short-term leases (as is the case for this lease) and leases for which the underlying asset is of low value which have been accounted for per the IFRS 16 *Leases* recognition exemptions and have become onerous fall within the scope of IAS 37. In other situations, IFRS 16 requires a lease liability to be recognised so no provision is required to reflect amounts that the lessee has an obligation to pay.

5.17 The correct answer is: To make the users of financial statements aware of the potential adverse impact on cash flows and profit

It is not the objective of accounting standards to maximise disclosures as this could lead to information overload for the users of financial statements, confusing them rather than assisting them. Instead, the objective of disclosures is to only include information that would be helpful to users of financial statements in making decisions.

It would not be very ethical if the motivation of directors in disclosing information in the financial statements were to prevent the auditors from conducting their audit properly.

A contingent liability could lead to a possible outflow, not inflow, on settlement.

5.18 The correct answers are:

- A brief description of its nature and an estimate of its financial effect
- An indication of the uncertainties relating to the amount or timing of any outflow
- The possibility of any reimbursements

There is no requirement to provide comparative information for contingent liabilities, nor to disclose the names of the parties involved in the transactions.

5.19 The correct answers are:

- The contingent asset relates to a court case regarding copyright infringement
- If CD wins the court case, lawyers estimate that damages of $150,000 will be awarded

IAS 37 requires a brief description of the nature of the contingent asset and, at the end of the reporting period, where practicable, an estimate of its financial effect. There is no requirement to disclose the percentage likelihood of the inflow occurring although the inflow must be probable for a contingent asset to exist. There is no requirement to disclose uncertainties nor a detailed description of the contingent asset.

5.20 The correct answer is: Dr Provision $100,000, Dr Profit or loss $20,000; Cr Cash $120,000

The provision is a liability and therefore a credit balance. On settlement, the provision must be reversed with a debit. There is no need to recognise the full $120,000 settled, as an expense of $100,000 was previously recognised in 20X4 when the original provision was created. Only the extra $20,000 paid needs to be recognised as an expense in profit or loss. Cash is an asset and therefore a debit balance. It is reduced by the amount paid with a credit entry.

6 Financial instruments

6.1 The correct answer is: These assets are remeasured to fair value and gains and losses are recognised in other comprehensive income.

Financial assets that are held **both** to **collect** the contractual cash flows **and to sell** are measured after initial recognition at fair value through other comprehensive income. Gains/losses recognised in OCI are reclassified to profit or loss on derecognition of the asset.

Financial assets that are held solely in order to collect the contractual cash flows associated with the asset, and not to sell, are measured at amortised cost.

Investments in equity instruments that are not held for trading can be measured subsequent to initial recognition at fair value through OCI if the investor irrevocably elects to do so at initial recognition. Gains/losses are not reclassified to profit or loss on derecognition of the asset.

All other financial assets are carried at fair value through profit or loss.

6.2 The correct answer is: The dividend payable will be included in ZX's finance cost as a period expense.

Financial instruments are recognised according to their substance, not their legal form. These redeemable preference shares have an obligation to pay cash; thus they must be classified as a liability, irrespective of the fact they are named shares and may have share certificates attached to them.

The dividend or cost attached to the share should be treated in the same way as the share itself. If the share is classified as a liability the dividends will be treated as finance costs in the SPLOCI not as a deduction from retained earnings.

6.3 The correct answer is: $20,073,690

	$
Fair value of net proceeds [(290,000 × $66) – 22,200]	19,117,800
Interest at 5%	955,890
	20,073,690

This is a financial liability because PP is the issuer of the bonds so has an obligation to repay the principal to the bondholder at the redemption date. Therefore, it should be initially recognised at its fair value (proceeds: 290,000 × $66 = $19,140,000) less transaction costs (issue costs of $22,200). Subsequently, it should be measured at amortised cost because it is not at fair value through profit or loss since the bonds are not held for short-term profit ('held for trading') nor are they a derivative.

6.4 The correct answer is: $27,450

This instrument is convertible debt, containing elements of debt (obligations to pay interest and repay the principal) and equity (the right to a share). Therefore, the proceeds need to be split into the component parts. The debt component is calculated as the present value of future cash flows (interest and principal) discounted at the market rate of non-convertible debt. The equity component is calculated as the residual (ie the proceeds less the debt component).

	$	$
Proceeds (1,500 bonds × $500 par value)		750,000
Financial liability component:		
Present value of interest ($750,000 × 5% × 1.808)	67,800	
Present value of principal ($750,000 × 0.873)	654,750	
		(722,550)
Equity component		27,450

6.5 The correct answer is: $311,000

Convertible debt must be split into its liability and equity component parts. The liability element (which is given here) is calculated as the present value of future cash flows (interest and capital), discounted at the market rate of non-convertible debt. The equity component is the residual (ie the proceeds less the liability component).

	$
Proceeds	4,000,000
Liability component (given)	(3,689,000)
Equity component (residual)	311,000

6.6 The correct answer is: Dr Finance costs $142,800; Cr Financial liability $142,800

	$
Net proceeds (6,000 – 120)	5,880,000
Finance costs (6% × 5,880)	352,800
Interest paid (3.5% × 6,000)	(210,000)
Balance at 31 December 20X3	6,022,800

The effective interest of $352,800 should have been recorded in profit or loss rather than the interest paid of $210,000. Therefore an extra $142,800 needs to be added to the finance costs and the financial liability needs to be increased by the same amount.

6.7 The correct answer is:

Heading	Statement of financial position	Statement of profit or loss and other comprehensive income	Statement of changes in equity
	Non-current liability	Finance cost	N/A
Amount (in $)	1,211,642	61,642	N/A

As these preference shares are redeemable and cumulative, they contain an obligation to repay the principal and to pay the dividends. Therefore they should be treated as a financial liability rather than equity. As the redemption date is not until 31 March 20Y8, the liability should be non-current. The classification of the dividends should be consistent with the classification of the shares themselves and therefore a finance cost should be recorded in profit or loss rather than a dividend in the statement of changes in equity. As the shares are not held for trading, the liability should be measured at amortised cost. It is the effective interest (which includes the dividend paid and part of the issue costs/premium on issue/premium on redemption) which should be recorded in profit or loss, rather than the dividend paid.

The other options in the question are incorrect for the following reasons:

- $1,250,000 – this is the amount payable on redemption ($1 million nominal value plus 25% premium) rather than the year end amortised cost.
- $1,190,000 – this is the amount that the financial liability should be initially measured at on 1 April 20X8 rather than the carrying amount at 31 March 20X9.
- $60,000 – these are the issue costs which should be deducted from the initial financial liability rather than recognised as an expense in profit or loss.
- $40,000 – this is the amount of dividends paid but the amount that should be recognised in profit or loss is the effective interest of 5.18% applied to the outstanding liability. The accounting entry for the dividends paid is: Dr Financial liability $40,000; Cr Cash $40,000, so there is no profit or loss effect.

6.8 The correct answer is: Gain to OCI $9,856.

The investment should be measured initially at fair value plus transaction costs. Subsequent measurement is at fair value through other comprehensive income as AP has made the irrevocable election, permitted in IFRS 9, to measure investments in equity instruments that are not held for trading in this way.

Initial measurement at 1.1.X2

	$
Fair value (40,000 × $2.12)	84,800
Transaction costs (3% × $84,800)	2,544
	87,344

Remeasurement gain at 31.3.X2

	$
Fair value (40,000 × $2.43)	97,200
Previous carrying amount	(87,344)
	9,856

It would be incorrect to expense the transaction costs as IFRS 9 *Financial Instuments* requires them to be added to the financial asset rather than expensed (unless the financial asset is classified as at fair value through profit or loss which is not the case here). It would also be incorrect to recognise the remeasurement gains in profit or loss as, on initial recognition, AP made the irrevocable election to present changes in fair value in other comprehensive income. The amount of $12,400 is incorrect because it is based on the investment initially measured at its fair value ($84,800) rather than its fair value plus transaction costs ($87,344).

6.9 The correct answers are:

Initial measurement	Subsequent measurement
Fair value plus transaction costs	Fair value through other comprehensive income

PZ intends to hold this investment for the long term; therefore, the investment is not held for trading. PZ's policy is to take gains and losses to other comprehensive income (OCI) wherever this is permitted by IFRS. As such, on initial recognition, PZ would make the irrevocable election to present changes in fair value of the investment in OCI as permitted by IFRS 9. As the investment is classified as measured subsequently through OCI, the investment should be recognised initially at fair value plus transaction costs.

A financial asset may only be subsequently measured at amortised cost if the entity's business model were to collect contractual cash flows comprising solely payments of principal and interest. This is not the case here as this is an investment in equity instruments rather than an investment in debt instruments.

6.10 The correct answers are:

Initial measurement	Subsequent measurement
Fair value	Fair value through profit or loss

The fact that BX intends to realise the investment within a few months means that it is held for trading and the option to elect to measure the investment at fair value through other comprehensive income is not available. The investment must be recognised initially at fair value (transaction costs are expensed) and then subsequently measured at fair value through profit or loss.

A financial asset may only be subsequently measured at amortised cost if the entity's business model were to collect contractual cash flows comprising solely payments of principal and interest. This is not the case here as this is an investment in equity instruments rather than an investment in debt instruments.

6.11 The correct answers are:

Liability

	$
Opening balance	3,800,000
Plus finance cost	319,200
Less interest paid	(X)
Closing balance	X

Transaction costs are deducted from the initial nominal value of a debt instrument ($4,000,000 – $200,000).

The finance costs are calculated at the effective interest rate on the opening balance ($3,800,000 × 8.4%).

6.12 The correct answer is: $22,842

Convertible debt must be split into its liability and equity component parts. The liability element is calculated as the present value of future cash flows (interest and capital), discounted at the market rate of non-convertible debt. The equity component is the residual (ie the proceeds less the liability component).

	$	$
Proceeds (3,000 bonds × $100 par value)		300,000
Liability component:		
Present value of interest ($300,000 × 6% × 2.531)	45,558	
Present value of principal ($300,000 × 0.772)	231,600	
		(277,158)
Equity component (residual)		22,842

6.13 The correct answer is: Dr Investment $2,020,000; Cr Bank $2,020,000

Under IFRS 9's business model approach, the instrument is measured initially at its fair value (the amount paid to purchase the debt instrument of $2,000,000) plus transaction costs ($20,000). Transaction costs are only recognised as an expense if the financial asset is classified as at fair value through profit or loss. This is not the case here because EM intends to hold the investment to maturity to collect the contractual cash flows which are solely principal and interest, rather than to make short-term profit. At each subsequent year end, the investment in the debt instrument will be measured at amortised cost.

It would be incorrect to deduct the transaction costs from the investment. Transaction costs are deducted from financial liabilities (unless they are at fair value through profit or loss). Therefore, the issuer of the debt instrument (rather than the purchaser) should recognise a financial liability and deduct any transaction costs incurred.

6.14 The correct answer is: A financial liability is any liability that is a contractual **obligation** to deliver **cash**, or a financial asset to another entity, or to exchange financial assets or liabilities under potentially **unfavourable** conditions.

This definition comes from IAS 32 *Financial Instruments: Presentation*.

6.15 The correct answer is: Dr Financial asset $7,000; Cr Profit or loss $7,000

This futures contract is a speculative derivative and therefore is categorised as measured at fair value through profit or loss.

Its classification at 31 December 20X6 depends on whether it is standing at a gain (a financial asset) or a loss (a financial liability).

The fair value of a derivative is calculated by comparing the agreed rate in the contract to the equivalent market rate for a contract settling at the same date. Therefore, at the commitment date (here 30 September 20X6), most derivatives have a fair value of zero because the rate agreed by the entity in the contract is the market rate at that date. However, at the year end, the market rate has moved; therefore the derivative will be standing at a gain or loss which will be the fair value of the financial asset or financial liability.

	$
At year end rate (100 ounces × $1,370)	137,000
At MC's agreed forward rate (100 ounces × $1,300)	(130,000)
Gain = financial asset	7,000

This futures contract is standing at a gain because, under MC's contract, MC will only have to pay $130,000 for the gold but if it had entered into an equivalent contract at the year end, it would have had to pay $137,000. Therefore, effectively MC has made a saving of $7,000 and $7,000 is what a third party would be prepared to pay MC to purchase the futures contract. As it is standing at a gain, this is a financial asset.

The journal required is:

Debit	Financial asset	$7,000	
Credit	Profit or loss		$7,000

6.16 The correct answer is: Fair value through profit or loss.

This speculative option contract is a derivative. Under IFRS 9 *Financial Instruments* speculative derivatives should be categorised as measured at fair value through profit or loss.

6.17 The correct answer is: In relation to this forward contract, QR should record **a financial liability** at 30 September 20X1 at the amount of **A$25,000**.

Under IFRS 9 *Financial Instruments*, speculative derivatives should be measured at fair value through profit or loss. The year-end fair value is the difference between the contracted rate in the contract and the year-end equivalent market rate. If the contract is favourable and standing at a gain, it should be recorded as a financial asset. If the contract is unfavourable and standing at a loss, it should be recorded as a financial liability.

For this contract it is calculated as:

	A$
At year-end rate (B$900,000/4.5)	200,000
At QR's agreed forward rate (B$900,000/4)	(225,000)
Loss = financial liability	(25,000)

This contract is not cash because it is simply an agreement to purchase cash in a foreign currency in the future. Nor is it a provision because a derivative is a type of financial instrument and financial instruments are covered under a different accounting standard (IFRS 9) to provisions (defined as 'a liability of uncertain timing or amount' in IAS 37).

6.18 The correct answers are:

- It is settled at a future date.
- Its value changes in response to an underlying variable.
- It requires no or little initial net investment.

IFRS 9 contains a three-part definition of a derivative comprising these three characteristics. The derivative is typically a contract where the entity commits to or has a right to buy or sell something at a fixed rate at a future date. The underlying variable could be, for example, a specified interest rate, financial instrument price, commodity price or foreign exchange rate. Apart from options, where a small premium is usually paid when the contract is entered into (the commitment date), typically no money changes hands on the commitment date.

Forwards, futures, options and swaps are examples of derivatives but are not an exhaustive list of all types of derivative and are not specifically included in the definition of a derivative in IFRS 9.

'It is acquired or incurred principally for the purpose of selling or repurchasing it in the near term' is IFRS 9's definition of 'held for trading' and not part of the specific definition of a derivative.

'It is a contractual obligation to deliver cash or another financial asset to another entity' is part of the broader definition of a financial liability rather than a derivative. A derivative

may be a financial liability if it is standing at a loss at the reporting date. Equally it may be a financial asset if it is standing at a gain at the reporting date.

6.19 The correct answer is: When the entity becomes party to the contractual provisions of the financial asset

While an entity usually becomes party to the contractual provisions of the financial asset on purchase of the instrument (which is normally when cash is exchanged), this is not always the case. For example, when a derivative contract is entered into, the derivative should be recognised from the commitment date even though no cash is usually exchanged until the settlement date.

6.20 The correct answers are:

- A trade receivable
- A purchase of bonds
- An acquisition of ordinary shares in another entity

An issue of redeemable preference shares and a loan from the bank are both classified as financial liabilities as there is an obligation to repay the principal (and to pay dividends in the case of the preference shares if they are cumulative and interest in the case of the bank loan).

An issue of ordinary shares is classified as equity as there is no obligation for the entity to pay dividends or to repay the principal.

7 Intangible assets

7.1 The correct answer is: GK spent $12,000 researching a new type of product. The research is expected to lead to a new product line in three years' time.

Research expenditure can never be capitalised and must be recognised as an expense in the statement of profit or loss in accordance with IAS 38.

7.2 The correct answer is: Internally developed brands must not be capitalised.

Negative goodwill must firstly be reassessed to ensure that it has not resulted due to an error and should then be credited to profit or loss in the period in which it arose.

Purchased goodwill must be capitalised as an intangible non-current asset and reviewed annually for impairment. Unlike most other intangible assets, it should not be amortised.

Internally generated goodwill cannot be recognised in the financial statements and may definitely not be revalued.

7.3 The correct answers are:

- The costing system is not sufficiently detailed to reliably measure the expenditure.
- Funds are unlikely to be available to complete the development.

In order to capitalise development expenditure, an entity must demonstrate its ability to measure the cost reliably.

The company must have adequate resources to fund the completion of the development project for it to be capitalised.

The development phase does not need to be complete before expenditure can be capitalised. Nor does the development have to relate to a single product.

Future economic benefits may be generated through use or sale of the asset, in the form of future cost savings or revenue. Therefore, IAS 38 requires an entity to demonstrate its intention and ability to **use or sell** an asset.

7.4 The correct answer is: $56,000

The $12,000 spent on devising processes for converting seaweed should not be capitalised as no commercial use has been discovered for chemicals X and Y and therefore probable future economic benefits cannot be demonstrated.

The $60,000 relating to the headache pill must be capitalised, as the IAS 38 capitalisation criteria have been met (probable economic benefits, intention to complete the asset, resources available to complete the development, ability to use or sell the asset, technically feasible and expenditure can be measured reliably). Amortisation must start once commercial production begins on 1 April 20X6 and amortisation is $1,000 per month ($60,000/5 years/12 months).

The carrying amount at the year end represents $60,000 less four months' amortisation from 1 April 20X6 to 31 July 20X6 ($60,000 – [4 months × $1,000]).

7.5 The correct answer is: $35,000

The IAS 38 capitalisation criteria for development costs appear to have been met for the $38,000 cost of developing new distilling techniques as they are to be put in place shortly (so appear to be technically feasible, likely to be completed with available resources and likely to be used) and will cut the production costs of making whisky (probable future economic benefits). Therefore, they should be recognised as an intangible asset rather than an expense in profit or loss. No amortisation is charged on the development costs as the new distilling techniques are not yet in use.

The $27,000 research costs are not directed towards a confirmed outcome and so should be recognised as an expense.

The $8,000 market research costs suggest that probable future economic benefits have not yet been demonstrated and so the capitalisation criteria have not yet been satisfied. Therefore, these costs should be recognised as an expense.

This results in a total expense of $35,000 ($27,000 + $8,000) being recognised in profit or loss.

7.6 The correct answer is: $0

According to IAS 38 *Intangible Assets*, development costs should only be recognised if all the 'PIRATE' criteria are met.

In this scenario, the future of the project is in doubt, and therefore EF may not have 'resources adequate to complete the asset' or be able to demonstrate that 'probable future economic benefits will be generated by the asset'.

If either of these is in doubt then EF would not satisfy all of the criteria necessary in order to be able to capitalise the development expenditure.

Amortisation of an intangible asset should commence only once the asset is generating economic benefits, so that the income and costs can be matched with each other.

7.7 The correct answer is: $65,000 spent on developing a special type of new packaging for a new energy efficient light bulb; the packaging is expected to be used by MN for many years and is expected to reduce MN's distribution costs by $35,000 a year

This expenditure appears to satisfy the IAS 38 capitalisation criteria and so the $65,000 should be recognised as an intangible asset.

The $120,000 spent on the train system relates to a project which is not yet viable. The costs are therefore research costs and cannot be capitalised.

The $50,000 paid to the local university is for research and therefore cannot be capitalised.

The customer dissatisfaction with the performance levels of the electric bicycle raise doubts over whether it will be successfully launched. Therefore, future economic benefits cannot be demonstrated with any certainty meaning that the IAS 38 capitalisation criteria have not been met.

7.8 The correct answer is: KJ purchased the copyright and film rights to the next book to be written by a famous author for $75,000 on 1 March 20X1.

The copyright and film rights to the book appear to satisfy the IAS 38 definition of an intangible asset as it appears that:

- Future economic benefits will flow to the entity; and
- The asset can be reliably measured.

The $50,000 advertising costs should be recognised as an expense in the statement of profit or loss as future economic benefits are not guaranteed. IAS 38 specifically requires expenditure on advertising expenditure to be recognised as an expense rather than an intangible asset.

The legal action may give rise to a potential asset but this is still uncertain. Since the IAS 38 probable economic benefits recognition criteria have not been met, no asset should be recognised at 31 January 20X2.

The brand is internally generated and IAS 38 specifically prohibits capitalisation of internally generated brands. Therefore, it may not be recognised as an intangible asset.

7.9 The correct answer is: Capitalise development costs of $180,000, start to amortise on 1 May 20X6.

CD should capitalise $180,000 development costs at 30 April 20X6. Amortisation should begin on 1 May 20X6 (once the process is implemented) and continue over the expected life of the process.

7.10 The correct answers are:

- Patents
- Copyrights
- Licences

An intangible asset is defined by IAS 38 as 'an identifiable non-monetary asset without physical substance'.

Purchased patents, copyrights and licences meet this definition as they are non-monetary and do not have physical substance.

A purchased bond is a monetary asset and qualifies as a financial asset under IFRS 9 *Financial Instruments*. Therefore, it is not an intangible asset.

Both properties and inventories have physical substance so are not intangible assets.

7.11 The correct answers are:

- A franchise purchased by an entity
- A publishing title acquired as part of a business combination
- Computer software bought by an entity

Separately acquired intangibles (the franchise and computer software) and those acquired as part of a business combination (the publishing title) should always be capitalised as an intangible asset as the recognition criteria (probable economic benefits and reliable measurement) are always presumed to be met.

IAS 38 prohibits capitalisation of internally generated customer lists.

Expenditure to gain new scientific knowledge is classified as research expenditure by IAS 38. IAS 38 requires research expenditure to be recognised as an expense in profit or loss rather than capitalised as an intangible asset, as probable future economic benefits cannot be demonstrated.

IAS 38 specifically requires expenditure on staff training activities to be recognised as an expense rather than an intangible asset.

7.12 The correct answer is: $129,000

For purchased intangibles, IAS 38 requires the following costs to be capitalised:

- The purchase price; and
- Any directly attributable costs in preparing the asset for its intended use.

In determining the purchase price, trade discounts (but not prompt payment discounts) are deducted. Therefore, the purchase price is $100,000 rather than the $90,000 actually paid.

Directly attributable costs include costs of employee benefits arising directly from bringing the asset to its working condition (the $20,000 of overtime paid to the IT department), professional fees (the IT consultant's fee of $4,000) and costs of testing whether the asset is functioning properly ($4,000).

However, administration and general overheads are not considered to be directly attributable and should be excluded from the cost of the asset.

Therefore, the cost of the intangible asset to be recognised in relation to the computer software is calculated as follows:

	$
Purchase price	100,000
Directly attributable costs:	
IT department overtime	20,000
External consultant's fee	4,000
Costs of testing	5,000
Cost of intangible asset	129,000

7.13 The correct answer is: $800,000

IAS 38 requires an intangible asset acquired as part of a business combination to be measured initially at fair value. Fair value is defined by IFRS 13 as 'the price that would be received to sell an asset or paid to transfer a liability in an orderly transaction between market participants at the measurement date'. Therefore the customer list should be recognised in AB's consolidated statement of financial position as at 31 December 20X0 at its fair value of $800,000 rather than the cost of $500,000. The directors' valuation of $1,000,000 should not be used as it is too subjective.

7.14 The correct answer is: $145,000

Expenditure can only be capitalised from the date on which the IAS 38 capitalisation criteria are met, which is 30 June 20X8. Therefore, the $490,000 costs incurred prior to the criteria being met must be recognised as an expense rather than being capitalised. It is only permitted to capitalise directly attributable costs necessary to create, produce and prepare the asset to be capable of operating in the manner intended by management. Therefore, while materials and staff costs should be capitalised, staff training costs should be expense rather than capitalised.

The amount that should be recognised as an intangible asset is calculated as follows:

	$
Materials used in developing the tool	80,000
Staff costs on developing the tool	65,000
	145,000

7.15 The correct answer is: $230,000

As an active market exists and LM wishes to hold intangible assets under the revaluation model where possible, the taxi licence should be revalued to its fair value of $230,000 at 31 December 20X4.

At 31 December 20X4, prior to the revaluation, the licence would have been amortised by $20,000 ([$200,000/5 years] × 6/12), resulting in a carrying amount of $180,000 ($200,000 − $20,000). Therefore, a revaluation gain of $50,000 arises ($230,000 − $180,000). As this taxi licence has not been revalued previously, the revaluation gain is recognised in other comprehensive income (and the revaluation surplus in the statement of financial position):

Debit   Intangible asset $50,000
Credit Other comprehensive income (and revaluation surplus) $50,000

7.16 The correct answer is:

- Recognise $5,000 in other comprehensive income and $10,000 in profit or loss

IAS 38 requires a decrease in value of an intangible asset to be recognised in other comprehensive income to the extent of any credit balance in the revaluation surplus in respect of that asset (here $5,000). Any excess should then be recognised in profit or loss (here $10,000).

7.17 The correct answers are:

- Brands
- Patents
- Music publishing rights

IAS 38 only permits intangible assets to be held under the revaluation model when an active market exists. It specifically states that an active market cannot exist for brands, newspaper mastheads, music and film publishing rights, patents or trademarks, because each such asset is unique.

7.18 The correct answer is: 30 September 20X2

IAS 38 requires an intangible asset to be derecognised on disposal or when no future economic benefits are expected from its use.

7.19 The correct answer is: $320,000

The gain on derecognition is calculated as:

	$
Net disposal proceeds (proceeds less selling costs) ($975,000 − $15,000)	960,000
Less carrying amount of intangible asset ($800,000 × 8/10)	(640,000)
Gain on derecognition (recognise in profit or loss)	320,000

Don't forget to deduct two years of amortisation (for 20X5 and 20X6) from cost when calculating the carrying amount at the date of derecognition. Another common error is to forget to deduct selling costs from the sales proceeds.

7.20 The correct answer is: Dr Profit or loss $675,000; Cr Intangible asset $675,000

An intangible asset can only be recognised in relation to development expenditure when the IAS 38 criteria for capitalisation have been met. If this ceases to be the case, the intangible asset should be derecognised. IAS 38 requires a gain or loss on derecognition to be recognised in profit or loss.

An asset is a debit balance so it is derecognised with a credit. The other side of the accounting entry is to recognise an expense in profit or loss with a debit.

8 Income taxes

8.1 The correct answers are:

	$
Property	500,000
Deferred tax liability	**60,000**
Revaluation surplus	**140,000**

The deferred tax liability is calculated as follows:

	$
Temporary difference (= revaluation gain) ($500,000 – $300,000)	200,000
Deferred tax liability (30% × $200,000)	60,000

The double entry to record this deferred tax is:

		$	$
Debit	Other comprehensive income (and revaluation surplus)	60,000	
Credit	Deferred tax liability		60,000

Therefore the balance on the revaluation surplus at the year end is calculated as follows:

	$
Revaluation gain ($500,000 – $300,000)	200,000
Less deferred tax on revaluation gain	(60,000)
Balance on revaluation surplus at 31 December 20X8	140,000

8.2 The correct answer is: $42,750

This is calculated by comparing the carrying amount to the tax base as at 30 September 20X4 to find the temporary difference. This temporary difference is then multiplied by the tax rate of 30% to calculate the deferred tax liability.

The carrying amount is calculated as follows:

	$
Cost	600,000
Less accumulated depreciation (X3, X4) [2/10 × 600,000]	(120,000)
Carrying amount at 30 September 20X4	480,000

The tax base is calculated as follows:

	$
Cost 1 October 20X2	600,000
Tax allowance (25% × 600,000)	(150,000)
Tax written down value 30 September 20X3	450,000
Tax allowance (25% × 450,000)	(112,500)
Tax written down value 30 September 20X4	337,500

Therefore, the temporary difference is $480,000 – $337,500 = $142,500.

The deferred tax liability is 30% × $142,500 = $42,750.

8.3 The correct answer is:

Items	Yes	No
Differences between accounting depreciation and tax allowances for capital expenditure	X	
Expenses charged in the statement of profit or loss and other comprehensive income but disallowed for tax		X
Revaluation of a non-current asset	X	
Unrelieved tax losses	X	

A temporary difference arises when an item is recognised in both the accounts and by the tax authorities but in different periods.

With the accounting depreciation and the tax allowances for capital expenditure, the full asset will have been recognised in both the accounts and the tax computation by the end of the asset's life but at different rates, making it a temporary difference.

The revaluation is recognised in the accounts at the date of revaluation but not by the tax authorities until the asset is sold or the carrying amount of the asset is recovered through use, generating taxable income in excess of tax allowance. Therefore this is also a temporary difference.

Unrelieved losses arise in the account immediately but no tax relief is granted by the tax authorities until sufficient future taxable profits arise, again making this a temporary difference.

However, where expenses are charged in the accounts but disallowed for tax purposes, this is a permanent rather than a temporary difference.

8.4 The correct answers are:

- Accrued expenses that will never be deductible for tax purposes
- Accrued expenses that have already been deducted in determining the current tax liability for current or earlier periods
- Accrued income that will never be taxable

Where accrued expenses will never be deductible for tax purposes, this is a permanent difference, so the tax base is made the same as the carrying amount of the liability so that the temporary difference comes to zero. The same applies to accrued income that will never be taxable.

With accrued expenses that have already been deducted in determining the current tax liability for current or earlier periods, the treatment in the accounts and by the tax authorities is effectively the same; ie the item is recognised in the accounts and granted tax relief on an accruals basis. Therefore, the carrying amount and the tax base are the same.

For the following, the carrying amount and tax base differ giving rise to a temporary difference:

- Accrued income that will be taxed on a receipts basis – the carrying amount is the accrued income and the tax base is zero, as the income has not yet been recognised by the tax authorities.
- A property that is revalued but the revaluation has no effect on taxable profit – the carrying amount will include the revaluation gain but the tax base will exclude it. Therefore, the carrying amount and tax base will differ giving rise to deferred tax. This is considered to be a temporary difference because the future recovery of the carrying amount of the property will result in a taxable flow of economic benefits.
- Fixtures and fittings on which the accounting and tax depreciation rates differ – the carrying amount of the fixtures and fittings will be cost less accumulated accounting depreciation and the tax base will be cost less accumulated tax depreciation. As the accounting and tax depreciation rates differ, the carrying amount and tax base will differ.

8.5 The correct answers are:

	Account reference	Amount in $
Debit	Deferred tax liability	630
Credit	Deferred tax expense (P/L)	630

Workings

1 Temporary difference

	Carrying amount $	Tax base $
Cost	60,000	60,000
Depreciation/tax depreciation	(12,000)	30,000
Balance at 31.3.X7	48,000	30,000
Depreciation/tax depreciation	(9,600)	(7,500)
Balance at 31.3.X7	38,400	22,500

2 Deferred/tax depreciation

	$
At 31.3.X7 [(48,000 – 30,000) × 30%]	5,400
Movement (to P/L)	(630)
At 31.3.X8 [(38,400 – 22,500) × 30%]	4,770

Note. As there is a reduction to the deferred tax liability, it must be debited. The other side of the double entry is to credit the deferred tax expense in profit or loss.

8.6 The correct answer is: $287,500

	$
Taxable temporary differences b/f	850,000
Accelerated tax allowances (500,000 – 450,000)	50,000
Revaluation surplus	250,000
Taxable temporary differences c/f	1,150,000
Deferred tax liability at 25%	287,500

8.7 The correct answer is: Accrued expenses nil, interest receivable nil

The accrued expenses will all be deductible for tax purposes, so the tax base is nil.

When the interest is received it will all be subject to tax, so the tax base is nil.

8.8 The correct answer is: Asset, which will be included in the statement of financial position at the amount that is expected to be able to be recovered from future expected profits

Tax losses can be carried forward to reduce current tax on future profits, representing a tax saving and thus a deferred tax asset (less tax payable in the future). These can only be recognised to the extent that it is probable the losses can be used before they expire.

8.9 The correct answer is: A deferred tax liability would still be necessary on the revaluation gain as the property will generate taxable income in excess of the depreciation allowed for tax purposes.

Under IAS 12 deferred tax must be recognised for all temporary differences between the tax base of assets and the amount at which they are carried in the statement of financial position. This is true even if there is no intention to sell the asset.

8.10 The correct answer is: -$4,000

Look at the deferred tax account over the years:

	Year 1	Year 2	Year 3	Year 4	Year 5
	$'000	$'000	$'000	$'000	$'000
Carrying amount	180	160	140	120	100
Tax base	150	100	50	0	0
Taxable temporary difference	30	60	90	120	100
Opening deferred tax liability	0	6	12	18	24
Deferred tax expense	6	6	6	6	(4)
Closing deferred tax liability @ 20%	6	12	18	24	20

A shortcut is to compare the accounting depreciation for Year 5 of $20,000 ($200,000 /10 years) to the tax depreciation in Year 5 which is zero (because the machinery is depreciated at 25% per annum straight-line for tax purposes so it is fully depreciated for tax purposes by the end of Year 4). The difference is then multiplied by the tax rate of 20%:

	$
Accounting depreciation ($200,000/10 years)	20,000
Tax depreciation (fully depreciated)	(0)
Reversal of temporary difference	20,000
Reversal of deferred tax liability	20% × 20,000
	= 4,000

A deferred tax liability arises when tax depreciation is greater than accounting depreciation which is the case here in Years 1 to 4. The deferred tax liability then reverses when accounting depreciation becomes greater than tax depreciation which is the case here in Years 5 to 10. Therefore, in Year 5, the deferred tax liability is reversing:

Debit   Deferred tax liability
Credit Deferred tax expense

The credit to deferred tax expense results in income in profit or loss.

8.11 The correct answer is: As F is expected to make **profits** in the future, a deferred tax **asset** of **$1.12 million** can be recorded in the financial statements for the year ended 31 December 20X7.

A deferred tax asset is created as the tax payable in the future will be reduced by the losses that F can carry forward. The deferred tax asset is calculated as the losses carried forward that can be used multiplied by the tax rate of 28%. Here there are losses of $5 million but only $4 million of taxable profits are expected in the carryforward period. Therefore, a deferred tax asset can only be recognised on the $4 million of the $5 million losses that are expected to be recoverable. This is calculated as: $4m × 28% = $1.12m.

8.12 The correct answers are:

	Account reference	$
Debit	Deferred tax liability	270,000
Credit	Tax expense	270,000

The deferred tax liability at 31 December 20X7 is calculated as:

	$
Carrying amount	1,900,000
Less tax base	(1,300,000)
Temporary difference	600,000
Tax rate	× 30%
Deferred tax liability	= 180,000

The journal entry should be made for the movement in the deferred tax liability in the year:

	$
Opening deferred tax liability (1.1.X7)	450,000
Movement (balancing figure)	(270,000)
Closing deferred tax liability (31.12.X7)	180,000

The deferred tax liability is a credit balance so it is reduced with a debit. An expense is a debit balance so the tax expense is reduced with a credit.

8.13 The correct answer is: Recognise a deferred tax asset of $10,000

There is a temporary difference here as the expenses are recognised in the financial statements when they are accrued in 20X0 but they will not be recognised in the tax computation until 20X1 (or later) when they are paid.

This gives rise to a deferred tax asset in relation to the future tax relief that MJ will receive on these expenses. It is calculated as follows:

	$
Carrying amount of accrual (in accounting SOFP)	(50,000)
Less tax base (value for tax purposes)	0
Temporary difference	(50,000)
Deferred tax asset (always opposite sign to temporary difference) (20% × 50,000)	10,000

8.14 The correct answer is: Dr Deferred tax expense $28,500; Cr Deferred tax liability $28,500

Deferred tax is calculated as follows:

	$
Carrying amount of asset (in accounting SOFP)	95,000
Less tax base (value for tax purposes)	(0)
Temporary difference	95,000
Deferred tax (liability) (always opposite sign to temporary difference) (30% × 95,000)	(28,500)

It is a deferred tax liability (created with a credit) because KW has an obligation to pay tax on the income when it is received in future periods. The other side of the double entry is to record a deferred tax expense with a debit in profit or loss.

8.15   The correct answer is: $145,000

This is calculated as follows:

	$
Current tax expense for the current period	150,000
(Over provision) in relation to the previous period (135,000 – 130,000)	(5,000)
	145,000

The current tax expense (and liability) recognised in the prior year was too high. Therefore, a reduction to the current tax expense is required in 20X5 to rectify this.

The accounting entry on settlement of the previous year's liability is:

Debit (↓)	Deferred tax liability	$135,000	
Credit (↓)	Cash		$130,000
Credit (↓)	Deferred tax expense		$5,000

8.16   The correct answer is: A current tax asset of $20,000

IAS 12 requires an entity to recognise a current tax asset for amounts paid in excess of amounts due. Here $20,000 has been paid in excess of amounts due ($460,000 – $440,000).

8.17   The correct answer is: A current tax liability of $145,000

IAS 12 requires a current tax liability to be recognised for unpaid amounts. As at 30 June 20X4, QP still owes the tax authorities for its final two instalments which amount to $145,000 ($290,000 × 2/4).

A current tax asset would only be recognised for amounts paid in excess of amounts due which is not the case here.

8.18   The correct answer is: Dr Current tax liability $50,000, Dr Profit or loss $9,000; Cr Cash $59,000

There has been an under-provision of $9,000 ($59,000 – $50,000) in respect of the prior year (20X0). This should be recognised as an additional expense in the current year (20X1).

It would be incorrect to record the whole amount paid of $59,000 as an expense in 20X1 as $50,000 has already been recognised in profit or loss in 20X0. Therefore, only the additional expense needs to be recognised in 20X1 (with a debit), cash which is an asset must be reduced by the amount paid (with a credit) and the current tax liability derecognised as it has now been settled (with a debit).

8.19   The correct answer is:

Statement of profit or loss	Statement of financial position
Current tax expense of $710,000	Current tax liability of $750,000

There has been an over-provision of $40,000 ($640,000 – $600,000) in respect of the prior year (20X2). This should be deducted from the tax expense in the current year (20X3). The current year tax expense is therefore $710,000 ($750,000 – $40,000).

The current year tax will not be paid until 9 months and 1 day after the year end and is therefore recorded as a current liability.

8.20 The correct answer is: $373,000

This is calculated as follows:

	$
Current tax expense for the current period	380,000
(Over-provision) in relation to the previous period	(20,000)
Increase in deferred tax liability (50,000 – 37,000)	13,000
	373,000

9 Consolidated statement of financial position I

9.1 The correct answer is: $303,000

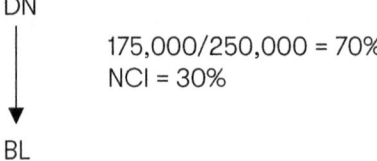

DN
↓ 175,000/250,000 = 70%
  NCI = 30%
BL

The acquisition was on 31 May 20X8, so only three months of BL's profits for the year ended 31 August 20X8 arose post-acquisition.

	$
NCI at acquisition (fair value)	300,000
NCI share of post-acquisition retained earnings (30% × 40,000 × 3/12)	3,000
NCI at 31.8.20X8	303,000

9.2 The correct answer is: $70,000

DN
↓ 175,000/250,000 = 70%
  NCI = 30%
BL

The acquisition was on 31 May 20X8, so nine months of BL's profits for the year ended 31 August 20X8 arose pre-acquisition.

Working: Goodwill

	$	$
Consideration transferred		700,000
NCI at acquisition (fair value)		300,000
Net assets at acquisition		
Share capital	250,000	
Pre-acquisition retained earnings		
At 1.1.X7	650,000	
To 31.5.X8 (40,000 × 9/12)	30,000	
		(930,000)
		70,000

9.3 The correct answer is: $1,330,000

	$	$
Consideration transferred		3,250,000
Non-controlling interests (at fair value)		1,960,000
Less net assets at acquisition		
Share capital	1,000,000	
Retained earnings	2,760,000	
		(3,760,000)
		1,450,000
Impairment		(120,000)
		1,330,000

9.4 The correct answer is: EF only.

Only AB has 40% of the voting rights and 80% of the non-voting rights in CD; therefore AB does not have control of CD.

AB has a minority of the voting rights (40%) of EF but it has control in that it has the power to appoint and remove directors, therefore EF is a subsidiary of AB.

9.5 The correct answer is: $24,800

	$
NCI at acquisition at fair value	14,800
NCI share of post-acquisition reserves 25% ($115,000 – $65,000)	12,500
Less NCI share of impairment losses (25% × $10,000)	(2,500)
	24,800

9.6 The correct answer is: $131,250

	$
NCI at acquisition 25% × ($310,000 + $165,000)	118,750
NCI share of post-acquisition reserves 25% × ($215,000 – $165,000)	12,500
	131,250

9.7 The correct answer is: $39,600

	$
Consideration transferred	280,800
Non-controlling interest	64,800
Net assets	(306,000)
Goodwill	39,600

9.8 The correct answer is: $25.0 million

	CD $m	MB $m
At the year end	26	12
At acquisition		(7)
		5
Group share of post-acquisition reserves (60% × $5 million)	3	
Less impairment loss	(4)	
	25	

9.9 The correct answer is: Carried at cost, with an annual impairment review.

Positive goodwill should be recognised as an intangible asset which should be carried at cost and reviewed annually for impairment. Revaluations of goodwill are not permitted by IAS 38 *Intangible Assets*.

9.10 The correct answer is: $3.04 million

	$m
Non-controlling interest at acquisition 40% × ($4.4m + $2.3m)	2.68
Non-controlling interest share of post-acquisition reserves 40% × ($3.2m – $2.3m)	0.36
	3.04

9.11 The correct answer is: $2.46 million

	$m
Non-controlling interests at acquisition at fair value	2.3
NCI share of post-acquisition reserves 10% × ($7.9m – $6.3m)	0.16
	2.46

9.12 The correct answer is: $96.4 million

	TR $m	SD $m
At the year end	81.0	54
At acquisition		(32)
		22
Group share of post-acquisition revaluation surplus (70% × $22m)	15.4	
	96.4	

9.13 The correct answer is: $223,200

	QZ $	FT $
At the year end ($140,000 + $80,000)/($60,000 + $40,000)	220,000	100,000
At acquisition		(60,000)
		40,000
Group share of post-acquisition reserves (80% × $40,000)	32,000	
Less group share of impairment loss (80% × $36,000)	(28,800)	
Consolidated retained earnings	223,200	

9.14 The correct answer is: $540,000

	$'000	$'000
Consideration transferred		6,000
Non-controlling interest at fair value (per Q)		4,000
Net assets at acquisition represented by:		
Share capital of subsidiary	1,000	
Retained earnings at acquisition	4,500	
		(5,500)
Goodwill at acquisition		4,500
Impairment of goodwill (20% × $4,500,000)		(900)
Goodwill after impairment		3,600

Impairment of goodwill attributable to the shareholders of the parent company is the group share (60%) because the full goodwill method has been adopted (NCI is measured at fair value at acquisition).

Group share of impairment loss on goodwill = 60% × $900,000 = $540,000

9.15 The correct answer is: $46 million

	FL $m	KT $m
At the year end	58	15
At acquisition		(20)
		(5)
Group share of KT post-acquisition (80% × (5))	(4)	
Group share of impairment of goodwill (80% × 10)	(8)	
	46	

9.16 The correct answer is: $85,000

	$	$
Consideration transferred		400,000
Non-controlling interest (10% × $350,000)		35,000
Fair value of net assets at acquisition:		
Share capital	300,000	
Retained earnings	50,000	
		(350,000)
Goodwill		85,000

9.17 The correct answer is: Immediate recognition as a gain in the statement of profit or loss

When the purchase price is less than the fair value of net assets acquired, negative goodwill arises. This is treated as a bargain purchase and should be credited to profit or loss immediately.

9.18 The correct answers are:

- CD – AB has a management contract under which it directs the activities of CD in return for 95% of the profits and 100% of the losses of CD.
- EF – AB owns 80% of the ordinary shares in EF but chooses not to exercise its voting rights.

IFRS 10 defines a subsidiary as 'an entity that is controlled by another entity'. Control exists if all of the parent has all of:

- Power to direct the relevant activities;
- Exposure, or rights, to variable returns; and
- The ability to use its power to affect the amount of returns.

With CD, the management contract gives AB the power to direct the relevant activities. AB has exposure to variable returns in the form of 95% of profits and 100% of the losses. The management contract gives AB the ability to use its power to affect the amount of returns. Therefore, CD is a subsidiary of AB.

With EF, owning the majority of the ordinary shares in EF gives AB the power to direct the relevant activities of EF and exposure to variable returns (dividends and movement in share price). Even though AB does not exercise its voting rights, it has the ability to do so. Therefore, EF is also a subsidiary of AB.

The other entities are not subsidiaries of AB for the following reasons:

- GH – even though AB has the half of the voting rights in GH, it has no representation on the board of directors so does not have the power to direct the relevant activities of GH.
- JK – AB has joint control of JK with YZ as unanimous consent is required for decisions over the relevant activities. This means JK is a joint arrangement of AB rather than a subsidiary.
- LM – preference shares have no voting rights so do not give AB control of LM.

9.19 The correct answers are:

- At cost
- At fair value
- Using the equity method

9.20 The correct answer is: $580,000

IAS 27 *Separate Financial Statements* offers a choice of **three possible methods to measure** this investment:

- At **cost**; or
- At **fair value** (as a financial asset under IFRS 9 *Financial Instruments*); or
- Using the **equity method**.

Here, PQ elects to measure the investment in SV as a financial asset under IFRS 9. Per IFRS 9, an investment in equity instruments must always be measured at fair value with gains or losses in profit or loss (or other comprehensive income if the parent takes up the irrevocable election under IFRS 9).

It is not permissible to measure the investment at present value so $535,000 is not an allowable option.

PQ would be permitted to measure the investment at its cost of $500,000 if this had been the method chosen by PQ. PQ would also be permitted to measure the investment at $572,000 using the equity method (cost $500,000 + group share of post-acquisition reserves 90% × [$440,000 − $360,000]) if this had been PQ's chosen method.

10 Consolidated statement of financial position II

10.1 The correct answer is: $3,136,500

	$
Cash	1,200,000
Deferred consideration (500,000 × 0.873 [2 year 7% discount factor])	436,500
Shares in MN	1,500,000
	3,136,500

10.2 The correct answer is: The existence of contingent liabilities in the books of the subsidiary at the acquisition date

The normal rule of IAS 37 *Provisions, Contingent Liabilities and Contingent Assets* of disclosing rather than recognising a contingent liability does not apply on acquisition of a subsidiary. Where there is a present obligation arising from past events and the fair value can be measured reliably, IFRS 3 *Business Combinations* requires a contingent liability to be recognised.

The purpose of fair value adjustments is to record true goodwill at the acquisition date. Therefore post acquisition changes in net assets are not relevant. Nor should a provision be recognised for post-acquisition reorganisation costs or anticipated losses as no obligation exists at the acquisition date.

10.3 The correct answer is: $180,000

	$	$
Consideration transferred		450,000
Fair value of non-controlling interest ($3.75 × 20,000)		75,000
Fair value of net assets:		
Share capital	100,000	
Retained earnings	165,000	
Fair value adjustment	80,000	
		(345,000)
Goodwill		180,000

10.4 The correct answer is: $10,080,000

	$
Cash 80% × 3,000,000 × $1.20	2,880,000
Shares 80% × 3,000,000 × 2 × $1.50	7,200,000
	10,080,000

The fair value of cash consideration is simply the cash amount paid. For consideration given in the form of shares, the fair value (market value of the share) as at the acquisition date should be used. IFRS 3 requires that any costs related to the acquisition, such as professional fees, are written off immediately to profit or loss, so these are not included in the consideration figure.

10.5 The correct answer is: $18,060,000

	$
ZA	16,000,000
PJ	1,750,000
FV uplift (2,200,000 – 1,890,000)	310,000
	18,060,000

10.6 The correct answer is: $660,000

		$
Consideration transferred		3,700,000
Non-controlling interest acquired		1,140,000
Fair value of net assets acquired		
Share capital	2,000,000	
Retained earnings	1,770,000	
FV of PPE	310,000	
		(4,080,000)
		760,000
Less impairment losses on goodwill to date		(100,000)
		660,000

10.7 The correct answer is: $397,500

Working: Retained earnings of PJ

	$
Retained earnings at the year end	2,400,000
Retained earnings at acquisition	(1,770,000)
	630,000
Group share of HJ's post acquisition retained earnings: (630,000 × 75%)	472,500
Less impairment loss on goodwill: (100,000 × 75%)	(75,000)
	397,500

10.8 The correct answers are:

- It will be included at its fair value on acquisition plus share of post-acquisition earnings of PJ.
- It will be included as a separate component of equity.
- 25% of the impairment in the goodwill arising on acquisition will be debited to it.

Post-acquisition earnings will be credited to non-controlling interest, not debited. Non-controlling interest is included in the equity of the ZA group, not non-current liabilities.

10.9 The correct answer is: $15 million

	$m
Consideration transferred	50
Non-controlling interests (at fair value)	30
Less fair value of net assets at acquisition	(65)
	15

The provision for reorganisation costs cannot be included in the goodwill calculation because it reflects the acquirer's intentions, rather than an actual liability of EF at the date of acquisition (IFRS 3 and IAS 37).

10.10 The correct answer is: $11,218,000

AJ owns 4 million of BK's 5 million shares; ie an 80% shareholding.

	AJ	BK
	$	$
At the year end	11,000,000	2,000,000
PUP (100,000 × ¾ × 25/125)		(15,000)
At acquisition		(1,600,000)
		385,000
Group share of BK post-acquisition		
(385,000 × 80%)	308,000	
Impairment	(90,000)	
	11,218,000	

Note. All of the impairment loss has been deducted because it is the partial goodwill method (NCI is measured at NCI % of net assets at acquisition). If it had been the full goodwill method (NCI measured at fair value at acquisition), the group share (80%) of the impairment loss would have been deducted with the NCI share being deducted in the NCI working.

10.11 The correct answer is: $840,000

Goodwill is calculated as follows:

	$	$
Consideration transferred		1,800,000
Non-controlling interests (1,600,000 × 40%)		640,000
Less fair value of net assets at acquisition		
Per question	1,500,000	
Fair value adjustments:		
▪ PPE ($430,000 – $370,000)	60,000	
▪ Brand	80,000	
▪ Contingent liability	(40,000)	
		(1,600,000)
Goodwill on acquisition (at 1 July 20X1)		840,000

IFRS 3 *Business Combinations* requires identifiable assets acquired and liabilities assumed to be recognised at fair value in the goodwill calculation even if they have not been recognised in the subsidiary's own financial statements. Therefore, the brand and contingent liability must be recognised in full as a fair value adjustment at acquisition. The PPE is already included in the subsidiary's statement of financial position so simply has to be uplifted to its fair value.

Note. No provision should be made for potential reorganisation costs because it is merely an intention rather than an obligation at the acquisition date.

10.12 The correct answer is: Deduct $6,000 from consolidated receivables and $4,000 from consolidated payables, and include cash in transit of $2,000.

As the intra-group balances do not agree, first you need to account for cash in transit by increasing cash by $2,000 and deducting $2,000 from receivables. The intra-group receivables balance now amounts to $4,000 ($6,000 – $2,000) so agrees with the intra-group payable balance of $4,000. These balances may now be eliminated. The end effect is a deduction of $6,000 from consolidated receivables (cash in transit of $2,000 then cancellation of the remaining $4,000) and a deduction of $4,000 from consolidated payables (to eliminate the intra-group balance).

10.13 The correct answer is: Dr Retained earnings of YZ $1,500; Cr Consolidated inventory $1,500

Dr Retained earnings of YZ (33⅓/133⅓ × $6,000) $1,500; Cr Consolidated inventory $1,500

10.14 The correct answer is: $80,000

Goods in transit should be accounted for at the year end by pushing the goods towards the recipient. This results in an increase in inventory of $100,000 and an increase of payables of $100,000 (the intra-group receivable and payable are then eliminated on consolidation).

Unrealised profit should then be eliminated on goods in inventory at the year end because inventory should be measured at the lower of cost and net realisable value to the group. Unrealised profit is calculated as $100,000 × 25%/125% (as there has been a 25% mark-up on cost). This amounts to $20,000. Once this unrealised profit has been eliminated, inventory amounts to $80,000 ($100,000 less $20,000 unrealised profit).

10.15 The correct answer is: $3,100 added to consolidated cash.

The payment sent by SV (the parent company) to its subsidiary TU should be included as cash in transit on consolidation. It should be pushed forward to the recipient by adding the amount of $3,100 to consolidated cash and deducting it from consolidated receivables. The intra-group receivable balance will then amount to $3,600 ($6,700 – $3,100) making the intra-group receivable and payable now agree. The intra-group receivable and payable will then be eliminated.

The amount of $2,325 is incorrect because it represents the group share of the cash in transit (75% × $3,100). However, on consolidation, 100% of the subsidiary's assets and liabilities are added to the parent's to show control. Therefore, 100% of the cash in transit balance of $3,100 must be included in consolidated cash.

10.16 The correct answer is: Reduce group inventory by $10,000 and reduce parent's profits by $10,000 to eliminate the unrealised profit in inventory

This is because the parent made the sale. The adjustment is $10,000 which is (20% × $100,000 × 50%).

10.17 The correct answer is: $3,296,000

	MX $'000	FZ $'000
At 31 December 20X9	3,200	1,100
Less unrealised profit (W)		(60)
At acquisition		(920)
		120
Group share (80% × $120,000)	96	
Consolidated retained earnings	3,296	

Working: Provision for unrealised profit

Intra-group sales by FZ $300,000

Margin ($300,000 × 20%) = $60,000 (adjust FZ's retained earnings as FZ made the sale)

10.18 The correct answer is: $3,144,000

	$'000
NCI at acquisition (at fair value)	2,844
NCI share of post-acquisition retained earnings (W1)	300
NCI recognised in the consolidated SOFP at 31 December 20X4	3,144

Workings

1 NCI share of post-acquisition retained earnings

	$'000
Retained earnings of SH at 31 December 20X4	5,700
Less pre-acquisition retained earnings	(4,650)
Less provision for unrealised profit (W2)	(50)
	1,000
NCI share ($1,000,000 × 30%)	300

2   *Provision for unrealised profit (PUP)*

During the year SH sold goods worth $600,000 to PL and half of these are left in inventory at the year end. SH applies a mark-up of 20% on cost.

Therefore PUP = $600,000 × 20/120 × 50% = $50,000.

For the intra-group trading, as SH (the subsidiary) is the seller, the NCI in SH must be allocated their share of the unrealised profit (see W2). If PL (the parent) had been the seller, no adjustment would be required to NCI.

10.19 The correct answer is: $251,000

	$'000
XY	160
PQ	90
Inventory in transit	10
Provision for unrealised profit ([20 + 10] × 30%)	(9)
	251

10.20 The correct answer is: $145,000

The cash in transit of $5,000 must be pushed forward to the recipient by increasing cash by $5,000 and decreasing AB's trade receivables by $5,000. This brings the intra-group trade receivable down to $17,000 ($22,000 – $5,000).

The goods in transit of $3,000 must be pushed forward to the recipient by increasing inventories by $3,000 and increasing trade payables of CD by $3,000. This brings the intra-group payable up to $17,000 ($14,000 + $3,000).

Now that the intra-group receivable and payable agree at an amount of $17,000, they must be eliminated.

This results in consolidated trade receivables calculated as follows:

	$
AB	105,000
CD	62,000
Less cash in transit	(5,000)
Less intra-group receivable	(17,000)
	145,000

11 Consolidated statement of profit or loss and other comprehensive income

11.1 The correct answer is: $44,000

	$
Total comprehensive income of CD per the question	238,000
FV adjustment - additional depreciation in the year	(8,000)
Goodwill impairment (as NCI is measured at fair value at acquisition)	(10,000)
	220,000
NCI share	× 20%
	= 44,000

11.2 The correct answers are:

- Revenue will need to be reduced by $1,000,000 to reflect the intra-group trading.
- Cost of sales will need to be reduced by $1,000,000 to eliminate the intra-group purchase.
- Cost of sales will need to be increased by $100,000 to remove the unrealised profit from closing inventory.
- Non-controlling interest will need to be adjusted to reflect the unrealised profit in closing inventory.

The intra-group sales price of $1,000,000 must be eliminated from revenue and cost of sales so that only third-party revenue and cost of sales are shown in the group accounts. Cost of sales will also need to be increased to remove the unrealised profit from closing inventory. A common mistake is to deduct unrealised profit from cost of sales but this would have the unwanted effect of increasing rather than decreasing profit.

As S charges a mark-up of 25% on sales, cost of sales is 100% and sales 125%. Unrealised profit is therefore calculated as:

$1,000,000 × 1/2 in inventory × 25/125 mark-up = $100,000

If it had been incorrectly calculated using a 25% margin, the incorrect answer of $125,000 would have been reached ($1,000,000 × 1/2 × 25/100 margin).

As the subsidiary is the seller, the unrealised profit must be deducted from the subsidiary's profit and total comprehensive income in the non-controlling interests working.

11.3 The correct answer is: $400,000

	$
JF	250,000
PR	180,000
Intra-group trading	(30,000)
	400,000

11.4 The correct answer is: Remove $7.8 million from revenue and cost of sales. Increase cost of sales and reduce inventory by the profit on the goods remaining in inventory at the year end.

11.5 The correct answer is: Dr Revenue $100,000; Cr Cost of sales $100,000

Intra-group revenue and cost of sales of $100,000 must be eliminated in full. As there is no unsold inventory at the year end, there is no unrealised profit to eliminate. If goods had been left in inventory at the year end, unrealised profit would have been eliminated by increasing cost of sales and reducing inventory by the amount of the unrealised profit.

11.6 The correct answer is:

Profit attributable to the owners of the parent	Non-controlling interest
Reduced by $3,000	Reduced by $2,000

The provision for unrealised profit is $5,000 ($30,000 20/120).

The subsidiary has sold to the parent; therefore the unrealised profit has arisen in the accounts of the subsidiary and must be allocated between the group and the non-controlling interest (NCI).

The amount of unrealised profit that must be allocated to NCI is $2,000 ($5,000 unrealised profit × 40% NCI share).

The amount of unrealised profit that must be allocated to the owners of the parent is the remaining $3,000 ($5,000 – $2,000). This can also be calculated as the group share of the unrealised profit (60% × $5,000).

If the parent had sold the goods to the subsidiary, the full unrealised profit of $5,000 would have been allocated to the owners of the parent and none to the NCI.

11.7 The correct answer is: $100.

	$
Profit attributable to:	
Owners of the parent (balancing figure)	5,000
Non-controlling interests 20% × ($1,100 – $600)	100
Profit for the year ($4,600 × $1,100 – $600)	5,100

Note. The NCI are only allocated their share of the impairment loss on goodwill because NCI were measured at fair value at acquisition. If NCI had been measured at the proportionate share of net assets at acquisition, no goodwill would have been recognised in relation to the NCI so no impairment loss on goodwill would have been allocated to NCI.

11.8 The correct answer is: $7,650,000

	$'000
Profit attributable to:	
Owners of parent (balancing figure)	7,650
Non-controlling interest (30% × $1,980,000)	594
Consolidated profit for the year ($7,020,000 + $1,980,000 – $756,000)	8,244

Note. As the non-controlling interests (NCI) are measured at the proportionate share of net assets, no goodwill is recognised in relation to NCI so none of the impairment loss on goodwill should be allocated to NCI.

11.9 The correct answer is: $31,600,000

Firstly aggregate the revenue and cost of sales figures in the companies' statements of profit or loss.

The consolidated financial statements should only show the transactions of the group with third parties, not between group members, and so $8,000,000 should be deducted from both revenue and cost of sales, since this will have been recognised as revenue for PR and cost of sales for SY, but the goods have not left the group. This adjustment will not, however, affect the gross profit.

If the goods have been sold to third parties, the group can recognise the profit in the consolidated financial statements. However, where goods are still in the group at the year end, the profit recognised by the seller should be removed, as the group has not yet made that profit. In this case, $2,000,000 worth of goods are still in group inventories at the year end. The unrealised profit on this amount is:

$2,000,000 × 25/125 = $400,000

This should be added to group cost of sales in the consolidated statement of profit or loss, and deducted from the value of group inventories in the consolidated statement of financial position:

	$'000
Revenue (84,000 + 26,000 – 8,000)	102,000
Cost of sales (56,000 + 22,000 – 8,000 + 400)	(70,400)
Consolidated gross profit	31,600

A shortcut would have been to aggregate the two companies' gross profit figures then eliminate the unrealised profit ($28,000,000 + $4,000,000 – $400,000), as the cancellation of intra-group revenue and cost of sales has no net effect on consolidated gross profit.

11.10 The correct answer is: Reduce revenue by $25,000 and gross profit by $2,000

Revenue should be reduced by the full amount of intra-group sales of $25,000.

Gross profit should be reduced by the unrealised profit on goods left in inventory at the year end ($10,000 × 25/125 mark-up).

11.11 The correct answer is: $60,000

This is calculated as DM's profit for the year of $240,000 multiplied by the NCI share of 25% ($240,000 × 25% = $60,000).

The elimination of the unrealised profit on the intra-group sales between PA and DM has no impact on non-controlling interests as the sale was made by the parent (PA) rather than the subsidiary (DM).

11.12 The correct answer is: $10.75 million

	$'000
SB's profit for the year	55,000
Less provision for unrealised profit ($15,000 × 20/120 × ½)	(1,250)
	53,750
NCI share (20%)	10,750

11.13 The correct answer is: $'000 6,140

	$'000
Consolidated profit for the year $7,700 + (9/12 × $3,200) – $3,000	7,100
Profit attributable to:	
Owners of the parent (balancing figure)	6,140
Non-controlling interests 40% × ($3,200 × 9/12)	960
	7,100

11.14 The correct answer is: $1,420,000

In a consolidated statement of profit or loss, the parent and 100% of the subsidiary's income and expenses are aggregated line by line. The subsidiary's figures are not multiplied by the group share.

The dividend income recorded in the parent's statement of profit or loss relating to its share of the subsidiary's dividend must be eliminated on consolidation as it is an intra-group transaction.

Therefore, the consolidated profit for the year figure is calculated as follows:

	$
HJ's profit for the year	900,000
KL's profit for the year	600,000
Less intra-group dividend income (80% × $100,000)	(80,000)
	1,420,000

11.15 The correct answer is: $2,195,000

This is calculated as follows:

	$
PH	1,300,000
GF	860,000
Add impairment loss on goodwill for the year	35,000
	2,195,000

Note. All of the impairment loss is charged to the consolidated administrative expenses with the NCI being allocated their share of the impairment loss separately as part of the NCI in profit for the year calculation.

11.16 The correct answer is: $1,158,000

This is calculated as follows:

	$
MN – profit for the year	750,000
PQ – profit for the year	410,000
Fair value adjustments – movements in the year:	
Inventories – sold in year	(20,000)
Contingent liability – settled in the year	18,000
Consolidated profit for the year	1,158,000

The other answers are incorrect for the following reasons:

- $1,122,000 – the settlement of the contingent liability has been deducted from rather than added to profit.

- $1,140,000 – this answer ignores the movement in the contingent liability. The contingent liability was disclosed in PQ's financial statements but should be recognised in full in the group accounts at the acquisition date of 1 January 20X0. However, at the subsequent year end, as the liability has been settled, it is reversed and this post-acquisition movement should be posted to the consolidated statement of profit or loss.

- $1,198,000 – this answer incorrectly adds the movement in inventory to profit rather than deducting it.

11.17 The correct answer is: $1,950,000

This is a mid-year acquisition. QR obtained control of VB four months prior to the year end. Therefore, the results of VB must be pro-rated and only 4/12 of VB's income and expenses should be consolidated to reflect the number of months QR controlled VB in the year ended 31 December 20X4.

Therefore, consolidated distribution costs are calculated as follows:

	$
QR	1,650,000
VB – from 1 September 20X4 to 31 December 20X4 ($900,000 × 4/12)	300,000
	1,950,000

11.18 The correct answer is: $186,000

This is calculated as follows:

	Profit for the year (PFY)
	$
Per question	970,000
Consolidation adjustments affecting the subsidiary's profit:	
Impairment loss on goodwill (as NCI is measured at fair value at acquisition) (10% × 120,000)	(12,000)
Provision for unrealised profit (as the subsidiary is the seller) (50,000 × 40% × 1/2)	(10,000)
Fair value adjustments – additional depreciation in the year (360,000 × 1/20)	(18,000)
	930,000
NCI share	× 20%
	= 186,000

11.19 The correct answer is: $35,000

Other comprehensive income is consolidated like any other income and expense – all (not just the group share) of the subsidiary's other comprehensive income is added to the parent's.

However, here there is a mid-year acquisition. As the subsidiary has only been owned for three months (1 October 20X2–31 December 20X2), the other comprehensive income should only be included for the three months that YC controlled MX and so must be pro-rated accordingly. Therefore, consolidated other comprehensive income is calculated as:

	$
YC's other comprehensive income	30,000
MX's other comprehensive income (1 October 20X2– 31 December 20X2) (20,000 × 3/12)	5,000
	35,000

11.20 The correct answer is: $96,000

The impairment of goodwill has no impact on non-controlling interests (NCI) because NCI is measured at the proportionate share of net assets at acquisition which means that the partial goodwill method has been adopted and no goodwill is recognised in relation to NCI.

The provision for unrealised profit has no effect on NCI because the parent (rather than the subsidiary) was the seller.

Therefore, NCI in total comprehensive income for the year is calculated as follows:

	$
Total comprehensive income of KX (before any consolidation adjustments)	400,000
Additional depreciation on fair value adjustment on property	(16,000)
	384,000
NCI share	× 25%
	= 96,000

12 Associates and joint arrangements

12.1 The correct answer is: $407,030

With an associate, the group share of the unrealised profit needs to be removed at the year end:

Unrealised profit = $10,000 × 3/4 in inventory × 20/100 margin × 30% = $450

The adjustment should be made in the parent's column (even though the associate is the seller) to avoid multiplying the unrealised profit by the group share twice.

The consolidated retained earnings working is as follows:

	EF group	SR
	$	$
At the year end	390,000	90,000
Provision for unrealised profit	(450)	
At acquisition		(22,000)
		68,000
Group share of SR's post acquisition retained earnings (68,000 × 30%)	20,400	
Less impairment of investment in associate	(2,920)	
	407,030	

12.2 The correct answer is: $126,900

	$
Cost of associate	75,000
Share of post-acquisition reserves [($270,000 - $50,000) × 30%]	66,000
	141,000
Impairment (10% × $141,000)	(14,100)
	126,900

12.3 The correct answers are:

- A joint venture is always structured through a separate vehicle.
- A joint venture must have a contractual arrangement.

A **joint operation** is a joint arrangement whereby the parties that have joint control have **rights to the assets and obligations for the liabilities** relating to the arrangement (IFRS 11: Appendix A).

A **joint venture** is a joint arrangement whereby the parties that have joint control have **rights to the net assets** of the arrangement (IFRS 11: Appendix A).

A joint venture must be structured through a separate vehicle. However, an arrangement that is structured through a separate vehicle may also be a joint operation, depending on the terms and the circumstances (ie whether the parties have rights to the assets and obligations for the liabilities **or** rights to the net assets).

Both joint ventures and joint operations need to have a contractual arrangement and joint control. This is what distinguishes them from associates.

12.4 The correct answers are:

- In the group accounts of the joint venturer, the equity method must be applied to its interest in the joint venture.

- Joint operations are accounted for by including the investor's share of assets, liabilities, income and expenses as per the contractual arrangement.

In the investor's separate financial statements, there is a choice of three possible methods to account for an investment in a joint venture. An investment in a joint venture may be accounted for at cost, in accordance with IFRS 9 or using the equity method. (IAS 27: para. 10)

12.5 The correct answer is: $'000 135

Investment in associate:	$'000
Cost of associate	60
Share of post-acquisition reserves (40% × [220 – 30])	76
Unrealised intra-group profit (40% × 10 × 25%)	(1)
	135

Note. The unrealised profit is deducted from the investment in the associate rather than inventory as the associate holds the inventory at the year end.

12.6 The correct answer is: Dr Share of profit of associate $8,750; Cr Inventories $8,750

Provision for unrealised profit	=	$500,000 × 25/125
	=	$100,000 × ¼
	=	$25,000
Adjust for the parent share in the associate	=	$25,000 × 35%
	=	$8,750

Reduce the profit in associate (as it has made the profit on the sale) and reduce the inventory in the parent (included in the consolidation) as the inventory held by the parent is overvalued.

12.7 The correct answer is: Include 25% of the assets and liabilities of UV and 25% of the revenue and expenses generated by UV

On consolidation no further entries are required as the 25% share of UV has already been included in the accounts of T.

If UV was a joint venture then it would be included in T's individual financial statements under one of three possible methods: either at cost; in accordance with IFRS 9; or using the equity method. A joint venture would then be included in the group accounts using the equity method.

12.8 The correct answer is: $570,000

	$'000
Cost of investment	650
Share of post-acquisition retained earnings (1,600 - 720) × 25%	220
Impairment	(300)
	570

12.9 The correct answer is: $222,270

	$
Group share of profit for the year (721,000 × 35%)	252,350
PUP (240,000 × 40% × 30%) × 35%	(10,080)
Impairment loss	(20,000)
	222,270

Note. The group share of the PUP is deducted because the associate (CK) is the seller. If the parent (HL) had been the seller, group cost of sales would have been increased instead.

12.10 The correct answer is: AB and CD have joint control of XY.

The combined shareholdings of AB and CD amount to 75%. Due to the contractual arrangement between AB and CD to vote together, and the fact that a majority of voting rights (at least 50%) is required for decisions, AB and CD have joint control. Even if investors owning the remaining 30% vote against them, this would not stop a decision by AB and CD going ahead. Therefore, the remaining 30% do not share control. The parties sharing control are AB and CD alone. XY is a joint arrangement. Whether it is a joint operation or joint venture of AB and CD depends upon whether AB and CD have rights to the assets and obligations for the liabilities or whether they have rights to the net assets of XY.

XY is not an associate of AB and CD as these two entities have joint control of XY rather than significant influence. To be a subsidiary, either AB or CD would need outright control of XY which is not the case here.

12.11 The correct answers are:

- PC will be treated as a joint venture in this case but only because key policy decisions require the consent of at least five of the directors and each of the investors has rights to the net assets of PC.
- SG should equity account for PC in its consolidated financial statements.
- In SG's own financial statements, the investment in PC should be held at cost in accordance with IFRS 9 *Financial Instruments,* or using the equity method as described in IAS 28 *Investments in Associates and Joint Ventures.*

To be a joint arrangement, joint control is required so simply owning one-third of the shares each is not enough. Unanimous consent is required and as all three investors' votes are needed here, there is joint control.

PC is a joint venture rather than a joint operation as SG has rights to the net assets of PC. The correct accounting treatment in the individual financial statements for a joint venture is to record the investment at cost, in accordance with IFRS 9 (at fair value with gains/losses in P/L or OCI if irrevocable election is taken up), or using the equity method. The correct accounting treatment in the consolidated financial statements is to equity account.

Accounting for SG's share of PC's assets, liabilities, expenses and revenue is incorrect because this would be the accounting treatment for a joint operation.

12.12 The correct answer is: AB and SL.

CD has the largest shareholding in AB and a board seat, which allow CD to exercise significant influence over AB, making AB an associate.

Significant influence is presumed when an entity holds 20% or more of the voting power. As CD holds 20% of the equity shares in SL, this threshold has been met. It is supported by the interchange of management personnel.

As mentioned above, significant influence is presumed when an entity holds 20% of more of the voting power. This would imply that WR is also an associate. However, the substance of the arrangement also needs to be considered. As CD does not have any representation on the board of WR and there is a majority shareholder that is the only shareholder with seats on the board, in substance, CD does not have significant influence over WL. Therefore, WL is not an associate of CD.

12.13 The correct answer is: $960

EF is a joint venture because the three parties have joint control over the arrangement. Therefore, EF must be accounted for in the RS group accounts using the equity method. Under this method, the group share of any unrealised profit in inventory must be eliminated.

	$
Profit on sale ($160,000 × 25/125)	32,000
Unrealised profit on goods left in inventory ($32,000 × 10%)	3,200
Group share (30% × 3,200)	960

12.14 The correct answer is: $16,250

GH is a joint venture of AB as AB has joint control over the arrangement and the parties sharing control have rights of the net assets of GH. Therefore, the equity method must be applied. This is a mid-year acquisition. Therefore, the share of the joint venture's profit should only be included for the nine months that AB had joint control over GF (1 October 20X8 to 30 June 20X9).

Share of profit of joint venture	$
25% × ($100,000 × 9/12)	18,750
Unrealised profit (W)	(2,500)
	16,250

Working: Unrealised profit

GH (joint venture) sells to AB (parent)

$80,000 × 25% × ½ = $10,000

Group share $10,000 × 25% = $2,500 deducted from the share of joint venture's profit (if the parent had been the seller, the adjustment would have been to increase cost of sales rather than decrease the share of joint venture's profit).

12.15 The correct answer is: $25,900

AF is a joint venture of HC. Therefore, the equity method must be applied. This involves recognising an investment in the joint venture which is calculated as follows:

	$'000
Cost of investment	25,000
Share of post-acquisition reserves 30% × ($6,500 – $3,500)	900
	25,900

Remember, retained earnings increase by profit for the year but decrease by dividends paid. As HC has only owned its shareholding in AF for one year, post-acquisition reserves comprise the current year's profit less the current year's dividend.

12.16 The correct answer is: $141,000

HQ is a joint venture of RY. Therefore, the equity method must be applied. This involves calculating the investment in joint venture for inclusion in the consolidated statement of financial position as follows:

	$'000
Cost of investment	120
Share of post-acquisition retained earnings 40% × (140 – 80)	24
Unrealised profit 30 × 25% × 40%	(3)
Investment in associate	141

The group share of the unrealised profit is eliminated by reducing the investment in the joint venture as the joint venture holds the inventory at the year end. However, if the joint venture (rather than the parent) had been the seller and the parent (rather than the joint venture) had held the inventory at the year end, the unrealised profit would have been eliminated from inventory rather than the investment in the joint venture.

12.17 The correct answer is: $1,500

An adjustment needs to be made to eliminate the group share of the unrealised profit as EF is a joint venture (AB has joint control and rights to the net assets of EF). The unrealised profit only relates to goods left in inventory at the year end. Therefore, the total unrealised profit is $5,000 ([$80,000 – $60,000] × 25% in inventory). The group share of the unrealised profit which must be eliminated amounts to $1,500 (30% × $5,000).

As the parent holds the inventory at the year end, the accounting entry required to eliminate the group share of the unrealised profit is the consolidated statement of financial position is:

Debit	Consolidated retained earnings	$1,500	
Credit	Inventories		$1,500

This accounting entry was not required to answer the question but has been included for your understanding.

12.18 The correct answers are:

- At cost
- At fair value
- Using the equity method

12.19 The correct answer is: As an associate

Although at first glance QR does not appear to have significant influence over LP because it owns less than 20% of the voting rights, there are other indicators of significant influence:

- QR has representation on the board of LP
- QR participates in policy-making processes because some decisions require unanimous consent
- There has been interchange of management personnel between QR and LP
- QR has provided LP with technical information

Therefore, LP appears to be an associate of QR. It is not a joint venture as not all decisions require unanimous consent; nor is it a subsidiary, as QR does not have outright control.

12.20 The correct answers are:

- A joint venture is always structured through a separate vehicle.
- A joint venture must be accounted for using the equity method in the consolidated financial statements.
- A contractual arrangement and two or more parties sharing control are the key characteristics of a joint arrangement.

The other answers are incorrect because:

- A joint operation may be structured through a separate vehicle.
- There is no requirement for the parties sharing control to have equal shareholdings – instead, unanimous consent regarding decisions over relevant activities is required
- To be a joint arrangement, unanimous consent of all shareholders is not mandatory – it is possible for only unanimous consent of only some of the shareholders to be required and for these parties only to have joint control.

13 Foreign transactions and foreign subsidiaries

13.1 The correct answer is: A$496,250

The exchange loss is arrived at by comparing the increase in net assets to the retained profit for the year. The increase in net assets is calculated as the closing net assets at the closing rate less the opening net assets at the opening rate. The retained profit is the profit at the average rate less the dividend at the actual rate.

	A$	A$
Closing net assets at closing rate (B$6,510,000/1.6)		4,068,750
Opening net assets at opening rate (B$4,557,000/1.4)		(3,255,000)
		813,750
Profit for the year (B$2,325,000/1.5)	1,550,000	
Dividend (B$372,000/1.55)	(240,000)	
		(1,310,000)
		(496,250)

Note. Other comprehensive income should include 100% of this loss (whereas consolidated reserves would include the group share of the loss).

The incorrect answers result from taking the group share of the exchange loss in error (A$397,000), translating the dividend at the average rather than the actual rate (A$488,250) and ignoring the dividend (A$736,250).

13.2 The correct answer is: $7,027,000

	€'000
Consideration transferred	20,000
Non-controlling interests (at fair value)	4,200
	24,200
Fair value of net assets	(19,000)
Goodwill	5,200
Translated at closing rate	
€0.74 to $1	7,027

13.3 The correct answer is: $70,720

The total effect of the acquisition on group reserves includes:

- The group share of the subsidiary's post acquisition reserves
- The group share of exchange differences on net assets and profit

The subsidiary was acquired partway through the current period. Therefore the post-acquisition reserves are going to comprise the profit for the nine months in the year the subsidiary was owned (1 April 20X7 to 31 December 20X7). This figure is given in the question as 97,920 crowns and should be divided by the average rate for the period of 1.7, giving post-acquisition profits of $57,600 (97,920 crowns/1.7).

The group share of exchange differences on net assets and profit is calculated as follows:

	$
Closing net assets at closing rate (489,600 crowns/1.6)	306,000
Opening net assets at opening rate (391,680 crowns/1.8)	(217,600)
	88,400
Less retained profit translated at average rate (97,920 crowns/1.7)	(57,600)
Exchange gain	30,800

The total amount to be recognised in group reserves is calculated as follows:

	$
Group share of post-acquisition reserves (57,600 × 80%)	46,080
Group share of exchange differences (30,800 × 80%)	24,640
Total amount to be recognised in group reserves in relation to EF	70,720

13.4 The correct answers are:

- It is the currency of the entity's year-end financial statements.
- The entity may choose which presentation currency to use.

The currency of the primary economic environment is the definition of the functional currency of an entity. The currency that mainly influences the entity's sales price is one of the factors IAS 21 requires to be considered when determining the functional currency.

The currency of the year-end financial statements and the currency the entity may choose both relate to the presentation currency which is defined as the currency in which the

financial statements are presented. IAS 21 allows the entity to choose its own presentation currency.

Whilst many entities choose to present their year-end financial statements in their functional currency, in certain circumstances (such as a listing on a foreign stock exchange or a parent preparing group financial statements in a different currency), an entity may choose to adopt a presentation currency which is different from their functional currency.

13.5 The correct answer is: When a foreign subsidiary has a different functional currency from the presentation currency of the group financial statements, **all** assets and liabilities of the subsidiary must be translated at the **closing rate**, income and expenses at the **average rate** and exchange differences should be reported in **other comprehensive income**.

13.6 The correct answer is: A$204,000

Goodwill is retranslated at each year end:

B$510,000/2.5 = A$204,000

13.7 The correct answer is: $5,099,000

	$'000
HM	3,200
OS (3,000/1.58)	1,899
	5,099

The consolidated statement of profit or loss and other comprehensive income of the foreign subsidiary is translated at the average rate.

13.8 The correct answers are:

	$'000
On translation of net assets	
Closing net assets at closing rate	10,691
Less opening net assets at opening rate	9,814
	X
Less total comprehensive income as translated	285
	X
Translation difference on goodwill	54
	X

Workings

1   *Calculation of exchange differences for the year*

	$'000
On translation of net assets	
Closing net assets at closing rate (15,800,000 + 450,000)/1.52	10,691
Opening net assets at opening rate (15,800,000/1.61)	(9,814)
	877
Less profit (450,000/1.58)	(285)
	592
Translation differences on goodwill (W2)	54
	646

2   *Calculation of exchange difference on goodwill*

	$'000
Goodwill at acquisition (1,680,000/1.61)	1,043
Impairment [(1,680,000 × 20%)/1.58]	(213)
Exchange gain to OCI (balancing figure)	54
Goodwill at 31 December 20X1 [(1,680,000 × 80%)/1.52]	884

Note. The goodwill calculation has been included as a learning exercise. This working was not necessary to answer the question as exchange differences on goodwill were provided in the question.

13.9 The correct answer is: $1,155,000

	Group $'000	Owners of HM $'000	NCI (20%) $'000
HM	580	580	–
OS (450/1.58)	285	228	57
Impairment [(1,680 × 20%)/1.58]	(213)	(170)	(43)
Exchange gains	646	517	129
	1,298	1,155	143

13.10 The correct answer is: A and C.

IAS 21 defines the functional currency as the currency of the primary economic environment in which the entity operates. One of the indicators that a subsidiary's functional currency is its own local currency is that its activities are carried out with a significant degree of autonomy.

Both A and C operate largely autonomously; therefore, their functional currencies will be their own local currency. However, B's activities are carried out as an extension of its parent. Therefore its primary economic environment is that of the parent, and its functional currency is the parent's currency (rather than its own local currency).

13.11 The correct answer is: $1,902,000

Translation of MO's SOFP:

	Unit'000	Rate	$'000
Other assets	1,260	2.5	504
Share capital	500	2.0	250
Pre-acquisition reserves	220	2.0	110
Post-acquisition reserves (460 – 220)	240	Bal.	24
			384
Liabilities	300	2.5	120
			504

Consolidated reserves:

	RA	MO
	$'000	Unit'000
Per question/translation working (110 + 24)	1,900	134
Less pre-acquisition		(110)
		24
Share of MO's post acquisition reserves (24 × 75%)	18	
Exchange losses arising on goodwill (given)	(16)	
	1,902	

Note. 100% of the exchange losses on goodwill have been deducted as it is the partial goodwill method (NCI is measured at the proportionate share of net assets) meaning that all of the goodwill and all of the associated exchange differences belong to the group.

13.12 The correct answers are:

- The functional currency of OP will be determined by the currency that dominates the primary economic environment in which OP operates.
- OP operates autonomously and raises its own finance which indicates that its functional currency should be ludd.

Functional currency is determined by the primary economic environment within which it operates. Companies within the same group can have different functional currencies, the functional currency of a subsidiary is not determined by the functional currency of the parent. Presentational currency can be any currency an entity chooses to use.

13.13 The correct answers are:

- If a subsidiary is autonomous, its functional currency will be its own local currency.
- If the level of intra-group transactions with a foreign subsidiary is high, this is an indicator that the functional currency of the subsidiary is the parent's currency.
- If the cash flows of a foreign subsidiary are sufficient to service its own debt, the functional currency of the subsidiary is likely to be the subsidiary's local currency.

These answers are all correct because the functional currency is determined by the entity's primary economic environment.

The other answers are incorrect because:

- The functional currency is the currency of the entity's primary economic environment. An entity may **not** choose its functional currency.
- The functional currency of a subsidiary is **not** chosen by its parent. It is dictated by the entity's primary economic environment.
- If the subsidiary's cash flows directly affect the parent this implies that the subsidiary is dependent on the parent's economic environment and the functional currency of the subsidiary would be the parent's currency rather than the subsidiary's local currency.

13.14   The correct answer is: A$11,800

	A$
TCI translated at the average rate: (C$450,000)/4.5	100,000
Impairment of goodwill (as NCI is measured at fair value): C$30,000/5	(6,000)
Exchange loss on translation of net assets	(25,000)
Exchange loss on translation of goodwill (as NCI is measured at fair value)	(10,000)
	59,000
NCI share	× 20%
	= 11,800

13.15   The correct answer is: A$283,750

	A$
NCI at acquisition (B$600,000/3)	200,000
NCI share of post-acquisition reserves (A$260,000 × 25%)	65,000
NCI share of exchange differences on goodwill (as NCI measured at FV at acquisition) (B$450,000/2 – B$450,000/3) × 25%	18,750
	283,750

13.16   The correct answers are:

- Loan
- Trade payable
- Cash

These are all monetary items – 'units of currency held and assets and liabilities to be received or paid in a fixed or determinable number of units of currency' (IAS 21). IAS 21 requires monetary assets and liabilities to be retranslated at the closing rate at the year end.

Non-monetary assets include non-current assets (here, the property and the licence) and inventory. These items should remain at the historical rate and not be retranslated at the year end unless they are held at fair value which is not the case here. Non-monetary assets held at fair value are retranslated at the date of remeasurement to fair value.

13.17   The correct answer is: Recognise an exchange loss of A$1,000 in profit or loss

The trade receivable should initially be recorded at the spot rate at the date of the transaction – this is the exchange rate of A$1:B$10 on 1 November 20X2. This results in recognition of a trade receivable of A$11,000 (B$110,000/10).

As the trade receivable is a monetary asset, IAS 21 requires it to be retranslated at the closing rate of A$1:B$11 at the year end of 31 December 20X2. This results in a revised trade receivable balance of A$10,000 (B$110,000/11). As the trade receivable balance has fallen, this results in an exchange loss equal to the decrease in the balance of A$1,000 (A$10,000 – A$11,000). IAS 21 requires this to be recognised in profit or loss:

Debit   Profit or loss   A$1,000
Credit Trade receivable   A$1,000

13.18 The correct answer is: Dr Trade payable A$200,000; Cr Cash A$180,000, Cr Profit or loss A$20,000

The foreign currency trade payable is initially translated at the spot rate at the date of the transaction of A$1:B$4 on 15 December 20X4 which results in an initial trade payable of A$225,000 (B$900,000/4).

As this is a monetary balance, it is retranslated at the closing rate of A$1:B$4.5 at the 31 December 20X4 year end which results in a restated trade payable of A$200,000 (B$900,000/4.5) and an exchange gain of A$25,000 (A$225,000 – A$200,000) which is recorded as follows:

Debit	Trade payable	A$25,000	
Credit	Profit or loss		A$25,000

On 10 January 20X5, the amount paid is translated using the exchange rate on that date of A$1:B$5 resulting in a reduction of A$180,000 (B$900,000/5) in the cash balance. The difference between the amount paid and the outstanding trade payable balance, which amounts to A$20,000 (A$200,000 – A$180,000), is recognised as an exchange gain in profit or loss:

Debit	Trade payable	A$200,000	
Credit	Cash		A$180,000
Credit	Profit or loss		A$20,000

13.19 The correct answer is:

Amount of gain in A$:	Recognise gain in:
15,000	Other comprehensive income

The land is a non-monetary asset. Non-monetary assets held at fair value are retranslated every time they are revalued.

The land must initially be recorded on 1 January 20X0 at the spot rate of A$1:B$5. This results in land of A$60,000 (B$300,000/5) being recognised.

On 31 December 20X2, the land is revalued and must also therefore be retranslated at the rate at the date of the revaluation of A$1:B$6. This increases the value of the land to A$75,000 (B$450,000/6) and results in a gain of A$15,000 (A$75,000 – A$60,000) which must be recognised in other comprehensive income. There is no need to separate this A$15,000 into the amount due to the increase in market value of the land and the amount due to movements in the exchange rate as both are required to be recognised in other comprehensive income.

The calculation is summarised below:

	A$
Revalued amount (B$450,000/6)	75,000
Less carrying amount of land (B$300,000/5)	(60,000)
Revaluation gain (including exchange gain)	15,000

13.20 The correct answer is:

Foreign transactions should initially be translated at the **spot rate** at the date of the transaction. At the year end all **monetary** assets and liabilities should be retranslated at the **closing rate**. Exchange differences must be recognised in **profit or loss**.

14 Consolidated statement of changes in equity

14.1 The correct answer is: $1,100,000

The dividends to include in the consolidated statement of changes in equity are:

	$
Attributable to the owners of the parent (SP's dividend)	1,000,000
Non-controlling interests (AX's dividend × NCI%) [400,000 × 25%]	100,000
Total	1,100,000

Note. The group share of the associate's dividend, ie 30% × $200,000 = $60,000, is excluded as it cancels on consolidation. Instead the group share of the associate's profit and other comprehensive income would be included in the consolidated statement of profit or loss and other comprehensive income when equity accounting for the associate.

14.2 The correct answer is:

TCI for owners of parent	TCI for non-controlling interests
$278,400	$19,600

	$
Consolidated total comprehensive income	298,000
($200,000 + $100,000 – [PUP: $15,000 × 2/3 in inventories × 20/100 margin])	
Total comprehensive income attributable to:	
Owners of the parent (balancing figure)	278,400
Non-controlling interests ([$100,000 – PUP $2,000] × 20%)	19,600
	298,000

14.3 The correct answers are:

- Issue of share capital
- Total comprehensive income for the year
- Dividends

A gain on revaluation of a property forms part of the total comprehensive income for the year figure so would not require separate line disclosure. Total comprehensive income for the year comprises both profit for the year and other comprehensive income; therefore, they do not need separate disclosure in their own right.

14.4 The correct answer is: As an increase to the equity attributable to the owners of the parent of $1,000,000

The equity attributable to the owners of the parent includes the parent's share capital and premium and consolidated reserves. Therefore, both the increase to share capital (500,000 × 50 cents = $250,000) and the increase to share premium (500,000 × $1.50 = $750,000) should be recorded as an increase to the equity attributable to the owners of the parent.

This is not an intra-group transaction as the shareholders of the parent are outside the group.

There is no impact on non-controlling interests as the shares have been issued by the parent rather than the subsidiary.

14.5 The correct answers are:

	Non-controlling interests $
Balance at 1 January 20X4 (10% × 100,000 × $2.20)	22,000
Total comprehensive income for the year (10% × $25,000)	2,500
Less dividends paid (10% × $5,000)	500
Balance at 31 December 20X4	24,000

14.6 The correct answer is: $105,880,000

The equity attributable to the owners of the parent at the year end is calculated as:

	$'000
Share capital (parent's only)	2,900
Consolidated retained earnings (see below)	102,980
	105,880

Consolidated retained earnings is calculated as:

	P $'000	S $'000	A $'000
At 31 December 20X7	78,200	38,500	16,000
PUP [($1.4m – $1m) × ¼ in inventory]		(100)	
Less pre-acquisition		(12,300)	(3,000)
		26,100	13,000
Group share of S post-acquisition (80% × 26,100)	20,880		
Group share of A post-acquisition (30% × 13,000)	3,900		
	102,980		

The other answers are incorrect for the following reasons:

- $102,980,000 – this figure only includes consolidated retained earnings but equity attributable to the owners of the parent should also include the parent's share capital.
- $105,640,000 – this figure has incorrectly deducted unrealised profit on all intra-group sales in the year rather than just those left in inventory.
- $105,860,000 – this figure has incorrected deducted unrealised profit from the parent's column in the consolidated retained earnings when it should have been deducted from the subsidiary's column, as the subsidiary was the seller.

14.7 The correct answers are:

- It is a primary statement required by IAS 1 *Presentation of Financial Statements*.
- The total comprehensive income for the year row comes from the ownership reconciliation in the consolidated statement of profit or loss and other comprehensive income.
- It reconciles equity from the prior year's consolidated statement of financial position to equity from the current year's consolidated statement of financial position.

While a consolidated statement of changes in equity is relevant to the parent's shareholders, it is also relevant to the external shareholders in subsidiaries (non-controlling interests).

The group share of the subsidiary is included in the equity attributable to the owners of the parent column. The NCI share of the subsidiary is included in the non-controlling interests column.

While associates are included in the consolidated statement of changes in equity (the group share of post-acquisition reserves), they will be included in the equity attributable to the owners of the parent column rather than a separate column in their own right.

14.8 The correct answer is: $5,812,500

Consolidated reserves at 1 January 20X5:

	LK $	SW $
Reserves at 1 January 20X5 per question	4,500,000	500,000
Less pre-acquisition reserves		(350,000)
		150,000
Share of SW post-acquisition (150,000 × 75%)	112,500	
	4,612,500	

Equity attributable to the owners of the parent comprises:

	$
Parent's share capital	1,000,000
Parent's share premium	200,000
Consolidated reserves	4,612,500
	5,812,500

14.9 The correct answer is: It includes dividends paid by the parent and dividends paid by the subsidiary to its external shareholders.

The equity attributable to the owners of the parent column includes the parent's dividends and the non-controlling interests column includes dividends paid by the subsidiary to the NCI.

Dividends paid by the parent to the subsidiary are cancelled on consolidation as they are an intra-group item.

Dividend income from subsidiaries and associates will be included in the parent's total comprehensive income figure. As they are intra-group items, they must be cancelled as a consolidation adjustment before entering the total comprehensive income line into the consolidated changes in equity.

14.10 The correct answers are:

- It should include the share capital and share premium of the parent and the year-end consolidated reserves figure.
- It should come to the same figure as equity before non-controlling interests in the year-end consolidated statement of financial position.
- It can be calculated as the broughtdown equity attributable to the owners of the parent, plus total comprehensive income for the year attributable to the owners of the parent, less the parent's dividends paid plus any share issues by the parent in the year.

The other answers are incorrect because unrealised profit on intragroup trading is cancelled on consolidation, the share capital and share premium of the subsidiary are excluded from the consolidated statement of financial position and the non-controlling interests relate to the subsidiary not the owners of the parent.

14.11 The correct answer is: $'000 34,400

	$'000
NCI at acquisition (fair value)	24,000
NCI share of post-acquisition reserves [(159,700 – 107,700) × 20%]	10,400
NCI at 31 March 20X8	34,400

14.12 The correct answer is: $483,000

This is calculated as follows:

	AB $	CD $
Equity at 1 January 20X9	420,000	175,000
Equity at acquisition		(105,000)
		70,000
Group share of CD's post-acquisition equity (90% × $70,000)	63,000	
	483,000	

Note. You did not need to add in the parent's share capital and share premium as the equity figure of $420,000 used in the above working already includes these balances.

14.13 The correct answer is: $759,200

This is calculated as follows:

	EF $	GH $
Equity at 31 December 20X4	720,000	260,000
Provision for unrealised profit ($20,000 × 40% margin × 3/4 in inventory)		(6,000)
Equity at acquisition		(170,000)
		84,000
Group share of GH's post-acquisition equity (80% × $84,000)	67,200	
Group share of impairment of goodwill (80% × $35,000)	(28,000)	
	759,200	

Notes

1 You did not need to add in the parent's share capital and share premium as the equity figure of $720,000 used in the above working already includes the parent's share capital and share premium.

2 The impairment of goodwill is multiplied by the group share because non-controlling interests are measured at fair value at acquisition.

14.14   The correct answer is: $3,500,000

The accounting entry on this share issue is:

Debit	Cash (1m × $3.50)	$3,500,000	
Credit	Share capital (1m × $1)		$1,000,000
Credit	Share premium (1m × $2.50)		$2,500,000

Both share capital and share premium are reported within equity. Therefore, the total increase in the parent's equity is $3,500,000 ($1,000,000 + $2,500,000).

14.15   The correct answer is: $724,000

	$
NCI at acquisition (40% × (1,000,000 + 200,000 + 440,000 + 90,000))	692,000
NCI share of post-acquisition retained earnings **up to the start of the year** (40% × (510,000 − 440,000))	28,000
NCI share of post-acquisition revaluation surplus **up to the start of the year** (40% × (100,000 − 90,000))	4,000
	724,000

14.16   The correct answer is: $860,000

The fair value adjustment on LM's property at acquisition is $40,000 ($190,000 fair value − $150,000 carrying amount). Five years have passed since the acquisition date (20X0, 20X1, 20X2, 20X3 and 20X4). Therefore, five years of additional depreciation need to be charged on the fair value adjustment to LM's property. This amounts to $20,000 ($40,000 × 5/10).

The provision for unrealised profit is calculated as: $200,000 × 25/125 mark-up × 1/4 in inventory = $10,000. As the subsidiary is the seller, this must be adjusted for in the NCI working.

	$
NCI at acquisition	520,000
NCI share of post-acquisition retained earnings (40% × (1,760,000 − 20,000 FV depreciation − 10,000 PUP − 880,000))	340,000
	860,000

14.17   The correct answer is: $391,500

This is calculated as follows:

	$
Total comprehensive income (pro-rated for mid-year acquisition) (1,200,000 × 9/12)	900,000
Consolidation adjustments affecting the subsidiary's profit:	
Fair value adjustment − movement in year (inventory sold)	(30,000)
	870,000
NCI share	× 45%
	= 391,500

Note that the intra-group sale of goods does not impact non-controlling interests as the parent, PW, was the seller.

14.18 The correct answer is: $827,000

This is calculated as follows:

	$
Total comprehensive income of parent (650,000 + 30,000)	680,000
Group share of total comprehensive income of subsidiary (70% × [235,000 + 15,000])	175,000
Less group share of impairment loss on goodwill for the year (70% × 40,000)	(28,000)
	827,000

14.19 The correct answers are:

- Parent's share capital
- Parent's share premium
- Consolidated reserves

The subsidiary's share capital and share premium are eliminated on consolidated. Non-controlling interests represent external shareholders in the subsidiary which is presented separately in the consolidated statement of changes of equity.

14.20 The correct answer is: $807,000

A consolidated statement of changes in equity should include the parent's dividend ($750,000) plus the non-controlling interest's share of the subsidiary's dividend (15% × $380,000). This amounts to $807,000 ($750,000 + [15% × $380,000]).

The dividend payable by the subsidiary to the parent is intra-group and is therefore eliminated on consolidation.

15 Consolidated statement of cash flows

15.1 The correct answer is: $135,000

You need to draw up a non-controlling interests working to find the dividends paid to NCI as a balancing figure:

	$
B/d (from 20X4 SOFP)	525,000
TCI attributable to NCI	60,000
NCI in subsidiary acquired (400,000 × 25%)	100,000
	685,000
Dividends paid to NCI (balancing figure)	(135,000)
C/d (from 20X5 SOFP)	550,000

The incorrect answers would have been arrived at by mixing up the b/d and c/d balances ($185,000), excluding NCI in the subsidiary acquired ($35,000) and deducting TCI attributable to NCI instead of adding it ($15,000).

15.2 The correct answer is: $767,000

Cash generated from operations is calculated as follows:

	$
Profit before taxation	775,000
Decrease in inventories (W)	5,000
Increase in receivables (W)	(33,000)
Increase in payables (W)	20,000
Cash generated from operations	767,000

Working: Movement in working capital

	Inventories $	Receivables $	Payables $
B/d	475,000	800,000	530,000
Acquisition of subsidiary	80,000	110,000	70,000
	555,000	910,000	600,000
Increase/(decrease) [bal. figure]	(5,000)	33,000	20,000
C/d	550,000	943,000	620,000

Be careful with the signs when posting the movements to the statement of cash flows. If inventory has decreased, we've sold some so it's a cash inflow. If receivables have increased, that means more credit sales which is bad for our cash flow so should be negative. But if payables have increased, it is good for our cash flow as we're not having to pay for cash purchases so it should be positive in the cash flow.

The incorrect answers would have arisen from ignoring the acquisition ($647,000), adjusting for the group share rather than 100% of the acquisition ($743,000) or using the wrong signs when adjusting for changes in inventories, receivables and payables ($783,000).

15.3 The correct answer is: $6,300

You need to complete an investment in associate working to find the dividends received as a balancing figure:

	$
B/d	107,900
Share of profit	10,000
Share of other comprehensive income	5,000
	122,900
Dividends received (balancing figure)	(6,300)
C/d	116,600

15.4 The correct answer is: Include under the heading 'operating activities' or 'financing activities'

Dividends paid can be shown under either operating activities or financing activities.

15.5 The correct answer is: $870,000

You need to complete a property, plant and equipment working to find additions as a balancing figure:

	$
B/d	3,700,000
Acquisition of subsidiary	500,000
Depreciation	(970,000)
	3,230,000
Additions (balancing figure)	870,000
C/d	4,100,000

Don't forget to include 100% of the PPE of the subsidiary acquired because this subsidiary will be consolidated for the first time this year and when we consolidate, we add across 100% of the assets and liabilities of the subsidiary (rather than the group share).

15.6 The correct answer is: $125,000

	$'000
Balance b/d	515
Revaluation gain	50
Depreciation	(60)
Acquisition of subsidiary	90
	595
Cash paid to buy PPE (balancing figure)	125
Balance c/d	720

15.7 The correct answer is: $375,000

	$
B/d	4,550,000
SPLOCI – TCI (395,000 + 30,000)	425,000
Acquisition of subsidiary (25% × 1,100,000)	275,000
Dividend paid (balancing figure)	(375,000)
C/d	4,875,000

15.8 The correct answer is: $120,000

	$'000
Balance b/d	6,600
Share of profit for the year (700 × 30%)	210
Share of other comprehensive income (200 × 30%)	60
	6,870
Dividends received (balancing figure)	(120)
Balance c/d	6,750

15.9 The correct answers are:

- Cash paid to acquire an interest in an associate
- Acquisition of equipment for cash
- Dividends received from an associate

Dividends paid to non-controlling interests are presented either under 'financing activities' (as per IAS 7 Illustrative Examples) or 'operating activities' (as an allowable alternative).

Under the indirect method, profit on sale of property, plant and equipment is shown as an adjustment to profit before tax in the 'operating activities' section of the statement of cash flows, as it is not a cash flow.

Interest paid on borrowings may either be presented as 'operating' or 'financing'.

15.10 The correct answer is: $4,000

You need to prepare a non-controlling interests working to find the dividends paid as a balancing figure:

	$
B/d	100,000
NCI in TCI	7,000
NCI in subsidiary acquired	8,000
	115,000
Dividends paid (balancing figure)	(4,000)
C/d	111,000

Note. The consolidated SPLOCI figure that you should use for the NCI working should be the NCI in total comprehensive income (not profit) as you need to include everything that makes NCI go up in the year (ie their share of profit and OCI).

15.11 The correct answer is: $230,000 outflow in one line

You only need to include the cash element of the consideration paid to buy the subsidiary which is $150,000 (the share element is non-cash). This is a cash outflow. You also need to add to this the subsidiary's overdraft of $80,000 which will be consolidated for the first time on acquisition of the subsidiary – this will cause group cash to fall so is also an outflow. IAS 7 requires these two cash flows to be aggregated, resulting in a total cash outflow of $230,000 (ie $150,000 + $80,000).

15.12 The correct answer is: ($535,000)

	$
Cash paid to buy shares	(500,000)
Cash balance consolidated	15,000
Overdraft consolidated	(50,000)
	(535,000)

The bank loan is not included as it does not fall within the definition of cash and cash equivalents.

15.13 The correct answer is: $40,000

Investment associate:

	$'000
Balance b/d	490
Share of profit for the year (300 × 25%)	75
Share of OCI (100 × 25%)	25
	590
Dividends received (balancing figure)	(40)
Balance c/d	550

15.14 The correct answer is: $146,000

	$
Opening balance (b/d)	685,000
Group share of joint ventures' profit for the year	219,000
Group share of joint ventures' other comprehensive income	51,000
Acquisition of joint venture	115,000
	1,070,000
Dividends received from joint ventures (balancing figure)	(146,000)
Closing balance (c/d)	924,000

15.15 The correct answer is: Include under the heading 'operating activities' or 'investing activities'.

Dividends received from associates can be shown under either operating activities or investing activities.

15.16 The correct answer is: ($718,000)

	$
Cash paid to buy the shares in MN	(759,000)
Cash balance consolidated	63,000
Overdraft consolidated	(22,000)
	(718,000)

15.17 The correct answer is: Deduct it from the profit before tax figure in 'operating activities'

Under the indirect method, the profit before tax figure is adjusted for non-cash items or items that should appear under a different heading in the statement of cash flows.

The group share of the associate's profit is not a cash flow. Therefore, it must be removed from the profit before tax by deducting it.

The cash flows for an associate may comprise dividends received from an associate, payments to acquire shares in new associates and receipts from selling shares in associates.

15.18 The correct answer is: $334,000

	$
Opening balance (b/d) (current + deferred) (800,000 + 150,000)	950,000
Current tax expense in P/L	400,000
Deferred tax expense in P/L	60,000
Deferred tax in OCI	30,000
Acquisition of subsidiary – current tax	70,000
Acquisition of subsidiary – deferred tax	24,000
	1,534,000
Tax paid (balancing figure)	(334,000)
Closing balance (c/d) (current + deferred) (1,000 + 200)	1,200,000

15.19 The correct answer is: An outflow of $28,000

	$
Opening balance (b/d)	389,000
Acquisition of subsidiary	56,000
	445,000
Increase in inventory (balancing figure)	28,000
Closing balance (c/d)	473,000

An increase in inventory means that inventory has been purchased in the year so this is a cash outflow. The incorrect amount of $47,600 arises if you wrongly include the group share of the inventory for the subsidiary acquired in the year. Remember, we add across 100% of the assets and liabilities of subsidiaries when we consolidate, in order to show control.

15.20 The correct answer is: $275,000

Goodwill:

	$
Opening balance (b/d)	775,000
Acquisition of subsidiary (W)	400,000
	1,175,000
Impairment of goodwill (balancing figure)	(275,000)
Closing balance (c/d)	900,000

Working: Goodwill on acquisition of GH

	$
Consideration transferred	
Shares (100,000 × $8.20)	820,000
Cash	300,000
Non-controlling interests (at fair value)	280,000
Less fair value of net assets at acquisition	(1,000,000)
Goodwill on acquisition of TU	400,000

16 Disclosure standards

16.1 The correct answer is: Arrangements entered into by the production director of the reporting entity to provide a review of the production facilities of a company controlled by his wife; the service will be provided at a full commercial price.

The director is a related party because he is considered to be key management personnel. The IAS 24 definition of a related party also extends to the close family of key management personnel. Close family includes children, spouse, domestic partner and dependants. Therefore, the director's wife is a related party. Under IAS 24, entities controlled by a related party also qualify as a related party. Therefore the company controlled by the director's wife is a related party. This is why the transaction requires disclosure.

The fact that a full price has been charged is irrelevant – all material related party transactions must be disclosed.

Trade unions in the normal course of their activities are not related parties (unless they have the capacity to control the entity).

Providers of finance and government departments and agencies are also deemed not to be related parties.

16.2 The correct answers are:

- The details of the transaction and a description of the nature of the relationships between the parties
- The amount involved

IAS 24 requires the disclosure of the details of the related party transactions including a description of the nature of the relationships between the related parties and the amount involved. However, there is no specific requirement to disclose either the name of the parties involved nor the date of the transaction. The only requirement regarding names is to disclose the controlling party and the ultimate controlling party.

There is no requirement to explain whether the transaction price was equivalent to the market value or not. Disclosures that related party transactions were made on terms equivalent to those that prevail in arm's-length transactions are made only if such terms can be substantiated.

16.3 The correct answers are:

- A person with a controlling shareholding in the parent company of WH
- An entity in which the wife of the finance director of WH owns a controlling stake
- A subsidiary of one of WH's associates

A person who has control over the entity meets the definition of a related party.

The finance director of WH would qualify as a related party as he is key management personnel and so would his wife as she is close family. The entity in which the finance director's wife has a controlling stake would also be a related party of WH.

Associates and joint ventures are related parties of their parent company. This definition also includes subsidiaries of the associate and joint venture. Therefore, a subsidiary of WH's associate qualifies as a related party of WH.

According to IAS 24, the following are not related parties:

- Two joint venturers simply because they share joint control over a joint venture
- A customer with whom the entity transacts a significant volume of business

16.4 The correct answer is: Shareholders of a large listed entity

Generally shareholders are not involved in the day-to-day running of a large listed entity. Therefore they need to be informed of any related party transactions.

However as directors are responsible for and employees are involved in the day-to-day running of the company, they should already be aware of related party transactions. Members of the same group qualify as related parties so will be aware of transactions among themselves.

16.5 The correct answers are:

- KL – an entity in which the controlling shareholder of HJ has a 30% shareholding and significant influence
- Mr Smith – the domestic partner of Ms Wilson who is a director of HJ
- WX – the defined benefit pension plan for the employees of HJ

Ms Green is not a related party of HJ as she is not key management personnel.

Trade unions do not qualify as related parties under IAS 24.

Under IAS 24, related parties, parent and subsidiaries, fellow subsidiaries, parent and associates, associates and joint ventures are all related. However, two associates in the same group are not related to each other as common significant influence is not considered sufficient.

Where a person who has control of the entity (and also their close family) has significant influence in another entity, that second entity is related to the first entity. This means that KL qualifies as a related party.

Key management personnel and their close family which includes domestic partners are considered to be related parties. This means that Mr Smith is a related party of HJ.

Post-employment benefit plans are also considered to be a related party to the entity. This means that WX would also be considered to be a related party.

16.6 The correct answer is: A close family member of the chief executive of NV purchased an asset from NV.

The chief executive of NV is a related party as they are key management personnel and close family of a related party is also considered to be a related party in their own right.

However, providers of finance (XYZ Bank), departments and agencies of a government that do not control/jointly control/significantly influence the reporting entity (government of Country X) and a supplier with whom an entity transacts a significant volume of business (YU) are not considered to be related parties.

16.7 The correct answers are:

- Purchase of inventory by a parent from an associate
- Sale of a company asset to the managing director of the reporting entity, at an externally agreed fair value
- Sale of an asset by Company A to an entity in which the wife of the managing director of Company A has a controlling interest

An associate, key management personnel, close family of key management and entities in which a related party has controlling interest are all related parties under IAS 24. Related party transactions must be disclosed even if they are at market value.

The other answers are incorrect because two associates, providers of finance (eg venture capital company) and suppliers with whom the entity transacts a large volume of business do **not** qualify as related parties under IAS 24.

16.8 The correct answers are:

- The chief executive officer of the BS board
- CD, an entity in which the husband of the chief executive officer of the BS board has a controlling shareholding

The CEO of the BS board is a related party as she is considered to be key management personnel. CD is a related party because it is an entity which a close family member of key management personnel controls.

TX is not a related party as IAS 24 states that a customer with whom an entity transacts a significant volume of business is not a related party simply by virtue of the resulting economic dependence. EF is not a related party because IAS 24 states that two joint venturers are not related simply because they share joint control of a joint venture. GH is not related as providers of finance are not considered to be related parties by virtue of their normal dealings with the entity.

16.9 The correct answers are:

- During the accounting period, George purchased a property from CB for $500,000. CB had previously declared the property surplus to its requirements and had valued it at $750,000.
- George's son, Arnold, is a director and controlling shareholder of a financial institution, FC. During the accounting period, FC advanced $2 million to CB as an unsecured loan at a favourable rate of interest.

As the chief executive officer, George is considered to be key management personnel and therefore a related party of CB, meaning that the sale of the property by CB to George needs to be disclosed.

Close family of a person who is a related party is considered to also qualify as a related party. The definition of close family includes children; therefore, as George is a related party, his son Arnold is also a related party of CB. Normally a provider of finance is not considered to be a related party but as a related party (Arnold) who has a controlling interest in FC, FC is also considered to be a related party and therefore the loan should be disclosed.

A customer with whom the entity transacts a significant volume of business is not a related party simply by virtue of the resulting economic dependence. Therefore, CB's sales to XC do not require disclosure as related party transactions.

Associates within the same group are not considered to be related parties as common significant influence is insufficient. Therefore, the sale of goods from CB to FG does not require disclosure.

Two entities are not related if they simply have a director in common. Therefore, CB and LK are not related parties and the cleaning services provided by LK do not require disclosure as related party transactions.

16.10 The correct answer is: The management fee payable by EF to AB

EF is a related party of AB as it is an associate of AB. Therefore, the management fee charged by AB should be disclosed.

However, two associates are not considered to be related parties under IAS 24. Therefore even though the sales by EF to GH are at cost, they are not required to be disclosed.

The question specifically asked about disclosure in EF's financial statements. Therefore, transactions between other group entities (ie sale of goods by CD to AB and management fee payable by CD and GH) are not relevant.

16.11 The correct answer is: The denominator of the earnings per share ratio is the weighted average number of ordinary shares outstanding during the period.

The other answers are incorrect because:

- Only an entity whose shares are traded in a public market (ie a listed entity) is required to disclose earnings per share.
- Earnings per share only represent the return for ordinary shareholders, not all capital providers.
- Preference dividends must also be deducted from profit after tax to arrive at earnings and the weighted average, not the year end total of ordinary shares, should be used.

16.12 The correct answer is: 17.7 cents

To restate comparatives, apply the reciprocal of the bonus fraction to the prior year.

$$\text{Bonus fraction} = \frac{\text{No. of shares after bonus issue}}{\text{No. of shares before bonus issue}} = \frac{3}{2}$$

EPS: 26.5 × 2/3 = 17.7 cents

16.13 The correct answer is: 5.1 million

Calculate the shares that are treated as being issued for nil consideration:

No. of shares under option		500,000
No. of shares that would have been issued at the average market price	$\frac{500{,}000 \times \$2.80}{3.50}$	(400,000)
No. of shares treated as issued for nil consideration		100,000

Shares used in EPS calculation = 5,000,000 + 100,000 = 5.1m

16.14 The correct answer is: $1.33

EPS = $120,000/90,476 (W1) = $1.33

Workings

1   Weighted average number of shares

Date	Narrative	No. of shares	Time	Bonus fraction	Weighted average
1.1.X6	B/f	80,000	8/12	1.5/1.4 (W2)	57,143
1.9.X6	1 for 4 rights issue	20,000			
		100,000	4/12		33,333
					90,476

2   Bonus fraction

= Fair value before rights issue/theoretical ex-rights price (TERP) = $1.5/$1.4 (W3)

3   Theoretical ex-rights price

	$
4 shares × $1.50	6
1 share × $1	1
5 shares	7

TERP = $7/5 shares = $1.4

16.15 The correct answer is: 35.2c

Diluted EPS = $\dfrac{\$2{,}852{,}964 \text{ (W1)}}{8{,}100{,}000 \text{ (W2)}}$ = 35.2 cents

Workings

1 *Diluted earnings*

	$
Basic earnings	2,763,000
Interest saving net of tax ($1,836,000 × 7% × 70%)	89,964
Diluted earnings	2,852,964

2 *Diluted number of shares*

	No. of shares
Basic	6,000,000
Maximum no. of shares on conversion (2m/100 × 105)	2,100,000
Diluted number of shares	8,100,000

The other answers are incorrect for the following reasons:

- 35.4 cents – this answer did not use the maximum number of shares on conversion so assumed a conversion rate of 103 shares per $100 of loan notes rather than 105 shares.
- 35.7 cents – this answer forgot to deduct the lost tax relief when calculating the interest saving in the diluted earnings working.
- 46.1 cents – this is the basic EPS but the question asked for the diluted EPS.

16.16 The correct answer is: 53.2c

Earnings

	$
Profit before tax	1,000,000
Tax	(200,000)
Non-controlling interests	(100,000)
Preference dividends on non-cumulative irredeemable preference shares (classified as equity)	(20,000)
Earnings attributable to the ordinary shareholders of the parent	680,000

= $\dfrac{\text{Earnings attributable to the ordinary shareholders of the parent}}{\text{Weighted average number of ordinary shares}}$

= $680,000/1,278,376

= 53.2c

Earnings are calculated as profits available for the ordinary shareholders. Therefore, earnings are profit after tax, NCI and preference dividends (on preference shares classified as equity as dividends are not already deducted in arriving at profit after tax).

The non-cumulative irredeemable preference shares are classified as equity since there is no obligation to pay dividends or to repay the principal. Therefore, the preference dividends are treated as an appropriation of profit and are deducted from retained earnings in the statement of changes in equity. This means that they have not already been deducted in arriving at the profit after tax figure so need to be removed when calculating earnings attributable to ordinary shareholders.

However, the cumulative redeemable preference shares contain an obligation to pay dividends and to repay the principal. Therefore, they are classified as a financial liability. This means that the dividends are classified as a finance cost so have already been accounted for in calculating profit before tax. Consequently they do not need to be deducted from profit before tax to arrive at the earnings figure.

Note. The ordinary dividends are not deducted because earnings should represent the amount available to the ordinary shareholders to either be distributed as dividends or to be reinvested in the business.

16.17   The correct answer is: 50.7c

$$\text{Basic EPS} = \frac{\$320,000 - \$20,000}{591,667 \text{ (W1)}} = 50.7c$$

Workings

1   Weighted average number of shares

Date	Narrative	No. of shares	Time	Bonus fraction	Weighted average
1.1.X3	B/f	500,000	2/12	11/10 (W2)	91,667
1.3.X3	Rights issue (1 for 5)	100,000			
		600,000	10/12		500,000
					591,667

2   Bonus fraction

$$= \frac{\text{Fair value per share immediately before rights issue}}{\text{Theoretical ex-rights price (W3)}}$$

$$= \frac{\$11}{\$10}$$

3   Theoretical ex-rights price

	$
5 shares × $11	55
1 share × $5	5
6 shares	60

TERP = $60/6 = $10

16.18 The correct answer is: 78.1 cents

$$EPS = \frac{\$8,200,000}{10,500,000} = 78.1 \text{ cents}$$

Weighted average number of shares:

Date	Narrative	Number of shares	Time	Weighted average
1 January 20X3	B/f	10,000,000	9/12	7,500,000
1 October 20X3	FMP issue	2,000,000		
		12,000,000	3/12	3,000,000
				10,500,000

16.19 The correct answer is: 17.9 cents

$$\text{Diluted EPS} = \frac{\$966,000 \text{ (W1)}}{5,400,000 \text{ (W2)}} = 17.9 \text{ cents}$$

Workings

1 *Diluted earnings*

	$
Basic earnings (1,040,000 − 270,000)	770,000
Interest saving net of tax (4,000,000 × 7% × 70%)	196,000
Diluted earnings	966,000

2 *Diluted number of shares*

	No. of shares
Basic	3,000,000
Maximum no. of shares on conversion	2,400,000
Diluted number of shares	5,400,000

16.20 The correct answer is: 72.7 cents

$$\text{Diluted EPS} = \frac{\$3,800,000}{5m + 225,000 \text{ (W1)}} = 72.7 \text{ cents}$$

Working: Number of shares issued at nil consideration

	No. of shares
No. of shares under option	1,000,000
No. that would have been issued at full market price	
(1,000,000 × $3.10)/$4	775,000
No. of shares for nil consideration	225,000

17 Integrated reporting and sustainability reporting

17.1 The correct answer is: To provide information to stakeholders on environmental, social and governance issues

Reporting of greenhouse gas emissions is covered in some sustainability reporting standards, such as IFRS S2 *Climate-related Disclosures* but sustainability reporting covers a wider range of environmental, social and governance topics.

Sustainability reporting is intended to complement financial reporting, and should be consistent where applicable, but it is not just an addition to financial reporting.

The combination of financial and non-financial information with a forward-looking perspective to help users understand the overall value of the business is the purpose of integrated reporting, not sustainability reporting. There are crossovers between the two types of reporting but integrated reporting covers a wider range of topics including financial reporting.

17.2 The correct answer is: To meet the information needs of investors

The ISSB has four key objectives:

(a) To develop standards for a global baseline of sustainability disclosures;

(b) To meet the information needs of investors;

(c) To enable companies to provide comprehensive sustainability information to global capital markets; and

(d) To facility interoperability with disclosures that are jurisdiction-specific and/or aimed at broader stakeholder groups.

An integrated report combines the different strands of reporting into a coherent whole that explains an organisation's ability to create and sustain value.

The purpose of an integrated report is to explain to providers of financial capital how an organisation creates value over time.

The standards issued by the International Sustainability Standards Board are optional rather than mandatory.

17.3 The correct answer is: A process founded on integrated thinking resulting in a periodic report about value creation, preservation or erosion over time

Integrated reporting is designed to go beyond an entity's financial statements to consider creation of value over the short, medium and long term.

An integrated report may include social, environmental and economic reporting but it is not restricted to this content and the focus should be on value creation, preservation or erosion.

The consideration by an organisation of the relationships between its various operating and functional units is part of the definition of 'integrated thinking'.

17.4 The correct answers are:

- Considering the relationships between an entity's operational and functional units and its capitals
- Making decisions and taking actions that promote the creation, preservation or erosion of value over the short, medium and long term

The definition of integrated thinking is:

'The active consideration by an organisation of the relationships between its various operating and functional units and the capitals that the organisation uses or affects. Integrated thinking leads to integrated decision-making and actions that consider the creation, preservation or erosion of value over the short, medium and long term.' (IIRC, 2021: p.53)

17.5 The correct answer is: To establish guidance principles and content elements that govern the overall content of an integrated report, and to explain the fundamental concepts that underpin them

The Framework adopts a principles-based rather than a rules-based approach to integrated reporting. An integrated report is primarily aimed at providers of financial capital although it might also assist other stakeholders in decision making. Although the Framework establishes content elements on what an integrated report should include, no fixed format is specified, which allows individual organisations to tailor the integrated report to their specific business models.

17.6 The correct answers are:

- Value creation, preservation or erosion
- The capitals
- The process through which value is created, preserved or eroded

The other three options are guiding principles of the Integrated Reporting Framework rather than fundamental concepts.

17.7 The correct answers are:

- Strategic focus and future orientation
- Reliability and completeness
- Consistency and comparability

The remaining four guiding principles are: connectivity of information, stakeholder relationships, materiality and conciseness.

17.8 The correct answers are: Research and development spending and Number of new products developed.

Intellectual capital is defined as 'organisational, knowledge-based intangibles'; therefore research and development spending and number of new products developed will be appropriate metrics to measure this type of capital.

ROCE will measure financial capital.

Internal quality inspections will measure manufactured capital.

CO_2 emissions will measure natural capital

17.9 The correct answer is: Integrated thinking

17.10 The correct answer is: Financial capital

Financial capital is defined as 'the pool of funds that is available to an organisation of use in the production of goods or the provision of services obtained through financing, such as **debt, equity or grants,** or generated through operations or investments.' (IIRC, 2021, p19)

17.11 The correct answers are:

- Intellectual capital
- Human capital
- Natural capital

The remaining three capitals are: financial, manufactured, and social and relationship.

17.12 The correct answers are:

- Air
- Water
- Biodiversity

Buildings qualify as manufactured capital, intellectual property as intellectual capital and shared norms as social and relationship capital.

17.13 The correct answers are:

- Governance
- Risks and opportunities
- Strategy and resource allocation

The remaining content elements are:

- Organisational overview and external environment
- Business model
- Performance
- Outlook
- Basis and presentation

17.14 The correct answer is: Performance

17.15 The correct answer is: To require an entity to disclose information about its sustainability-related risks and opportunities that is useful to the primary users of general purpose financial reporting is making decisions relating to providing resources to the entity

The other options are descriptions of some of the areas of core content that are required by IFRS S1 – governance, risk management and metrics and targets.

17.16 The correct answer is: Social and relationship capital

Social and relationship capital refers to relationships in place within an entity and between an entity and its stakeholders.

Intellectual capital includes an entity's formal research and development and the less formal knowledge that is gathered, used and managed by the entity.

Human capital refers to an entity's management and its employees and the skills they have.

Manufactured capital is the equipment and tools used in an entity's production process.

17.17 The correct answers are:
- Product obsolescence due to customer preference for a more environmentally friendly product
- Closure of a production site to meet carbon emission targets set by national government

Customer preference for more environmentally products is an example of a climate-related transition risk, which is the risk of transition to a lower carbon economy. Climate-related legislation, such as setting carbon emission targes is also an example of a transition risk.

A warehouse being damaged in a hurricane is an example of an acute climate-related physical risk due to a weather event. The lack of availability of raw materials due to biodiversity loss is an example of a chronic climate-related physical risk.

17.18 The correct answer is: The principles-based approach allows the report to be tailored to specific entities.

The Framework is not mandatory. It is a guidance document which should be applied to any communication claiming to be an integrated report and referencing the Framework.

It does not provide a prescribed format – instead it gives guidance on the content elements that an integrated report should address.

17.19 The correct answer is: It needs to be adapted for not-for-profit and public sector companies as it is primarily aimed at private sector for-profit companies.

The other answers are incorrect for the following reasons:

- Guidance is provided on the content elements of an integrated report.

- Although the Framework defines six capitals, it acknowledges that not all capitals are equally relevant or applicable to all organisations. An integrated report is not required to adopt the six categories or be structured in line with the capitals. Instead the capitals serve to underpin the concept of value creation and act as a guideline to ensure organisations consider all forms of capital they use or affect.
- An integrated report should focus on value creation over the short, medium and long term.

17.20 The correct answers are:

- Improved co-operation between different departments
- A better understanding of the business as a result of improved internal processes
- Increased engagement of senior management in the long-term sustainability of the business

The other answers are incorrect for the following reasons:

- An integrated report contains forward-looking information as its focus is the creation of value over the short, medium and long term. One of the content elements of an integrated report is an organisation's outlook.
- While an organisation's performance may improve due to more integrated thinking and management resulting in more effective capital allocation, this is not guaranteed and is unlikely to be instant. Preparing an integrated report for the first time involves significant time and cost.
- While an integrated report, if successful, should result in a better relationship with stakeholders as a result of improved dialogue between the organisation and providers of capital (and other stakeholders), a positive response is not guaranteed.

18 Working with financial statements I

18.1 The correct answer is: 1.26:1

(Receivables + short-term investments) are divided by (trade payables, overdraft, taxes payable + deposits in advance):

(158,000 + 18,000)/(61,000 + 64,000 + 10,000 + 5,000) = 1.26.

18.2 The correct answer is: 13%

The formula for calculating return on capital employed is:

$$= \frac{\text{Profit before interest and tax}}{\text{Equity + Interest-bearing borrowings - Non-current assets that do not contribute to operating profit}}$$

= $600/$4,550

= 13%

18.3 The correct answer is: PQ moved to an out-of-town location where the rent and employment costs were less than in the previous year.

Reclassifying expenses from administrative expenses to cost of sales will make gross margin fall but will have no impact on operating margin, because no matter whether the expenses are in cost of sales or administrative expenses, they will still need to be deducted in calculating the operating profit and therefore margin.

Rent and employment costs are operating costs, so reducing these costs will improve the operating margin.

Interest is a finance cost and therefore has no impact on operating profits.

The revaluation surplus on revaluation of the head office building should be presented in other comprehensive income and does not affect profit or loss. As the carrying amount of the head office has increased, the depreciation charge associated with the head office will also increase, so reducing profit and therefore reducing operating profit margin.

18.4 The correct answer is: The entity has purchased a property for cash.

This reduces current assets without a corresponding reduction in current liabilities.

The other answers are incorrect because:

Poor credit control would increase receivables and reduce cash so there would be no impact on current assets.

Inventory is excluded from quick ratio so there would be no impact.

Reducing the allowance for receivables would increase current assets and thus increase the quick ratio.

18.5 The correct answer is: 69.7%

Gearing = Debt/(Debt + Equity) × 100%

= (100,000 + 475,000)/(30,000 + 20,000 + 200,000 + 575,000)

= 69.7%

18.6 The correct answers are:

- Increased inventory obsolescence
- Slowdown in trading

If inventory is becoming obsolete then sales may fall, leading to a build-up of old inventory.

A slowdown in trading would probably affect inventory levels because the level of purchases would take a while to adjust to the lower levels of sales, leading to a build-up of inventory.

The following two options would **not** cause inventory days to increase:

- A marketing decision to reduce selling prices – a reduction in selling price would not directly affect either the purchase price or the level of inventory. If anything, it would be more likely to reduce inventory days, as the entity moves towards more of a low-margin, fast-turnover approach.

- Seasonal fluctuations in sales orders – this would affect inventory days, but it would not affect it from year to year (on the assumption that the 'seasonality' in question does not take place over more than one year!).

Changing supplier may change payables days etc but is unlikely to impact on average inventory days if the same inventory lines/products are being purchased/sold.

18.7 The correct answers are:

- WH's liquidity has deteriorated year on year
- WH is funding working capital using a bank overdraft nearing its limit

The other statements are incorrect for the following reasons:

- WH has a net current liability position of $638,000 in 20X7 ($430,000 + $3,860,000 + $12,000 – $4,660,000 – $228,000)

- As a result of this net current liability position, WH cannot afford to pay its current liabilities out of its current assets in 20X7

- The new department store contract has credit terms three times as long as WH's normal contracts with customers, thereby delaying receipt of cash from sales resulting in a negative impact on WH's liquidity

18.8 The correct answers are:

- GH made an unusually large sale just before the year end.
- GH paid its payables earlier than usual, because it had a positive cash balance.

Making a large sale before the year end would cause inventory to fall and trade receivables to increase. This will cause the current ratio to increase because inventory will fall by the cost of the goods but trade receivables will increase by the selling price which will be higher.

Paying payables earlier than usual out of a positive cash balance will cause current assets (cash) and current liabilities (payables) to fall by the same amount. However, as current liabilities are less than current assets (due to a current ratio of 1:2:1 prior to the transaction), this will have a greater impact on current liabilities than current assets causing the current ratio to increase.

The other answers are incorrect:

If GH paid its payables earlier than usual by making use of its bank overdraft facility, current liabilities would remain the same and there would be no impact on the current ratio.

Buying inventory for cash would have no overall impact on current assets or the current ratio because one current asset (cash) would fall and another current asset (inventory) would increase by the same amount.

Negotiating longer credit terms with suppliers would cause trade payables to increase. Even if this results in short-term reduction in GH's overdraft, the net effect on current liabilities is likely to be an increase or, at best, no change. Therefore, this would result in a decrease or no change to the current ratio.

18.9 The correct answers are:

- Increase in payroll costs due to staff bonuses
- Major investment in property, plant and equipment shortly before the year end
- A revaluation of property in the year resulting in a significant uplift in value

ROCE will fall when profit before interest and tax falls or when capital employed increases. Increases in the average interest rate and a large tax bill do not affect ROCE as they affect profit after interest and tax. A repayment of the long-term loan would improve ROCE as it will cause capital employed to fall.

18.10 The correct answer is: 3.24

$$\text{Interest cover} = \frac{\text{Profit before interest}}{\text{Interest}}$$

18.11 The correct answers are:

- It is calculated as earnings before interest, tax, depreciation and amortisation.
- It is useful in assessing an entity's performance.
- It is a non-GAAP financial measure.

EBITDA stands for 'earnings before interest, tax, depreciation and amortisation'. It excludes depreciation and amortisation from profit on the grounds that they are accounting adjustments rather than cash flows. Interest is excluded because it relates to an entity's financing decisions rather than its operating decisions. Tax is excluded as a non-discretionary item. The theory is that these adjustments to the GAAP-based profit figure reported in an entity's statement of profit or loss result in a better measure of an entity's underlying performance. EBITDA is a non-GAAP financial measure as its calculation is not covered by any IAS or IFRS. Therefore, it is a voluntary rather than mandatory measure.

The other statements are incorrect for the following reasons:

- EBITDA is often misunderstood to be a measure of cash flows but this is incorrect because financial statements are prepared on an accruals basis.

- It does not reflect an entity's financial position as it is calculated from statement of profit or loss rather than statement of financial position figures.
- It does not equate to an entity's gross profit figure as, in order to calculate EBITDA, any depreciation or amortisation in arriving at the gross profit figure must be removed by adding them back. Distribution costs and administrative expenses (excluding depreciation and amortisation) must be deducted.

18.12 The correct answer is: The cake shop has a higher level of wastage of inventory than the electrical store.

Given that both entities charge the same mark-up on cost per unit when they arrive at their selling price, wastage can be the only reason for the cake shop having a lower gross margin than the electrical store.

The other answers are incorrect for the following reasons:

- Although a trade discount would allow the electrical store to have a lower cost base, as both entities apply the same mark-up on cost, this should have no impact on the gross margin.
- The cake shop's higher inventory turnover just means that the cake shop is selling goods more quickly than the electrical store but as both stores charge the same mark-up on cost, this will have no impact on the gross margin.
- The level of volume does not impact margins. Margins are affected by change in prices and costs not volume.

18.13 The correct answers are:

- Return on capital employed will decrease.
- Net profit margin will decrease.
- Non-current asset turnover will decrease.

A revaluation will increase the revaluation and surplus therefore equity and capital employed, making ROCE decrease. As the assets are larger, the depreciation will increase, making profit lower and the net margin decrease. Non-current asset turnover is calculated as revenue/non-current assets; therefore, it too will decrease.

A revaluation will have no effect on the current ratio and will make gearing (debt/equity) decrease as equity has increased. Interest cover is likely to decrease because profit before interest and tax will fall due to the higher depreciation.

18.14 The correct answer is: Decrease in return on capital employed; increase in gearing

This lease is neither short-term nor for an underlying asset that is low value so the IFRS 16 *Leases* recognition exemptions cannot be applied.

Therefore, the normal IFRS 16 accounting treatment for a lessee must be applied and the accounting entry required by the lessee (YT) at the start of the lease is:

Debit   Right-of-use asset
Credit   Lease liability

Return on capital employed

$$= \frac{\text{Profit before interest and tax}}{\text{Equity + Interest-bearing borrowings − Non-current assets that do not contribute to operating profit}}$$

The new lease liability would be classified as interest-bearing borrowings so would cause capital employed to increase; hence return on capital employed would decrease.

There are two possible formulae for gearing:

$$\text{Debt/Equity} = \frac{\text{Long-term debt}}{\text{Equity}} \times 100\% \text{ or}$$

$$\text{Debt/(Debt + Equity)} = \frac{\text{Long-term debt}}{\text{Long-term debt + Equity}} \times 100\%$$

Whichever formula is used, the creation of a lease liability will cause long-term debt to increase and therefore gearing will increase.

18.15 The correct answers are:

- Gearing of RF has decreased due to the increase in total equity.
- Shares were issued at a premium to nominal value.
- RF may have paid a dividend to shareholders in 20X8.

Retained earnings may have fallen due to other factors such as dividends, not only due to a loss. Long-term borrowings may have increased due to a reclassification from short-term debt. Long-term borrowings could also have increased due to amortisation and effective interest in the year. Share capital may have increased due to a market share issue, not only a bonus issue.

18.16 The correct answer is: 57.4%

Gearing = Long-term debt/Equity = (100 + 40)/244

18.17 The correct answer is: XX is suffering from a worsening liquidity situation in 20X9.

This is true because the current ratio has fallen, customers are taking longer to pay, inventory is taking longer to sell and XX is paying its suppliers more quickly.

18.18 The correct answer is: S is less likely to be benefiting from economies of scale

As S's revenue is significantly lower than the other two companies, it is less likely to be benefiting from economies of scale which could explain why S has the lowest operating margin.

It would not be possible to determine the effects of control on administrative expenses alone, as the ratios do not identify the impact of just administrative expenses. If Y had secured better supply discounts than the other entities it would have the biggest gross profit margin. It would not be possible to determine the effects of the tax rate alone, as the ratios do not identify the impact of just tax. Gross profit and operating profit margins are both calculated on before-tax profit figures.

18.19 The correct answer is: X has a smaller proportion of productive assets than its competitor.

Carrying its non-current assets at historic cost would make X's asset turnover higher than its competitor as X would have a lower asset balance.

X embarked on a programme of capital investment in the previous year which should result in extra revenue in the current year thus making X's asset turnover ratio higher than its competitor's. Recruiting additional production staff would also make X's asset turnover ratio higher than its competitor's.

18.20 The correct answer is: Requiring external IT contractors to take an extra two weeks' holiday

External IT contractors would not be employees of UV. Therefore, taking an extra two weeks' holiday would result in UV not having to pay their fees for this period and this cost saving would therefore improve UV's profit and EBITDA.

The other answers are incorrect for the following reasons:

- Taking longer to pay suppliers would increase payables days, decrease the current ratio and potentially improve working capital but would have no direct impact on EBITDA.

- Increasing the useful life of non-current assets would result in a lower depreciation charge and improve the bottom line profit but would have no impact on EBITDA as it is based on earnings before depreciation.

- Renegotiating loans to pay a lower rate of interest would make the finance cost fall but as EBITDA is profit before interest, this would have no impact on EBITDA.

19 Working with financial statements II

19.1 The correct answer is: Make a rights issue of ordinary shares

This would increase both cash and share capital, increasing current (liquid) assets but without incurring any additional liabilities.

Offering a settlement discount to customers would make cash received lower than receivables which would cause the current ratio to decrease rather than increase.

Making a bonus issue of shares would generate no cash at all and would only affect QR's reserves, not its current ratio.

Selling current asset investments would just replace the investments with cash, having no effect on the current ratio.

19.2 The correct answer is: An increase in revenue

An increase in revenue will probably lead to an increase in operating profit. There will be no increase in capital employed.

Decreasing the level of dividends has no effect on ROCE in the short term. In the long term it would increase retained earnings and capital employed and therefore reduce ROCE.

Revaluing land and buildings upwards decreases ROCE, because it increases capital employed and reduces profits.

Issuing ordinary shares increases capital employed and decreases ROCE in the short term, although the issue proceeds can be used to generate additional profit and this may help to increase ROCE in the longer term.

19.3 The correct answers are:

- Switching slow paying customers to cash only
- Introducing a just-in-time ordering system for inventory
- Sending final demands to very overdue customers

The working capital cycle is calculated as:

Inventory days + Receivable days – Payable days

Switching slow paying customers to cash only should help reduce receivable days (provided the customers do not move to an alternative supplier) and, therefore, reduce the working capital cycle.

Introducing a just-in-time ordering system for inventory should result in a reduction in inventory days and therefore a reduction in the working capital cycle.

Sending final demands to very overdue customers should encourage them to pay more quickly, thereby reducing receivable days and the working capital cycle.

The other answers are incorrect because they would all increase the working capital cycle:

- Negotiating a longer credit term with customers will cause receivables and receivable days to increase, thereby increasing rather than reducing the working capital cycle.

- Taking advantage of settlement discounts with suppliers would result in paying suppliers more quickly, making payables decrease and payable days decrease. This would cause the working capital cycle to increase rather than decrease.
- Bulk purchasing inventory would result in higher inventory days and therefore cause an increase in the working capital cycle rather than a decrease.

19.4 The correct answer is:

Proposal 1   Proposal 2

decrease ratio   increase ratio

Proposal 1 will cause the acid test ratio to fall, because although receivables will convert into cash more quickly, the amount of cash received (net of the discount) will be less than the amount of the receivables. Current assets will fall, without any change in current liabilities, so the acid test ratio will fall.

Proposal 2 will cause the acid test ratio to rise by delaying the reduction in cash that would occur by paying suppliers. Since the acid test ratio is less than 1.0, anything that prevents an equal fall in current assets above the line and current liabilities below the line will boost the ratio.

This solution can be demonstrated with simple numbers. Suppose receivables = 200 and cash = 100, payables must be 750 (since the acid test ratio is currently 0.4).

Proposal 1: If all the receivables take the 2% discount, there will be receivables of 0, cash of (100 + 98% of 200) = 298 and payables of 750. Acid test ratio = 298/750 = 0.397 = lower.

Proposal 2: If payment of 100 is delayed to payables, cash will rise by 100 and so too will payables. There would therefore be cash of 200, receivables of 200 and payables of 850. Acid test ratio = 400/850 = 0.47 = higher.

19.5 The correct answers are:

- Published financial statements contain estimates such as depreciation.
- Accounting policies may vary between companies, making comparisons difficult.
- The nature and character of a business may change over time, making strictly numerical comparisons misleading.

Published accounts are frequently unreliable as a result either of fraud or of error on the part of management – this may be the case, but it is offset by the statutory requirement for them to represent a true and fair view, and by the fact that most investment decisions (for example) would involve an element of due diligence work to ensure that the accounts could in fact be relied upon.

There are no prior year figures to compare to current year figures – this is incorrect because in published financial statements comparatives must be shown.

The following are problems associated with inter-temporal analysis (ie analysis of the same company, over time):

- Changes in the nature of the business
- Unrealistic depreciation rates under historical cost accounting
- The changing value of the currency unit being reported
- Changes in accounting policies

The following are problems associated with cross-sectional analysis (ie analysis of different companies, at the same time):

- Different degrees of diversification
- Different production and purchasing policies
- Different financing policies
- Different accounting policies
- Different effects of government incentives

Although the nature of the business being volatile will impact the accounts, the volatility will affect all companies within the industry and thus ratio analysis will still be useful/meaningful to assess relative performance.

19.6 The correct answer is: Paying a supplier and taking an early settlement discount

Working capital is calculated as current assets less current liabilities.

Paying a supplier and taking an early settlement will reduce cash less than payables so will cause working capital to increase. Therefore this is the correct answer.

The other answers are incorrect for the following reasons:

Delaying a payment to trade payables would cause trade payables to increase and therefore working capital to decrease.

Reducing the credit period given to customers would cause receivables to fall and cash to rise with a nil effect on current assets and working capital.

Purchasing inventory on credit will cause current assets and current liabilities to increase by the same amount resulting in a nil effect on working capital.

19.7 The correct answer is: The failure of QW to raise long-term finance to fund its investing activities has resulted in a deterioration QW's financial adaptability and liquidity.

It is good financial management to finance long-term assets (investing activities) with long-term finance (financing activities). However, while QW has managed to finance some of its investing activities from its operating activities, it has failed to raise long-term finance to cover the remainder. Instead it has relied on an overdraft which is both expensive and risky.

The other statements are incorrect for the following reasons:

A negative cash flow in investing activities is indicative of expansion rather than decline. QW has not shown competent stewardship by financing long-term assets with an overdraft. As no prior year figures are given, it is not possible to conclude on whether QW's working capital management has improved or deteriorated.

19.8 The correct answer is: Increase sales.

An increase in sales will probably lead to an increase in operating profit. There will be no increase in capital employed.

Restructuring its long-term finance would have no impact on ROCE as overall capital employed will remain the same. Revaluing land and buildings upwards decreases ROCE, because it increases capital employed (revaluation surplus) and reduces profits (higher depreciation). Issuing ordinary shares increases capital employed and decreases ROCE in the short term, although the issue proceeds can be used to generate additional profit and this may help to increase ROCE in the longer term.

19.9 The correct answers are:

- One entity revalues its properties and the other entity holds its assets under the cost model.
- One entity has assets nearing the end of their useful life whereas the other entity has recently acquired new assets.
- One entity depreciates its assets over a much shorter useful life than the other entity.

All of these would cause the carrying amount of non-current assets to be comparatively higher in one entity than the other, thus causing a difference in their non-current asset turnover ratio.

Whether an entity buys assets for cash or leases the assets for the entirety of their useful life should have minimal impact on the non-current asset turnover ratio because in both instances the entity will record a non-current asset in its statement of financial position. If the asset is bought for cash, it will be recorded as property, plant and equipment. If the asset is leased, a right-of-use asset is recognised. Both a right-of-use asset and property, plant and equipment would be classified as non-current assets. The right-of-use asset is recorded at the present value of lease payments, and as the leases here are for the entirety of the assets' lives, the present value of the lease payments is likely to be very similar to the cash price of the asset.

Neither interest nor borrowings feature in the non-current asset turnover ratio so the rate of interest an entity pays is not relevant here.

To help with questions like this, think of the formula and what impacts the items on the top and bottom halves:

$$\frac{\text{Revenue}}{\text{Non-current assets}}$$

Gearing is the ratio of debt to equity or the ratio of debt to debt plus equity. Neither debt nor equity feature in the non-current asset turnover ratio so a company's level of gearing has no impact on non-current asset turnover.

19.10 The correct answers are:

- Search online for articles on LP, particularly in the financial press, and review these articles to assess the market's view of the future of LP.
- Review the narrative reports within the financial statements that give details of recent investment and related financing to assess if the business is undergoing expansion and likely to bring additional future returns.
- Review the financial report to establish the dividend per share paid over the last few years and to identify whether increased gearing has negatively impacted on investor returns.

It is unlikely that the individual would be able to gain access to board minutes or have direct discussions with the CFO due to issues of confidentiality.

19.11 The correct answers are:

- Gearing
- Return on capital employed
- Interest cover

Revaluing property, plant and equipment will impact on the value of net assets and increase the revaluation reserve, which will increase equity. The additional depreciation charges on the revalued assets will reduce profits.

Gearing will be affected by the increased equity.

Return on capital employed will be impacted by the change to operating profit and the higher equity within capital employed.

Receivable days will not be affected as the revaluation does not impact receivables or revenue.

The current ratio will not be affected as the revaluation will have no impact on current assets or current liabilities.

Interest cover will be affected due to the change in profit from the extra depreciation.

The quick ratio will not be impacted as the revaluation will not affect cash, receivables or current liabilities.

19.12 The correct answer is: LM's management has shown competent stewardship of the entity's resources by increasing long-term finance to partly fund investing activities.

The management of LM has generated funds from daily operations, but has invested a large amount in the continuing business, as seen by the large outflow in investing activities. This may be through the acquisition of property, plant and equipment, purchase of shares as a strategic investment or through investing in intangible assets. This demonstrates

strong stewardship and investment in the future of the business. A small net cash outflow is not a sign of a company in decline or of insolvency – it must be considered against the components of the cash flows.

19.13 The correct answers are:

- PR's largest segment has the best operating profit margin in 20X7.
- PR's smallest segment has the worst operating profit margin in 20X7.
- The segment with the best operating profit margin in 20X6 has the worst operating profit margin in 20X7.

In revenue terms, Europe is the largest segment, comprising 37.6% of the 20X7 revenue (25,146/67,510 × 100%) and Europe has the best operating margin at 14.4%. The Middle East is the smallest segment, comprising 12.9% of the 20X7 revenue (8,736/67,510 × 100%) and it has the worst operating profit margin in 20X7. The Middle East had the best operating margin in 20X6 (11.5%) but the worst operating margin in 20X7 (10.5%) demonstrating a significant decline in profitability.

The other answers are incorrect because:

- The largest revenue growth has been in the least profitable segment (the Middle East)
- Operating margin has only improved in three out of four segments (Europe, Asia and America)
- The smallest revenue growth has been in America which is the second worst operating margin (not the worst) so is not the least profitable segment (the Middle East is the least profitable segment in 20X7)

19.14 The correct answers are:

- Health is a new division, requiring start-up costs in its first year which could lead to a loss.
- JK is offering heavily discounted prices for its nursing and dentistry courses to win market share.

A new division is likely to be loss-making in its first year due to start-up costs such as recruiting new staff to teach the courses, creating course materials, renting premises to teach the courses from (unless there is room in existing premises) and marketing the new courses.

If JK offers discounted prices to win market share, this will cause the gross margin and therefore the operating margin to fall.

The other answers are incorrect because:

- A lower asset base would not in its own right cause a lower operating margin as depreciation would be low. Also, it is likely that the School of Health will have to invest in new assets such as specialist medical equipment to use in the classroom as well as new premises and classroom equipment (if accountancy and law course facilities are at full capacity). As the accountancy and law segments are well established, their assets are likely to be older and have a lower value.
- If there were little competition in the health market, JK could sell its courses at a price sufficiently high to ensure profitability in the segment.
- Having large clients in the accountancy and law market demanding low prices would keep operating margins in the accountancy and law segments down but would be unlikely to affect the health market as clients in the health market are likely to be very different from the accountancy and law market.

19.15   The correct answer is: Diagnostic

The question for descriptive is 'what happened?'. The question for predictive is 'what will happen?'. The question for prescriptive is 'what should I do?'.

19.16   The correct answer is: Future funds raised should be equity finance rather than debt finance to avoid increasing gearing further.

This is prescriptive analytics because it answers the question 'what should I do?'.

Stating that gearing has increased is descriptive analytics. Giving the reason for the increase is diagnostic analytics. Stating what would happen if profits decline is predictive analytics.

19.17   The correct answer is: Descriptive

This is descriptive analytics because it answers the question 'what happened?'.

19.18   The correct answer is: Predictive

This is predictive analytics because it answers the question 'what will happen?'.

19.19   The correct answer is: Diagnostic

This is diagnostic analytics because it answers the question 'why did it happen?'.

19.20   The correct answers are:

- The minimum wage is higher in C-land than B-land.
- C-land and B-land require the use of different national GAAPs.
- Import duties on parts are higher in C-land than B-land.

The different tax regimes and market rate of interest will have no impact on the operating margin because tax and interest are reported after operating profit (but they would impact the net margin). Differing liquidity of stock markets will affect an entity's capital structure, gearing and interest ratios rather than the operating margin.

Practice mock questions

Questions

1   Which of the following is a characteristic of deep discount bonds?

○ They carry a much lower rate of interest than conventional, fixed rate redeemable bonds.

○ They are often referred to as convertible bonds.

○ They do not have a par value.

○ They carry a much higher rate of interest than conventional, fixed rate redeemable bonds.

2   Which THREE of the following statements are TRUE?

☐ Ordinary shares are less risky for investors than redeemable debt.

☐ Preference shares always carry voting rights.

☐ Investors in unsecured bonds will generally want a higher yield than investors in secured bonds.

☐ Investors in ordinary shares expect a higher return than investors in preference shares or debt.

☐ Ordinary shareholders hold rights such as voting and attendance at general meetings, and receive a share of any dividend agreed.

☐ A rights issue is offered to the general public whether they hold shares in the entity or not.

3   Complete the sentences below by selecting the correct options from the pull down lists.

The role of the sponsor in an initial public offering (IPO) is to [▼1]. The role of the book runner is to [▼1]. Both of these roles are generally performed by a [▼2].

Pull down list 1

co-ordinate the overall IPO process and advise the company's board throughout

raise finance from investors on behalf of the company and help determine the appropriate pricing for the share

perform financial due diligence and provide tax advice

develop a communication strategy pre- and post-IPO

perform legal due diligence, draft the prospectus and provide legal opinions

Pull down list 2

management accountant
management consultant
small law firm
financial institution such as an investment bank

4   XN has $300 million 6% irredeemable bonds in issue. This debt was originally issued at its par value of $100 and is now trading at 95% of this value. XN pays corporate income tax at 25%.

What is XN's post-tax cost of debt? Give your answer as a percentage to two decimal places.

☐ %

---

5   PQ has just paid a dividend of 40 cents per share. The expected growth in dividends is 7% per annum. PQ's current share price is $6.11.

What is PQ's cost of equity (as a % to one decimal place)?

○ 6.5%
○ 13.5%
○ 14.0%
○ 14.5%

---

6   NM, a listed entity, has 5% coupon, $100 par value bonds in issue. The bonds are redeemable at a 10% premium in 10 years' time. The bonds are currently trading at $85 and NM currently pays tax on profits of 30%.

The net present value of the bond price, the annual coupon interest (after tax) and the final redemption value have been calculated as follows at discount rates of 5% and 10% respectively:

At 5%: $21.15
At 10%: -$11.81

What is the post-tax cost of debt for NM?

○ 8.21%
○ 9.14%
○ 14.63%
○ 16.32%

---

7   QV has in issue 5% convertible bonds with a nominal value of $100. The bonds are redeemable at a 10% premium or can be converted into shares at a ratio of $100 of bonds to 30 shares in three years' time, in Year 3. The current share price for QV is $5.49 and this is expected to grow by 3% per annum for the next three years.

What is the redemption value at the end of Year 3 that should be used in the internal rate of return calculation for the cost of debt to QV (to the nearest whole $)?

○ $100
○ $110
○ $165
○ $180

8   JZ has had the following dividends:

20X9	20X8	20X7	20X6
27c	23c	20c	18c

What is the historic growth of JZ's dividends? Give your answer as a percentage to one decimal place.

[ ] %

9   BG currently has a cost of equity of 15% and a pre-tax cost of debt (yield to maturity) of 10%. The market values of BG's equity and debt are $20 million and $5 million respectively. BG pays corporate income tax on profits of 30%.

What is BG's weighted average cost of capital (WACC)?

○ 14.0%
○ 13.4%
○ 8.6%
○ 11.0%

10 KT operates in the telecommunications industry. On 1 January 20X2, KT enters into a contract with a customer to provide a mobile phone handset and a combined data and calls package for two years. The customer collects the handset from KT's retail outlet on 1 January 20X2 and has immediate access to calls and data.

The total price of the contract is $1,800 payable in monthly instalments of $75 over two years. The standalone selling prices of each element of the contract are:

- Handset $800
- Data and calls package $600 per annum

How much revenue should KT recognise in relation to this contract for the year ended 31 December 20X2?

○ $720
○ $800
○ $1,260
○ $1,800

11 ZM, a construction company, entered into a two-year contract on 1 April 20X5 to construct a ten-storey office block for a customer on the customer's land. The contract specifies that control of the office block is transferred to the customer as it is constructed. The agreed contract price is $25 million. As at 31 March 20X6, costs incurred to date were $9 million and further costs to complete were estimated at $11 million. At this date, four of the ten storeys had been completed.

Which TWO of the following are correct in relation to this contract?

☐ Revenue should be recognised only when the construction of all ten storeys has been completed.
☐ The performance obligation is satisfied over time as ZM constructs the office block.
☐ Using an input method based on costs incurred, revenue of $12.5 million would be recognised in the year ended 31 March 20X6.
☐ Using an output method based on units produced, revenue of $10 million would be recognised in the year ended 31 March 20X6.
☐ Revenue should be recognised only to the extent of the $9 million costs incurred.

12 Complete the sentence below by selecting the correct options from the pull down lists.

A finance lease is a lease that transfers substantially all the [____▼1____] incidental to ownership of an underlying asset to the [____▼2____]; title may or may not be eventually transferred.

Pull down list 1

title documents
value
risks and rewards

Pull down list 2

lessor
lessee
third party

13 On 1 January 20X0, MN leased a property to LK under a four-year operating lease. On this date, MN paid LK a lease incentive of $4,000. Under the terms of the contract, LK must pay annual lease rentals of $20,000 commencing on 31 December 20X0.

On 1 January 20X0, the remaining economic life of the property was estimated to be 30 years. The present value of the annual lease rental payments was $64,800, discounted at the interest rate implicit in the lease of 9%. The fair value of the property was $750,000.

What should MN recognise in its statement of profit or loss for the year ended 31 December 20X0 in relation to this lease?

- ○ Lease rental income of $20,000
- ○ Lease rental income of $19,000
- ○ Finance income of $5,832
- ○ Finance income of $4,032

14 **Which of the following costs would be recognised as a provision in accordance with IAS 37 Provisions, Contingent Liabilities and Contingent Assets?**

- ○ Costs relating to the closure of a factory that has not yet been announced
- ○ Expected operating losses for the next financial year from a newly acquired subsidiary
- ○ Expected retraining costs of staff as a result of new legislation passed in the current year
- ○ The costs to remove an oil rig at the end of extraction where required by a licensing agreement

15 At the year end of 30 June 20X9, a court case is pending against JM. JM's lawyers believe that there is a 60% chance of JM winning the case and a 40% chance of JM losing the case. If JM loses the case, the lawyers believe that it will have to pay damages of $500,000.

What is the correct treatment of this court case in JM's financial statements for the year ended 30 June 20X9?

- ○ Do nothing
- ○ Recognise a provision
- ○ Disclose a contingent liability
- ○ Disclose a contingent asset

16 On 1 July 20X6 CA issued 6% convertible bonds with a nominal value of $100,000. The terms of the bonds stipulate that the holders can either redeem the bonds at par in three years' time or convert them into 25 ordinary shares at the redemption date. Coupon interest on the bonds is paid annually in arrears and the market interest rate for similar bonds without the conversion option is 9%.

The present value of the liability component of the bonds at 1 July 20X6 has been calculated correctly as $92,500 and the equity component of $7,500 has been calculated at the same date.

What is the carrying amount of the liability component of the convertible bonds as at 30 June 20X7?

- ○ $92,050
- ○ $94,825
- ○ $103,000
- ○ $95,500

17 **Complete the sentence below by selecting the correct options from the pull down lists.**

A financial asset is cash, an equity instrument of another entity or a contractual [▼1] to receive cash or financial asset from another entity, or to exchange financial assets or liabilities under potentially [▼2] conditions.

Pull down list 1

duty
obligation
right
responsibility

Pull down list 2

challenging
favourable
interesting
unfavourable

18 **Which THREE of the following should be recognised as intangible assets in accordance with IAS 38 *Intangible Assets*?**

☐ A purchased franchise

☐ The cost of activities aimed at obtaining new knowledge

☐ A customer list acquired as part of a business combination

☐ Goodwill arising on acquisition of a subsidiary

☐ A new product developed for which commercial production is not possible due to lack of funds

☐ An investment in staff training

---

19 AB has been developing a new production process. On 1 April 20X2, AB was able to demonstrate that the new production process was technically feasible and could be used in its operations. At that date, AB also demonstrated its intention to use the new process, the usefulness of the process in manufacturing inventory and the availability of resources to complete the development.

On 1 December 20X2, AB commenced the use of the new production process in manufacturing inventory for resale.

Costs incurred in relation to this development were as follows:

	$
1 January 20X2–31 March 20X2	345,000
1 April 20X2–1 December 20X2	120,000
	465,000

The directors of AB expect to be able to generate economic benefits from this new production process for 10 years from 1 December 20X2.

In relation to the development costs, what is the amortisation that AB should recognise in its statement of profit or loss for the year ended 31 December 20X2?

○ $1,000

○ $2,875

○ $3,875

○ $9,000

---

20 **Which of the following would result in a deferred tax asset being recognised in accordance with IAS 12 *Income Taxes*?**

○ Accrued expenses that are not deductible for tax purposes

○ Revaluation surplus on property, plant and equipment

○ Tax depreciation in excess of accounting depreciation

○ Interest payable that has been accrued in the financial statements, which will be deducted for tax purposes on a cash payments basis

21 MK operates in a tax regime in which corporate income tax is payable nine months and one day after the year end.

MK's tax computation for the year ended 31 December 20X1 calculated tax owing for the year of $195,000.

In MK's financial statements for the year ended 31 December 20X0, MK recognised a current tax liability and current tax expense of $140,000. The actual amount paid to settle the liability on 1 October 20X1 amounted to $148,000.

What is the total current tax expense that MK should recognise in its statement of profit or loss for the year ended 31 December 20X1?

- ○ $187,000
- ○ $195,000
- ○ $203,000
- ○ $343,000

22 **Which of the following statements is correct in relation to the accounting treatment of non-controlling interests (NCI) in the consolidated financial statements?**

- ○ NCI at acquisition must always be measured at fair value.
- ○ If NCI is measured at fair value then all of the goodwill impairment will be charged to group retained earnings.
- ○ If the subsidiary sells goods to the parent in the year and there is an unrealised profit on inventory left within the group at the year end then the NCI should not receive a share of it.
- ○ The NCI share of the subsidiary's post-acquisition reserves should be included in the calculation of NCI in the equity section of the group statement of financial position.

23 The accounting treatment of associates in the consolidated financial statements is governed by IAS 28 *Investments in Associates and Joint Ventures*.

Which TWO of the following statements are correct in relation to associates?

- ☐ The choice of treatments for an associate in the parent's individual financial statements is the same as for an investment in a subsidiary or joint venture.
- ☐ Significant influence can only be achieved by investing in at least 20% of the ordinary shares.
- ☐ When the parent sells goods to the associate, the group share of intra-group revenue and cost of sales must be eliminated.
- ☐ In the consolidated statement of profit or loss, the group share of the associate's profit before tax must be shown in a separate line.
- ☐ The group share of the associate's post-acquisition reserves must be included in the investment in associate and consolidated reserves.

24 Which of the following is the correct accounting treatment for a joint venture in the consolidated statement of financial position, in accordance with IAS 28 *Investments in Associates and Joint Ventures*?

　　○　The equity method

　　○　Investor's share of jointly held assets, liabilities, income and expenses

　　○　At cost or at fair value (as a financial asset)

　　○　Consolidate net assets in full on a line-by-line basis

---

25 JU acquired 60% of the $1 ordinary shares in HL on 1 April 20X2 for $20 million. At the date of acquisition, the carrying amount of HL's net assets was the same as the fair values with the following exceptions:

　　•　A property included in HL's statement of financial position at a carrying amount of $500,000 had a fair value $750,000. This is assessed as having a remaining useful life of ten years from the date of acquisition.

　　•　HL has a strong brand name in the industry in which it operates. On the date of acquisition this brand was deemed to have a fair value of $1 million and a remaining useful life of 20 years.

　　•　HL had disclosed a contingent liability in the notes to its financial statements for the year ending 31 December 20X1. Its fair value was $150,000 at acquisition. The liability was settled in October 20X2.

On 1 April 20X2 the carrying amount of HL's net assets were $15 million.

What is the fair value of net assets that should be included when calculating goodwill arising on the acquisition of HL for inclusion in JU's consolidated financial statements?

　　○　$16,100,000

　　○　$16,600,000

　　○　$16,250,000

　　○　$15,100,000

---

26 JU acquired 60% of the $1 ordinary shares in HL on 1 April 20X2 for $20 million. At the date of acquisition, the carrying amount of HL's net assets was the same as the fair value with the following exceptions:

　　•　A property included in HL's statement of financial position at a carrying amount of $500,000 had a fair value $750,000. This is assessed as having a remaining useful life of ten years from the date of acquisition.

　　•　HL has a strong brand name in the industry in which it operates. On the date of acquisition this brand was deemed to have a fair value of $1 million and a remaining useful life of 20 years.

　　•　HL had disclosed a contingent liability in the notes to its financial statements for the year ending 31 December 20X1. Its fair value was $150,000 at acquisition. The liability was settled in October 20X2.

On 1 April 20X2 the carrying amount of HL's net assets were $15 million.

Which TWO of the following statements are TRUE in relation to JU's consolidated financial statements for the year ended 31 December 20X2?

- [ ] Additional depreciation of $25,000 is to be included in the consolidated statement of profit or loss.
- [ ] The brand should never be amortised.
- [ ] Additional depreciation of $18,750 is to be included in the consolidated statement of profit or loss.
- [ ] The settlement of the contingent liability of $150,000 would be shown as income in the consolidated statement of profit and loss.
- [ ] Additional amortisation of $50,000 should be included in the consolidated statement of profit or loss.

27 MB acquired a 90% stake in YH on the 1 January 20X2 when the reserves of YH were $525,000.

The share capital and share premium of MB at 31 December 20X4 were $1,500,000 and $300,000 respectively.

Reserves of MB and YH on 31 December 20X4 stood at $6,750,000 and $1,750,000 respectively.

What is the equity attributable to the owners of the parent at 31 December 20X4 for inclusion in the consolidated statement of changes in equity of the MB group as at that date?

- ○ $7,975,000
- ○ $7,852,000
- ○ $8,872,500
- ○ $9,652,500

28 **Which TWO of the following may be presented under the heading 'cash flows from investing activities' in the consolidated statement of cash flows using the indirect method in accordance with IAS 7 Statement of Cash Flows?**

- [ ] Share of profit in associate
- [ ] Dividends paid to non-controlling interests
- [ ] Acquisition of subsidiary net of cash acquired
- [ ] Proceeds from long-term borrowings
- [ ] Dividends received from associates

29 DJ group has recently acquired 80% of the ordinary share capital in JM. DJ group primarily operates in B-Land and prepares its consolidated financial statements in B$.

JM operates in C-Land where the currency is the croma.

After the acquisition JM will continue to make its sales in C-Land in the croma. Existing employees will be retained and continue to be paid in croma, and raw materials will continue to be purchased from local suppliers in C-Land.

The level of intra-group transactions will be low and it is expected that JM will generate sufficient cash flows to be able to service its own loan finance.

The management of JM will continue to operate independently.

Which TWO of the following statements are true?

☐ JM must adopt the croma as its presentation currency.

☐ JM is a subsidiary of DJ group and therefore its functional currency must be the B$.

☐ JM operates autonomously, and has a low level of intra-group transactions with DJ group which indicates that its functional currency is the croma.

☐ JM makes its sales and purchases in C-Land and pays its employees in croma which indicates that its functional currency is the croma.

☐ The functional currency of JM will be the currency in which the financial statements are always presented.

30 MM acquired 90% of SA on 1 April 20X2 for 83,250 dinars. SA operates in D-Land and its functional currency is the dinar. At the date of acquisition the fair value of net assets of SA was 90,000 dinars. NM elected to measure non-controlling interests in SA at fair value at acquisition. The fair value of non-controlling interests in SA on 1 April 20X2 was 11,250 dinars. Goodwill on acquisition has been calculated as 4,500 dinars.

MM presents its group financial statements in A$ and its year end is 31 March each year.

The relevant exchanges rates are as follows:

1 April 20X2   A$1:4.5 dinars
31 March 20X3   A$1:4 dinars

Average exchange rate for the year ended

31 March 20X3   A$1:4.3 dinars

There has been no impairment of goodwill in SA in the post-acquisition period.

What is the exchange difference arising on the translation of goodwill that will be included in the calculation of exchange rate differences in the year which will be shown in MM's consolidated statement of profit or loss and other comprehensive income for the year ended 31 March 20X3?

○ A$17 gain

○ A$63 loss

○ A$78 loss

○ A$125 gain

31 PL is a publicly listed entity and is a subsidiary within a larger group of companies; their direct parent company is TJ. The directors of PL would like to know the possible related parties of their company according to IAS 24 *Related Party Disclosures*.

Which TWO of the following will normally be deemed as a related party of PL in accordance with IAS 24?

☐ Jed, who is the finance director of PL

☐ RY, PL's main supplier

☐ HB Bank, which has recently provided a substantial loan to PL

☐ UV, a charity (which is not part of the PL group), whose board includes Jed (the finance director of PL)

☐ QP, the parent of TJ and the ultimate parent of the group in which PL is included

32 NK owns 80% of SU. NK also owns 30% of CA, which it has significant influence over. NK shares joint control of TD, a separate company, with UJ in a joint venture. NK also operates a defined benefit pension plan for all of its employees.

Which of the following would be considered as related parties of NK in accordance with IAS 24 *Related Party Disclosures*?

○ SU, CA, UJ and the pension plan
○ SU, TD and UJ
○ SU, CA, TD and UJ
○ SU, CA, TD and the pension plan

33 Basic and diluted earnings per share (EPS) are required to be disclosed at the foot of the statement of profit or loss and other comprehensive income for most publicly listed entities. IAS 33 *Earnings per Share* standardises the calculation of these ratios to allow consistency in their calculation which enables comparisons to be made between entities.

Which TWO of the following instruments that an entity has recently issued would be included in denominator of only diluted EPS and not basic EPS?

☐ Convertible bonds
☐ Share options granted to executives
☐ Preference shares with no conversion rights
☐ Ordinary shares
☐ Redeemable bonds

34 ER has 1.6 million ordinary shares in issue on 1 January 20X0. On 1 September 20X0, ER made a 1 for 4 rights issue at $1.50 per share. The fair value of each share before the rights issue was $2.25.

ER has a number of subsidiaries. The consolidated profit before tax of the ER group for the year ended 31 December 20X0 was $3 million and its consolidated income tax expense was $900,000. Profit for the year attributable to non-controlling interests was $350,000.

What is the basic earnings per share of the ER group for the year ended 31 December 20X0? Give your answer in cents to one decimal place.

☐☐☐☐☐☐ cents

35 On 1 January 20X5, HF acquired 90% of MW's 1,000,000 $1 ordinary shares for $1,350,000. At that date, the fair value of MW's net assets was $1,200,000 and the market price of an ordinary share in MW was $1.40.

The directors of HF are trying to decide whether to measure non-controlling interests of MW at fair value or at the proportionate share of net assets.

What is the additional goodwill that will be recognised if the directors choose to measure non-controlling interests using the fair value method rather than the proportionate method? Give your answer to the nearest $.

$ ☐☐☐☐☐☐

36 BV acquired 75% of JK on 1 May 20X6.

The retained earnings in the financial statements of BV and JK as at 31 December 20X6 are $2,560,000 and $880,000 respectively. JK made a profit for the year of $144,000.

There has been no impairment to the goodwill since acquisition.

What are the consolidated retained earnings for inclusion in the consolidated statement of financial position of the BV group as at 31 December 20X6?

- ○ $2,623,000
- ○ $2,632,000
- ○ $2,641,000
- ○ $3,220,000

---

37 DX acquired 80% of RW on 1 August 20X4 for $468,000.

The statement of financial position for both entities for the year ended 31 March 20X5 is as follows:

	DX $	RW $
Investment in RW	468,000	
Other assets	540,000	370,000
	1,008,000	370,000
Share capital	300,000	150,000
Retained earnings at 1 April 20X4	510,000	124,000
Profit for year ended 31 March 20X5	128,000	63,000
Liabilities	70,000	33,000
	1,008,000	370,000

DX elected to measure the non-controlling interests in RW at their fair value of $35,000 at acquisition.

What is the amount of goodwill arising on the acquisition of RW?

- ○ $166,000
- ○ $202,750
- ○ $208,000
- ○ $213,250

38 AB has owned its 60% subsidiary, CD, for several years. In the year ended 31 December 20X4, AB sold goods to CD for $350,000 earning a margin of 20%. At the year end, one-quarter of these goods were left in inventory.

Cost of sales of AB and CD for the year ended 31 December 20X4 amounted to $1,200,000 and $870,000 respectively.

What is the consolidated cost of sales for inclusion in the consolidated statement of profit or loss of the AB group for the year ended 31 December 20X4? Give your answer to the nearest whole $.

$ _____

39 VQ has many subsidiaries. On 1 January 20X1, it acquired a 25% associate, AB, for $460,000. At that date, AB had retained earnings of $250,000 and a revaluation surplus of $80,000. As at 31 December 20X3, AB's retained earnings and revaluation surplus were $390,000 and $110,000 respectively.

In the year ended 31 December 20X3, VQ sold goods to AB for $60,000 at a mark-up of 50% on cost. At the year end, half of these goods were still in inventory.

What is the amount of the investment in the associate that should be included in the consolidated statement of financial position of the VQ group as at 31 December 20X3? Give your answer to the nearest $.

$ _____

40 **What of the following best describes the role of the International Sustainability Standards Board?**

○ To issue International Sustainability Disclosure Standards
○ To provide a fixed format for a sustainability report
○ To promote communication about value creation
○ To encourage dialogue between an entity and its stakeholders

41 **Which of the following is the International Integrated Reporting Council's (IIRC) definition of integrated thinking?**

○ The thought process involved in determining an organisation's objectives and strategy to achieve those objectives.
○ The active consideration by an organisation of the relationships between its various operating and functional units and the capitals that the organisation uses or affects.
○ The belief that all stakeholders of an organisation should be of equal importance and be communicated with regularly.
○ The opinion that the sustainability of an organisation is of equal importance to its financial performance and position.

42 **What is the objective of the Integrated Reporting Framework?**

   ○ To provide mandatory rules for organisations to follow when preparing an integrated report
   ○ To establish guiding principles and content elements for preparation of an integrated report
   ○ To increase the length of all organisations' integrated reports
   ○ To promote integrated reporting around the world

43 **Which THREE of the following are potential benefits of integrated reporting?**

   ☐ Improved co-operation between different departments
   ☐ Greater accuracy in preparation of financial statements
   ☐ Increased focus and awareness of management on sustainability
   ☐ Better articulation of an organisation's strategy
   ☐ Higher remuneration for the board of directors
   ☐ Savings from reducing employee headcount

44 **Patents, copyrights, software rights and licences are examples of which of the capitals according to the Integrated Reporting Framework?**

   ○ Financial
   ○ Human
   ○ Intellectual
   ○ Social and relationship

45 **Which THREE of the following statements are correct in relation to the principles of disclosure of the capitals in the Integrated Reporting Framework?**

   ☐ Disclosures about an entity's capitals must be categorised into financial, manufactured, intellectual, human, social and relationship, and natural capitals.
   ☐ The greater the quantity of disclosures, the more useful an integrated report will be to its stakeholders.
   ☐ All disclosures about significant movements in capitals must be quantitative not qualitative.
   ☐ Disclosures should be determined by the effects of the capitals on the organisation's ability to create value rather than whether they are owned by the organisation.
   ☐ An exhaustive account of the all the complex interdependencies between the capitals is not required.
   ☐ Disclosure is required of the trade-offs between the capitals and over time.

46 The following is an extract from PD's statements of financial position:

	$m
Equity	
Ordinary share capital issued	168
Share premium	103
Revaluation surplus	281
Retained earnings	1,640
Total equity	2,192

	$m
Non-current liabilities	
Long-term borrowings	331
Deferred tax liabilities	17
Total non-current liabilities	348

What is the gearing ratio (calculated as debt/equity) for PD? Give your answer as a percentage to one decimal place.

[ ] %

47 Entity A operates in A-land and Entity B operates in B-land. Both entities have similar capital structures, are of a similar size and operate in the same industry. The following ratios have been calculated for the current year:

	Entity A	Entity B
Operating profit margin	20%	20%
Net profit margin	5%	12%

Which TWO of the following independent options could explain why Entity A has a greater difference between its operating and net margins than Entity B?

☐ The market rate of interest is lower in B-land than in A-land.
☐ Labour costs are typically lower in B-land than in A-land.
☐ Companies have to pay a higher rate of tax in A-land than in B-land.
☐ Non-current assets usually have shorter useful lives in A-land than in B-land.
☐ Transport links are poor in B-land making delivery costs typically higher than in A-land.

48   The following are extracts from PD's financial statements:

Statement of profit or loss (extract) for the year ended 31 December 20X4

	$m
Share of profit in associate	20
Finance costs	(14)
Profit before tax	457
Income tax expense	(95)
Profit for the year	362

Statement of financial position (extract) at 31 December 20X4

	$m
Non-current assets	
Property, plant and equipment	230
Intangible assets	75
Investment in associates	201
Total non-current assets	506
Equity	
Ordinary share capital issued	168
Share premium	103
Revaluation surplus	281
Retained earnings	1,640
Total equity	2,192

	$m
Non-current liabilities	
Long-term borrowings	331
Deferred tax liabilities	17
Total non-current liabilities	348

What is the return on capital employed for PD for the year ended 31 December 20X4? Give your answer as a percentage to one decimal place.

[   ] %

49   The following are extracts from PD's financial statements:

Statement of profit or loss (extract) for the year ended 31 December 20X4

	$m
Revenue	2,562
Share of profit in associate	20
Profit for the year	362

Statement of financial position (extract) at 31 December 20X4

	$m
Non-current assets	
Property, plant and equipment	230
Intangible assets	75
Investment in associates	201
Total non-current assets	506
Non-current liabilities	
Long-term borrowings	331
Deferred tax liabilities	17
Total non-current liabilities	348

What is the non-current asset turnover for PD for the year ended 31 December 20X4? Give your answer to one decimal place.

[   ] times

50 The gross profit margin of LL has decreased from 25% to 10% in the year to 31 March 20X2.

Which TWO of the following would be realistic reasons for this decrease?

☐ LL announcing at the start of the year a price promise to undercut any of its competitor's prices

☐ LL signing a major contract to supply a single customer in the year, which was obtained after a very competitive tendering process

☐ LL increasing the credit period offered to its customers from one month to three months

☐ LL achieving economies of scale in the year

☐ LL not controlling its indirect costs

---

51 The following information is available for two potential acquisition targets. The entities have similar capital structures and both are toy manufacturers.

	SH	RV
Current ratio	4.3	7.5
Quick ratio	1.6	2.9
Inventory days	184 days	340 days
Receivable days	35 days	70 days
Payable days	56 days	27 days

Which of the following statements is a realistic conclusion that can be drawn from the above information?

○ Both entities are suffering from liquidity problems – both cannot pay their current liabilities as they fall due using their current assets.

○ RV's inventory days are considerably higher than SH's, implying a significant obsolescence risk to RV of changes in the popularity of toys compared to SH.

○ SH's receivable days are lower than RV's, implying that RV has a better credit control function.

○ RV pays its suppliers more quickly than SH, suggesting that RV has more favourable credit terms due to a shorter credit history.

---

52 The gearing ratio (calculated as debt/equity) of YY has increased from 43% to 140% in the year to 31 December 20X0.

Which TWO of the following are likely to be reasons for this increase?

☐ YY acquiring an expensive item of equipment in the year under a five-year lease

☐ YY making a substantial profit for the year, thereby increasing retained earnings at the year end

☐ YY having more taxable temporary differences in 20X0 which has increased the deferred tax liability substantially

☐ YY raising more finance in the year by issuing new ordinary shares to the market

☐ YY issuing redeemable preference shares in the year

53 The following ratios have been calculated from GJ's financial statements:

	31 March 20X3	31 March 20X2
Asset turnover	2.1	1.8
Gearing (debt/equity)	40%	40%

GJ has reported the same revenue and operating profit for both years in its statement of profit or loss.

Which of the following statements (in isolation), relating to GJ's activities in the year to 31 March 20X3, would explain the movements, if any, in both financial ratios?

○ The acquisition of an associate for cash at the end of the year

○ The issue of 1 for 4 bonus shares from reserves during the year

○ The consolidation of several existing bank loans into one long-term loan with a lower annual finance cost at the end of the year

○ The issue of new redeemable bonds to fully pay a cash dividend partway through the year

54 'AB should sell its trade receivables to a debt factoring company in order to decrease its receivables collection period.'

Which type of analytics is this statement according to Gartner's data analytics maturity model?

○ Descriptive

○ Diagnostic

○ Predictive

○ Prescriptive

55 MX has changed its accounting policy in the year and now values all inventory using first-in, first-out (FIFO) instead of weighted average cost.

Over the year, inventory prices have rapidly increased.

Which TWO of the following ratios would directly be affected by a change in this policy, therefore affecting the comparability of these ratios from last year to this year?

☐ Current ratio

☐ Non-current asset turnover

☐ Receivables days

☐ Gross profit margin

☐ Quick ratio (acid test)

56 The following ratios have been calculated for KL, a bespoke furniture manufacturer, from its financial statements:

	31 March 20X3	31 March 20X2
Cash operating cycle	300 days	170 days
Inventory days	85 days	30 days

Which of the following possible actions would be likely to improve the liquidity of KL?

○ Move from an economic order quantity ordering system to a just-in-time purchasing and production system

○ Reduce the credit terms offered to customers from three months to one month

○ Bulk buy all raw materials

○ Apply to the bank to reduce KL's existing overdraft facility

---

57 GH, a supermarket, has been struggling recently with increased competition and price pressure from other retailers in their domestic market.

In order for GH to survive, the directors have adopted a strategy to grow the business through the acquisition of international subsidiaries, in order to grow their market share in other markets. GH already has a high gearing level (calculated as debt/equity) which is currently at 70% and is close to breaching a loan covenant on an existing bank loan.

The directors of GH have found a potential acquisition target, AS. GH will need to raise more finance to be able to fund the acquisition of AS and the directors would like to know what the best possible source of finance is.

Which of the following is likely to be the most appropriate source of finance for GH to access to fund the acquisition of AS?

○ 10% redeemable bonds

○ 8% cumulative redeemable preference shares

○ 1 for 3 rights issue to existing ordinary shareholders

○ Bank overdraft

---

58 YU's statement of profit or loss for the year ended 31 December 20X8 is as follows:

	$'000
Revenue	780
Cost of sales	(490)
Gross profit	290
Distribution costs	(18)
Administration expenses	(40)
Finance costs	(16)
Share of profit of associate	70
Profit before tax	286
Income tax	(80)
Profit for the year	206

What is YU's interest cover for the year ended 31 December 20X8?

○ 14.5
○ 17.8
○ 18.1
○ 18.9

---

59 PJ and QW are of similar size and both operate in the pharmaceuticals sector. The return on capital employed for PJ and QW respectively is 44% and 38%.

Which of the following statements could explain the difference between PJ's and QW's return on capital employed?

○ QW holds its properties under the cost model whilst PJ holds its properties under the revaluation model.

○ PJ classifies its development expenditure amortisation as an administrative expense while QW classifies it as cost of sales.

○ QW obtains the right to use assets under leases while PJ buys its assets for cash.

○ QW acquires investments in associates for cash on the last day of the year whereas PJ does not have any investments in associates.

---

60 RC has recently changed its accounting policy from valuing its non-current assets using the cost model to using the revaluation model as permitted by IAS 16 *Property, Plant and Equipment*. In the year, RC revalued all of its property, plant and equipment upwards.

Which of the following statements correctly identifies the effect of the revaluation upwards on gearing and return on capital employed (ROCE)?

○ Reduces ROCE and increases gearing
○ Increases both ROCE and gearing
○ Reduces both ROCE and gearing
○ Increases ROCE and reduces gearing

Practice mock answers

Answers

1   The correct answer is: They carry a much lower rate of interest than conventional, fixed rate redeemable bonds.

One of the main attractions of deep discount bonds to investors is that they are issued at a large discount to the nominal value. Therefore, there is a large capital gain offered by the bonds, which is the difference between the heavily discounted issue price and the redemption value. Consequently, deep discount bonds will carry a much lower rate of interest than other types of bond because of this gain offered on redemption.

Convertible bonds are a different type of bond from conventional and deep discount bonds because they give the bondholders the right (but not the obligation) to convert their bonds at a specified future date into new equity shares of the company, at a conversion rate that is specified when the bonds are issued.

All bonds have a par or nominal value attached to them.

2   The correct answers are:

- Investors in unsecured bonds will generally want a higher yield than investors in secured bonds.
- Investors in ordinary shares expect a higher return than investors in preference shares or debt.
- Ordinary shareholders hold rights such as voting and attendance at general meetings, and receive a share of any dividend agreed.

Investors are likely to expect a higher yield (return) with unsecured bonds than with secured bonds to compensate them for the extra risk of not having a fixed or floating charge on the issuer's assets.

Ordinary shareholders are the ultimate bearers of risk as they are at the bottom of the creditor hierarchy in a liquidation. This means there is a significant risk they will receive nothing after the settlement of all the company's liabilities. This risk means that investors in ordinary shares expect the highest return of all long-term providers of finance. Redeemable debt holders will normally be one of the first creditors to get paid in a liquidation, followed by preference shareholders and finally ordinary shareholders. Therefore investors in redeemable debt and preference shares face less risk and expect a lower return.

Ordinary shareholders have rights as a result of their ownership of the shares. Voting rights, attendance at general meetings and an entitlement to receive a share of any agreed dividend are some of the various rights that they receive.

Preference shares generally do not carry voting rights. But they are paid dividends before ordinary shareholders and are just above ordinary shareholders in the creditor hierarchy in a liquidation (but below creditors).

A rights issue is an issue of new shares to existing shareholders. The general public are not invited to participate.

3   The correct answer is: The role of the sponsor in an initial public offering (IPO) is to **co-ordinate the overall IPO process and advise the company's board throughout**. The role of the book runner is to **raise finance from investors on behalf of the company and help determine the appropriate pricing for the share**. Both of these roles are generally performed by a **financial institution such as an investment bank**.

The reporting accountant will perform financial due diligence and provide tax advice for the issuing company in an IPO.

The role of the lawyer in an IPO is to perform legal due diligence, draft the prospectus and provide legal opinions.

A financial public relations firm will develop a communication strategy pre- and post-IPO.

Generally it will be a financial institution such as an investment bank that will perform the role of sponsor and book runner.

4   The correct answer is: 4.74%

The calculation for the cost of irredeemable debt is:

$$k_d = \frac{i(1-t)}{P_0}$$

$i = 6$

$(1-t) = 0.75$

$P_0 = 95$

$k_d = 6 \times 0.75/95 = 0.474$ or 4.74%

5   The correct answer is: 14.0%

$$k_e = \frac{d_1}{P_0} + g = \frac{40(1.07)}{611} + 0.07 = 14.0\%$$

The other answers are incorrect for the following reasons:

- 6.5% – this has ignored dividend growth
- 13.5% – this has used d_0 rather than d_1
- 14.5% – this has incorrectly deducted the dividend from the share price; as a dividend has just been paid, the share price given is already ex-div

6   The correct answer is: 8.21%

The post-tax cost of redeemable bonds is calculated using the internal rate of return (IRR) formula:

$$IRR = L + \left[\frac{NPV_L}{NPV_L - NPV_H} \times (H-L)\right]$$

$$= 5 + \left[\frac{21.15}{21.15 - -11.81} \times (10 - 5)\right]$$

$$= 5 + \left[\frac{21.15}{21.15 + 11.81} \times 5\right]$$

$$= 5 + 3.21$$

$$= 8.21\%$$

7   The correct answer is: $180

The redemption value at the end of Year 3 of the convertible bond should be the higher of:

Estimated value of the shares on conversion	($5.49 × 1.03³) × 30 shares	= $180
Cash payable on redemption	$100 × 1.10	= $110

8   The correct answer is: 14.5%

$$g = \sqrt[3]{\left(\frac{27}{18}\right)} - 1 = 0.145 \text{ or } 14.5\%$$

Note. Be careful in this question – although four years of dividends have been given, JZ has only experienced three years of growth (from 20X6 to 20X7, from 20X7 to 20X8 and from 20X8 to 20X9).

9　The correct answer is: 13.4%

$$\text{WACC} = k_{eg}\left(\frac{V_E}{V_E + V_D}\right) + k_d(1-t)\left(\frac{V_D}{V_E + V_D}\right)$$

$$\text{WACC} = 15\%\left(\frac{20}{20+5}\right) + 10\%(1-0.3)\left(\frac{5}{20+5}\right)$$

WACC = 12% + 1.4%

WACC = 13.4%

10　The correct answer is: $1,260

Under IFRS 15 *Revenue from Contracts with Customers*, revenue should be recognised as or when the performance obligation is satisfied. At the inception of a contract, an entity should identify each distinct promise to transfer goods or services as a separate performance obligation. In this contract, there are two performance obligations:

- To transfer the handset to the customer
- To give the customer access to the agreed data and calls each month

The transaction price should be allocated to these two performance obligations in proportion to their standalone selling prices as follows:

Performance obligation	Standalone selling price	% of total	Transaction price allocated
Handset	$800	40%	$720
Data and calls package	$1,200	60%	$1,080
Total	$2,000		$1,800

In the year ended 31 December 20X2, KT has transferred the handset to the customer so the full amount of revenue of $720 relating to this performance obligation should be recognised. Also, the customer has had access to one of the two years of data and calls in the contract so half of the $1,080 relating to data and calls should be recognised as revenue in the year ended 31 December 20X2. Therefore, the total correct amount of revenue to be recognised in the year ended 31 December 20X2 is:

$720 + (½ × $1,080) = $1,260

The other options are incorrect for the following reasons:

- $720 – this ignores the revenue earned from the provision of data and calls.
- $800 – this is the standalone selling price of the handset rather than the proportion of the total transaction price that relates to the transfer of the handset.
- $1,800 – this recognises all of the revenue in relation to the data and calls in the first year which is incorrect because KT has only fulfilled one of the two years required in the contract for the provision of data and calls.

11　The correct answers are:

- The performance obligation is satisfied over time as ZM constructs the office block.
- Using an output method based on units produced, revenue of $10 million would be recognised in the year ended 31 March 20X6.

As the office block is built on the customer's land and control is transferred to the customer as the asset is constructed, ZM's performance obligation is satisfied over time. Therefore, revenue should be recognised over time based on ZM's progress towards complete satisfaction of its performance obligation. Methods to recognise progress include input methods (based on the entity's efforts on inputs) and output methods (based on the value to the customer of goods or services transferred to date relative to the remaining goods or services promised under the contract).

Using an output method based on units produced, ZM has constructed four out of ten storeys, indicating that progress is 40% complete. Revenue calculated on this basis would amount to $10 million (40% × $25m).

The other options are incorrect for the following reasons:

- Revenue should not be recognised when the construction of all ten storeys has been completed because control of the asset is transferred to the customer as the asset is constructed indicating that the performance obligation is satisfied over time rather than at a point in time. Revenue should therefore be recognised over time as the asset is constructed.

- Using an input method based on costs incurred, ZM's progress would be measured as 45% complete ($9m/[$9m + $11m]). Revenue calculated on this basis would amount to $11.25 million (45% × $25m). The $12.5 million stated in the option is calculated on a time elapsed basis (one of the two years of the contract has been completed so revenue would be ½ × $25m). Time elapsed is a permissible input method but was not the method specified in this option.

- Revenue should only be recognised to the extent of recoverable costs incurred if the entity cannot reasonably measure the outcome of a performance obligation. This is not the case here as total costs can be estimated and the entity has already completed one of the two years of the contract.

12   The correct answer is: A finance lease is a lease that transfers substantially all the **risks and rewards** incidental to ownership of an underlying asset to the **lessee**; title may or may not be eventually transferred.

Under IFRS 16 *Leases*, for lessor accounting, leases must be classified either as finance leases or operating leases. Under a finance lease, risks and rewards are transferred to the lessee. Although transfer of legal title is an indicator that a lease may be a finance lease, it is not a mandatory criterion. Therefore, a lease may still be classified as a finance lease without transfer of legal title.

13   The correct answer is: Lease rental income of $19,000

This is an operating lease as the lease term is only for a short portion of the underlying asset's economic life and the present value of lease payments is significantly less than the fair value of the underlying asset.

Therefore, as the lessor (MN) retains the risks and rewards of ownership, it should continue to recognise the property and depreciate it as normal. Additionally it should recognise lease payments as income on a straight-line basis over the life of the lease:

$$= \frac{(\$20,000 \times 4\,\text{years}) - \$4,000}{4\,\text{years}}$$

= $19,000

The other answers are incorrect for the following reasons:

- Lease rental income of $20,000 – this does not take into account the $4,000 lease incentive.

- Finance income of $5,832 – if this had been a finance lease, MN would have recognised a lease receivable equivalent to the net investment in the lease and finance income on this lease receivable ($64,800 × 9% = $5,832).

- Finance income of $4,032 – as explained above, if this had been a finance lease, finance income would have been recognised. However, this would be the wrong amount as it is calculated having deducted the first instalment from the present value of lease payments (($64,800 – 20,000) × 9%).

14 The correct answer is: The costs to remove an oil rig at the end of extraction where required by a licensing agreement

The oil rig has been constructed and there is a legal obligation under the licensing agreement to remove the oil rig at the end of extraction. Therefore, there is a present obligation as a result of a past event. There is a probable outflow as the company is more likely than not to dismantle the oil rig otherwise it will be unlikely to be awarded any future licensing agreements. Reliable measurement should be possible on the basis of past dismantling costs. Therefore, the IAS 37 criteria for a provision have been met and a provision should be made for the best estimate of the dismantling costs. An equal amount should be added to the cost of the oil rig rather than recognised as an expense.

Costs relating to the closure of a factory that has not yet been announced – this is incorrect because no valid expectation has been created in those affected by the closure and therefore no constructive or legal obligation exists. No provision can be made for this.

Expected operating losses for the next financial year from a newly acquired subsidiary – this is incorrect because IAS 37 explicitly prohibits future operating losses to be provided for as no obligation exists.

No provision should be made for the staff retraining costs because the obligating event will be the retraining which has not yet taken place.

15 The correct answer is: Disclose a contingent liability

There is only a possible obligation and possible outflow as JM's lawyers believe that the probability of the company losing the court case is less than 50%. Therefore, no provision should be recognised. Instead, a contingent liability must be disclosed.

A contingent asset would only be relevant to a potential future inflow of cash rather than a potential future outflow and it would only disclosed if the likelihood of the inflow were probable.

16 The correct answer is: $94,825

		$
1.7.X6	Opening liability	92,500
30.6.X7	Finance costs (92,500 × 9%)	8,325
30.6.X7	Coupon interest paid (100,000 × 6%)	(6,000)
30.6.X7	Carrying amount of liability component	94,825

On initial recognition, the convertible bonds must be split into their liability and equity components. The liability is calculated as the present value of future cash flows (here the 6% coupon and the $100,000 repayable on redemption) discounted at the market rate of non-convertible debt (here: 9%). The equity component of $7,500 is calculated as the proceeds ($100,000) less the liability component ($92,500).

Subsequently, the liability component must be carried at amortised cost and the equity component remains unchanged.

The finance costs on the liability component of the convertible bond are accrued using the effective interest rate, which is the market rate of similar non-convertible bonds (ie 9%), as this is the rate the future cash flows on the bond would have been discounted at in order to arrive at the present value of the liability component of $92,500.

Coupon interest of 6% is paid annually in arrears and is always based on the par/nominal value of the bonds.

17 The correct answer is: A financial asset is cash, an equity instrument of another entity or a contractual **right** to receive cash or financial asset from another entity, or to exchange financial assets or liabilities under potentially **favourable** conditions.

This definition comes from IAS 32 *Financial Instruments: Presentation*.

18 The correct answers are:

- A purchased franchise
- A customer list acquired as part of a business combination
- Goodwill arising on acquisition of a subsidiary

The cost of activities aimed at obtaining new knowledge are research costs which IAS 38 requires to be recognised as an expense rather than an intangible asset.

The development costs for the new product do not meet IAS 38's capitalisation criteria because financial resources are not available to produce the asset for sale.

IAS 38 *Intangible Assets* prohibits the capitalisation of staff training costs. They should always be recognised as an expense.

19 The correct answer is: $1,000

Development costs should only be capitalised from the date that they meet the IAS 38 *Intangible Assets* capitalisation criteria, which occurs on 1 April 20X2. Therefore, the $345,000 incurred before this date cannot be capitalised. The $120,000 incurred from 1 April 20X2 until the new production process comes into use on 1 December 20X2 should be capitalised as an intangible asset.

IAS 38 requires amortisation to commence when the asset is available for use. Here this is on 1 December 20X2. Therefore, the $120,000 should be amortised over its ten-year useful life but only one month of amortisation should be recognised in the year ended 31 December 20X2. This is calculated as follows:

Amortisation = $120,000 × 1/10 × 1/12 = $1,000

20 The correct answer is: Interest payable that has been accrued in the financial statements, which will be deducted for tax purposes on a cash payments basis

Interest (and other expenses) that have been accrued for in the financial statements but will be tax deductible in the future do give rise to a temporary difference and therefore deferred tax must be recognised. This temporary difference will give rise to a deferred tax asset because when the expense is recognised by the tax authorities at a later date (when the interest is paid), this will reduce future taxable profits and therefore reduce the amount of tax that is payable by the entity.

Accrued expenses that are not deductible for tax purposes – this is incorrect as this creates a permanent difference between taxable and accounting profits so deferred tax cannot be provided for.

Revaluation surplus on property, plant and equipment – this is incorrect as this will give rise to a deferred tax liability. The revaluation will make the accounting carrying value of the asset greater than its tax base as the tax authorities will not recognise an increase in value until the asset is sold.

Tax depreciation in excess of accounting depreciation – this is incorrect as it will result in a deferred tax liability, as too much tax relief has been granted and this must be reversed with a deferred tax liability.

21 The correct answer is: $203,000

The total amount that MK should recognise is the current tax of $195,000 for the current year plus the underprovision of $8,000 ($148,000 – $140,000) in respect of the previous year. This amounts to $203,000 ($195,000 + $8,000).

The other answers are incorrect for the following reasons:

- $187,000 – the $8,000 underprovision in relation to the prior year has incorrectly been treated as an over-provision.
- $195,000 – this ignores the underprovision in respect of the prior year.
- $343,000 – this incorrectly recognises the full $148,000 paid this year in relation to the previous year; – $140,000 of this amount had already been recognised as an expense in the previous year's financial statements.

22 The correct answer is: The NCI share of the subsidiary's post-acquisition reserves should be included in the calculation of NCI in the equity section of the group statement of financial position.

When calculating the value of NCI to be included in the consolidated statement of financial position, the NCI share of the subsidiary's post-acquisition reserves is added to NCI at acquisition. NCI at acquisition may either be measured at fair value (full goodwill method) or at the NCI share of net assets (partial goodwill method).

Depending on the choice of measurement of NCI at acquisition, any impairment of goodwill will either be charged in full to the group retained earnings (partial goodwill method) or split between group retained earnings and NCI (full goodwill method).

If the subsidiary sells goods to the parent in the year and there is unrealised profit on the goods left in inventory at the year end, the NCI should take a share of this unrealised profit as a deduction from the subsidiary's profit for the year when calculating the NCI share of profit in the consolidated statement of profit or loss.

23 The correct answers are:

- The choice of treatments for an associate in the parent's individual financial statements is the same as for an investment in a subsidiary or joint venture.
- The group share of the associate's post-acquisition reserves must be included in the investment in associate and consolidated reserves.

In the parent's individual accounts, under IAS 27 *Separate Financial Statements*, an investment in a subsidiary, associate or joint venture may be held at cost, at fair value or using the equity method.

Equity accounting is required for an associate in the consolidated financial statements. This involves including the group share of the profit for the year (ie after tax) and the group share of the associate's other comprehensive income in the consolidated statement of profit or loss and other comprehensive income. In the consolidated statement of financial position, an investment in associates (cost plus group share of post-acquisition reserves less any impairment) is included in non-current assets and the group share of the associate's post-acquisition reserves are included in consolidated reserves.

Significant influence may be achieved through holding at least 20% of voting rights but other factors all need to be taken into consideration (eg representation on the board of directors, participation in policy-making, material transactions between the entity and investee, interchange of management personnel and provision of essential technical information).

For any transactions between the parent and associate, only the group share of any unrealised profit should be eliminated. Intra-group revenue, cost of sales, receivables and payables are not eliminated as the parent does not control the associate.

24 The correct answer is: **The equity method**

The equity method is required for recognition and subsequent measurement of a joint venture on consolidation. In the consolidated statement of financial position, the investment in joint venture will be held under non-current assets, measured as follows:

	$
Cost of joint venture	X
Share of post-acquisition retained earnings (and other reserves)	X
Less impairment losses on investment in joint venture to date	(X)
	X

The group share of post-acquisition retained earnings and the impairment losses on the investment in the joint venture to date will also be included in consolidated retained earnings in the consolidated statement of financial position.

Including the investor's share of jointly held assets, liabilities, income and expenses is the accounting treatment for a **joint operation** in the individual and consolidated financial statements.

Holding the investment at cost or at fair value (as a financial asset) are two of the three possible treatments for accounting for a joint venture in the investor's **individual** financial statements. The third option is the equity method.

Consolidating net assets in full on a line-by-line basis would be the correct accounting treatment for a **subsidiary** rather than an associate.

25 The correct answer is: **$16,100,000**

	$'000
Carrying amount of net assets	15,000
FV adjustments	
Property (750 – 500)	250
Brand	1,000
Contingent liability	(150)
Fair value of net assets at acquisition	16,100

Property — It should be the excess of the fair value over the carrying amount (already included in the financial statements) that should be adjusted for.

Brand — This would not have been previously recognised in HL's individual financial statements because it is an internally generated intangible asset which cannot be measured reliably. However, on acquisition of the subsidiary by the parent, it can now be measured reliably and therefore should be recognised in the consolidated financial statements and added in full to the net assets.

Contingent liability — This was only disclosed in the notes to HL's individual financial statements under IAS 37 *Provisions, Contingent Liabilities and Contingent Assets* and not provided for. However, IFRS 3 *Business Combinations* requires that on acquisition of the subsidiary by the parent, the contingent liability should be recognised in the consolidated financial statements in full as a fair value adjustment.

26 The correct answers are:

- Additional depreciation of $18,750 is to be included in the consolidated statement of profit or loss.
- The settlement of the contingent liability of $150,000 would be shown as income in the consolidated statement of profit and loss.

Property additional depreciation is calculated as $250,000 (fair value adjustment)/10 = $25,000. However, as it was a mid-year acquisition of HL, depreciation should be pro-rated for the nine months post-acquisition (1 April 20X2 to 31 December 20X2).

Therefore, the charge to the consolidated P/L is:

$25,000 × 9/12 = $18,750

A settlement of a contingent liability is income as the liability is being reduced; therefore $150,000 would be credited to the consolidated P/L.

The brand would be amortised over its 20-year remaining life giving an annual amortisation amount of $50,000. Again, this would need to be pro-rated for the year ended December 20X2 as it was a mid-year acquisition.

Therefore the charge to the consolidated P/L is:

$50,000 × 9/12 = $37,500

27 The correct answer is: $9,652,500

Consolidated reserves as at 31 December 20X4:

	MB	YH
	$	$
At year end	6,750,000	1,750,000
At acquisition		(525,000)
		1,225,000
Group share (1,225,000 × 90%)	1,102,500	
Reserves at year end	7,852,500	

Equity attributable to the owners of the parent comprises:

	$
Parent's share capital	1,500,000
Parent's share premium	300,000
Consolidated reserves	7,852,500
Total equity at year end	9,652,500

28 The correct answers are:

- Acquisition of subsidiary net of cash acquired
- Dividends received from associates

'Cash flows from investing activities' include cash items relating to the acquisition and disposal of non-current assets and investments and income from those investments (dividends and interest received). The acquisition of a subsidiary net of cash acquired (the consideration transferred to purchase the subsidiary less the subsidiary's cash balance at the date of acquisition) is always presented under 'investing activities'. However, for dividends and interest received, IAS 7 *Statement of Cash Flows* allows the cash flow to be presented either under 'investing activities' or 'operating activities'.

The other answers are incorrect for the following reasons:

- The share of profit in associate is an adjustment to profit before tax under the heading of 'cash flows from operating activities'.
- Dividends paid to non-controlling interests may be presented either as 'financing activities' or 'operating activities'.
- Proceeds from long-term borrowings are cash flows from 'financing activities'.

29 The correct answers are:

- JM operates autonomously, and has a low level of intra-group transactions which indicates that its functional currency is the croma.
- JM makes its sales and purchases in C-Land and pays its employees in croma which indicates that its functional currency is the croma.

Statement 1 is incorrect because the presentation currency can be any currency. It is likely that DJ group will encourage JM to select the B$ as its presentation currency as it is the currency of the group financial statements.

Statement 2 is incorrect because the functional currency cannot be chosen. It is the currency of the primary economic environment – here, the croma not the B$.

Statements 3 and 4 are correct because the functional currency is the currency of the primary economic environment. It is determined by looking at certain factors such as the currency that influences sales prices, raw materials and labour costs, as well as the currency from which receipts from operations are retained and funds from borrowing are generated.

In addition, along with the above, indicators of the functional currency for a foreign subsidiary include the degree of autonomy from the parent and the level of inter-group transactions with the parent to determine whether the subsidiary is carrying out activities as an extension of the parent, or whether it still operates largely independently from the parent.

Statement 5 is incorrect as this is the definition of presentation currency, not functional currency. An entity can choose the presentation currency of its year-end accounts whereas the functional currency must be the currency of the primary economic environment.

30 The correct answer is: A$125 gain.

	Dinar	Rate	A$
Consideration transferred	83,250		
Non-controlling interests	11,250		
Less fair value of net assets at acquisition	(90,000)		
Goodwill at 1 April 20X2	4,500	4.5	1,000
Exchange gain on goodwill in the year		Bal. fig	125
Goodwill at 31 March 20X3	4,500	4	1,125

Note. You did not need to calculate goodwill as it was given as 4,500 dinars. The full calculation is shown to help your understanding. You just needed to compare goodwill divided by the historic rate to goodwill divided by the closing rate. IAS 21 *The Effects of Changes in Foreign Exchange Rates* requires goodwill to be translated at the closing rate at each year end which gives rise to exchange differences.

31 The correct answers are:

- Jed, who is the finance director of PL
- QP, the parent of TJ and the ultimate parent of the group in which PL is included

Jed is a related party because he is a member of the key management personnel of PL. QP is related because it is a member of the same group as PL.

IAS 24 *Related Party Disclosures* gives specific examples of those parties that are not necessarily related to the reporting entity:

- Two entities simply because they have a director in common, meaning UV is not a related party
- Providers of finance – therefore HB Bank is not related to PL
- Customers and suppliers – therefore RY is not a related party of PL

32 The correct answer is: SU, CA, TD and the pension plan

According to IAS 24 *Related Party Disclosures*, entities that are typically related parties are those entities that are part of the same group. This includes parent, subsidiaries (ie SU), associates (ie CA) and joint ventures (ie TD). A post-employment benefit plan for the benefit of employees of an entity (ie the defined benefit plan for NK's employees) is also specifically mentioned in IAS 24 as a related party.

Two joint venturers are not necessarily related parties simply because they share joint control of a joint venture. Therefore UJ is not a related party of NK.

33 The correct answers are:

- Convertible bonds
- Share options granted to executives

The denominator of basic EPS is the weighted average number of ordinary shares. For diluted EPS, the weighted average number of ordinary shares must be adjusted for the effects of all dilutive potential ordinary shares.

Convertible bonds and share options are potential ordinary shares because both of these instruments can potentially convert into ordinary shares in the future. Therefore the number of potential dilutive shares issued should be included in the denominator of diluted EPS but, as they are not currently ordinary shares, they should not be included in the denominator of basic EPS.

Preference shares issued will not be included in the denominator of either basic or diluted EPS. This is because IAS 33 requires only ordinary shares to be included in the weighted average number of shares. As they are not convertible, they are not potential ordinary shares, so they should also be excluded from the denominator of diluted EPS.

Redeemable bonds will not be included in the denominator of either basis or diluted EPS. This is because they are classified as debt rather than equity (ordinary shares) so they must be excluded from the weighted average number of shares. As they are not convertible, they are not potential ordinary shares so they will not be included in the denominator of diluted EPS.

34 The correct answer is: 96.7 cents

$$\text{Basic EPS} = \frac{\text{Profit available to ordinary shareholders of the parent}}{\text{Weighted average number of ordinary shares}}$$

$$\text{Basic EPS} = \frac{(\$3,000,000 - \$900,000 - \$350,000)}{1,809,524 \,(\text{W1})}$$

Basic EPS = 96.7 cents

Profit (earnings) available to ordinary shareholders should be profit for the year less any preference dividends and profit attributable to non-controlling interests.

Workings

1 Weighted average number of ordinary shares

Date		Number of shares	Time fraction	Bonus fraction (W2)	Average
1.1.X0	Ordinary shares at start of year	1,600,000	× 8/12	× 2.25/2.10	1,142,857
1.9.X0	1 for 4 rights issue	400,000			
31.12.X0	Total	2,000,000	× 4/12		666,667
	Weighted average				1,809,524

2 Bonus fraction

Bonus fraction = Fair value prior to issue (cum rights price)/Theoretical ex-rights price (TERP)

$$= \frac{2.25}{2.10} \,(\text{W3})$$

3 TERP

4	× $2.25	=	$9.00
1	× $1.50	=	$1.50
5		=	$10.50
$10.50/5		=	$2.10 TERP

35 The correct answer is: $20,000

The difference between the 'full' goodwill method (where NCI is measured at fair value at acquisition) and the 'partial' goodwill method (where NCI is measured at the proportionate share of the fair value of net assets at acquisition) is the goodwill relating to the non-controlling interests.

This is calculated as follows:

	$
Fair value of NCI (10% × 1,000,000 shares × $1.40)	140,000
Less NCI share of net assets (10% × $1,200,000)	(120,000)
Goodwill relating to NCI	20,000

This is quicker than calculating the goodwill under both methods and working out the difference, and gives you the same answer:

	Full method $	Partial method $	Difference $
Consideration transferred	1,350,000	1,350,000	
NCI			
(10% × 1,000,000 × $1.40)			
(10% × $1,200,000)	140,000	120,000	
Less fair value of net assets	(1,200,000)	(1,200,000)	
Goodwill	290,000	270,000	20,000

36 The correct answer is: $2,632,000

	BV $'000	JK $'000
At 31 December 20X6	2,560	880
Pre-acquisition retained earnings (880 − (144 × 8/12))		(784)
		96
Group share (75% × $96,000)	72	
Consolidated retained earnings	2,632	

37 The correct answer is: $208,000

	$
Consideration transferred	468,000
Non-controlling interest at fair value	35,000
Fair value of net assets acquired:	
Share capital	(150,000)
Retained earnings at 1 April 20X4	(124,000)
Profit to 31 July 20X4 ($63,000 × 4/12)	(21,000)
	208,000

38 The correct answer is: $1,737,500

This is calculated as follows:

	$
AB	1,200,000
CD	870,000
Less intra-group cost of sales	(350,000)
Add unrealised profit (350,000 × 20/100 × 1/4)	17,500
	1,737,500

39 The correct answer is: $500,000

The investment in associate is calculated as follows:

	$
Cost of associate	460,000
Share of post-acquisition retained earnings (25% × [390,000 – 250,000])	35,000
Share of post-acquisition revaluation surplus (25% × [110,000 – 80,000])	7,500
Less group share of unrealised profit (25% × 60,000 × 50/150 × 1/2 in inventory)	(2,500)
	500,000

40 The correct answer is: To issue International Sustainability Disclosure Standards

There is no fixed format for sustainability reporting, it will depend on what an entity considers is material.

Integrated reports provide information about value creation.

Stakeholder relationships is an important part of sustainability reporting, but not the main role of the ISSB.

41 The correct answer is: The active consideration by an organisation of the relationships between its various operating and functional units and the capitals that the organisation uses or affects

This is the IIRC's definition of integrated thinking. The IIRC believes that integrated thinking leads to integrated decision making and actions that consider the creation of value over the short, medium and long term.

42 The correct answer is: To establish guiding principles and content elements for preparation of an integrated report

The Integrated Reporting Framework is principles-based rather than rules-based so that an integrated report can be tailored to individual organisations. A long integrated report is not necessarily a good one. The quality and usefulness to stakeholders is of greater importance.

The IIRC wishes to promote integrated reporting around the world. The Integrated Reporting Framework specifically provides guidance for those organisations that prepare an integrated report.

43   The correct answers are:

- Improved co-operation between different departments
- Increased focus and awareness of management on sustainability
- Better articulation of an organisation's strategy

An integrated report is a forward-looking document which goes beyond the traditional reporting of backward-looking financial statements.

While an integrated report could lead to improved performance, preparation of an integrated report requires significant time and cost so there is no guarantee of increased profit and therefore there is not an obvious link to the higher remuneration of directors. This is not a specific aim of integrated reporting.

An integrated report is concerned with an organisation's capitals, one of which is human capital. Therefore, it is seen as key to an entity's success. Reducing employee headcount is not consistent with this view although it might be seen to have the potential to increase financial capital.

44   The correct answer is: Intellectual

Intellectual capital is defined as:

'Organisational, knowledge-based intangibles, including:

- intellectual property, such as patents, copyrights, software, rights and licences
- organisational capital such as tacit knowledge, systems, procedures and protocols.' (IIRC, 2021: p.12)

45   The correct answers are:

- Disclosures should be determined by the effects of the capitals on the organisation's ability to create value rather than whether they are owned by the organisation.
- An exhaustive account of the all the complex interdependencies between the capitals is not required.
- Disclosure is required of the trade-offs between the capitals and over time.

The Integrated Reporting Framework's categorisation of capitals is not mandatory. An organisation may define its own capitals.

A greater quantity of disclosures in an integrated report does not necessarily increase its usefulness to stakeholders and may in fact confuse users as important information may be obscured.

If it is not practicable or meaningful to quantify significant movements in capital, an organisation may make qualitative disclosures instead.

46   The correct answer is: 15.1%

$$\text{Gearing} = \frac{\text{Long-term debt}}{\text{Equity}} \times 100\%$$

$$\text{Gearing} = \frac{331}{2{,}192}$$

Gearing = 15.1%

Note. Deferred tax is excluded from long-term debt as it is not interest-bearing nor a source of long-term finance.

47   The correct answers are:

- The market rate of interest is lower in B-land than in A-land.
- Companies have to pay a higher rate of tax in A-land than in B-land.

The difference between the operating and net margins relates to interest and tax. Therefore, if the market rate of interest is lower in B-land, Entity B is likely to pay less interest on its borrowings than Entity A, which explains why there is a smaller difference between Entity B's operating and net margin. Also, if companies have to pay higher tax in A-land, this explains why there is a greater difference between Entity A's operating and net margins.

Labour costs, delivery costs and depreciation of non-current assets will be reported within cost of sales, distribution costs and administration expenses. However, both operating and net profit are calculated after deducting these categories of operating expenses. Therefore, issues around these expenses do not explain why one entity has a greater difference between its operating and net margin than the other.

48   The correct answer is: 19.4%

$$\text{ROCE} = \frac{\text{Profit before interest and tax (excluding associate)}}{\text{Capital employed (excluding associate)}} \times 100\%$$

Profit before interest and tax (excluding associate) = 457 + 14 – 20

= 451

Capital employed (excluding associate) = Equity + Interest-bearing borrowings – Investment in associate

= 2,192 + 331 – 201

= 2,332

$$\text{ROCE} = \frac{451}{2,332} \times 100\%$$

ROCE = 19.4%

49   The correct answer is: 8.4 times

$$\text{Non-current asset turnover} = \frac{\text{Revenue}}{\text{Non-current assets (excluding investment in associate)}}$$

Non-current assets should exclude any investments in associates because the revenue figure does not include revenue generated from the associate.

$$\text{Non-current asset turnover} = \frac{2,562}{(230 + 75)}$$

Non-current asset turnover = 8.4 times

50   The correct answers are:

- LL announcing at the start of the year a price promise to undercut any of its competitor's prices
- LL signing a major contract to supply a large proportion of its output to a single customer in the year, which was obtained after a very competitive tendering process

By undercutting its competitors' prices, LL would be reducing its selling price in the year which would lead to a reduction in the gross margin.

Also, with LL securing a contract after a very competitive tender, it would have forced LL to reduce prices to win the contract and therefore it would have reduced its margin in the year.

By increasing credit terms, LL is likely to have an increase in volume of sales and is likely to increase sales volume rather than reduce the gross margin.

If LL achieves economies of scale it is likely to improve margins rather than deteriorate them.

If LL is not controlling its indirect costs, this would be reflected in a deteriorating operating profit margin, not the gross profit margin, which includes direct costs in cost of sales.

51   The correct answer is: RV's inventory days are considerably higher than SH's, implying a significant obsolescence risk to RV of changes in the popularity of toys compared to SH.

It is to be expected that toy manufacturers would have high inventory days, as their goods are not perishable. However, RV's inventory days are almost double that of SH's which means that RV is exposed to significant obsolescence risk from changes in popularity of certain toys compared to SH.

Option 1 is incorrect as both entities have current and quick ratios in excess of 1 – therefore they both have sufficient current assets to pay current liabilities as they fall due.

Option 3 is incorrect as SH has the lower receivables days and therefore we can presume that it would have better credit control than RV, not the other way around.

Option 4 is incorrect because although RV does pay its suppliers more quickly than SH, it is likely to be because they get **less favourable** (ie shorter) credit terms than SH, which means they have to pay their suppliers quicker. Also, to obtain favourable credit terms, a long rather than a short credit history is usually required.

52   The correct answers are:

- YY acquiring an expensive item of equipment in the year under a five-year lease
- YY issuing redeemable preference shares in the year

The new five-year lease does not qualify for the IFRS 16 *Leases* recognition exemptions as it is neither short term (as the lease term is greater than 12 months) nor is it for an underlying asset of low value. Therefore, the required accounting entry for the lessee (YY) is:

Debit   Right-of-use asset
Credit Lease liability

Debt in the gearing ratio includes all interest-bearing debt. Therefore, the new lease liability will increase the debt balance resulting in an increase in gearing.

The preference shares are a type of financial instrument. Since they are redeemable, they contain an obligation to repay the principal and, as such, should be classified as a financial liability rather than equity. This means that they are included in debt and would cause gearing to increase.

Option 2 is incorrect as this would decrease gearing in the year by increasing equity, the denominator in the gearing ratio.

Option 3 is incorrect because although deferred tax appears in the statement of financial position as part of non-current liabilities, it is not a part of long-term debt because it is not a source of funding for an entity.

Option 4 is incorrect as again this will have the effect of increasing equity, therefore reducing gearing.

53   The correct answer is: The acquisition of an associate for cash at the end of the year

Asset turnover is calculated as **revenue/capital employed**

where capital employed = equity + interest-bearing borrowings − non-current assets that do not contribute to operating profit (eg investment in associates).

In this case, if GJ were to acquire a new associate at the end of the year, the cost of investment would be debited to non-current assets and credited to cash. Therefore this increases the amount of investments that need to be stripped out from capital employed. This will not impact equity because the transaction was at the end of the year and therefore no share of profit after tax would have been included in profit.

This therefore will increase asset turnover by reducing the denominator in the formula and leave gearing unchanged.

Option 2 is incorrect as the bonus issue is debited to reserves and credited share capital with the same amount. The net effect of this transaction means that there is no movement in debt or equity in the year, therefore leaving gearing and asset turnover unchanged.

Option 3 is incorrect as the overall debt figure used in capital employed and in gearing would remain unchanged as a result of the consolidation of the debt.

Option 4 is incorrect as the issue of new redeemable bonds would increase gearing by increasing the numerator in that ratio and reduce asset turnover by increasing the denominator, the amount of capital employed.

54   The correct answer is: Prescriptive

This is prescriptive analytics because it answers the question 'what should I do?'.

55   The correct answers are:

- Current ratio
- Gross profit margin

$$\text{Current ratio} = \frac{\text{Current assets}}{\text{Current liabilities}}$$

$$\text{Gross profit margin} = \frac{\text{Gross profit}}{\text{Revenue}} \times 100\%$$

In times of rising prices, FIFO will give a higher closing inventory valuation than weighted average cost.

In the current ratio, inventory is included in the numerator. Inventory will be higher and therefore this will increase the current ratio if all other elements remain constant.

In the gross profit margin, inventory is included within cost of sales. A higher valuation of inventory will reduce cost of sales by a greater amount, therefore increasing gross profit and pushing up the gross profit margin if all other elements remain constant.

None of the other ratios include inventory in their formulae.

56 The correct answer is: Move from an economic order quantity ordering system to a just-in-time purchasing and production system

By moving to a just-in-time (JIT) system, KL will only buy in raw materials and produce furniture when it is needed (ie in response to a customer order). This means that KL will not be holding large amounts of inventory which will reduce inventory days and improve overall liquidity.

Reducing credit terms offered to customers will deter customers from buying from KL, meaning that inventory days may increase as a result. This will not improve overall liquidity.

Bulk buying raw materials will increase inventory days as KL will be holding the raw materials in stock for longer before they are issued into production.

Applying for a reduction in an overdraft facility will not improve liquidity and would not be a recommended course of action when the cash operating cycle is increasing and liquidity deteriorating.

57 The correct answer is: 1 for 3 rights issue to existing ordinary shareholders

This source of finance will be the most appropriate for GH given its high gearing levels and the fact that it is close to breaching a loan covenant. This share issue will reduce gearing by increasing equity.

The other options are not appropriate as they would increase gearing and would cause GH to breach its loan covenant, which could have the consequence of the bank recalling or withdrawing the loan. This means that GH may not be able to finance the acquisition of AS or be able to continue to survive into the future.

58 The correct answer is: 14.5

$$\text{Interest cover} = \frac{\text{Profit before interest and tax (PBIT)}}{\text{Interest expense}}$$

PBIT must exclude the share of the associate's profit or loss because the interest expense figure does not include any of the associate's interest. Therefore interest cover is calculated as:

$$\frac{\$286{,}000 - \$70{,}000 + \$16{,}000}{\$16{,}000} = 14.5$$

The other answers are incorrect for the following reasons:

17.8 – this is the answer if you forget to remove the share of the associate's profit and add back the finance costs to profit before tax.

18.1 – this is the answer if you use gross profit rather than profit before interest and tax.

18.9 – this is the answer if you forget to remove the share of the associate's profit from profit before tax.

59 The correct answer is: QW obtains the right to use assets under leases while PJ buys its assets for cash.

This would cause QW to have higher capital employed due to recognising a lease liability. However, the impact of interest from the lease on QW's profit is irrelevant as ROCE is based on operating profit before interest and tax. The higher debt and capital employed of QW should make its ROCE lower than PJ's.

Option 1 is incorrect because if PJ held its properties under the revaluation model, it would have higher capital employed due to the revaluation surplus in equity and lower profit due to a higher depreciation charge. This would make PJ's ROCE lower than QW's, not higher.

Option 2 is incorrect because the different classification of amortisation would have no impact on ROCE which is calculated on profit after all operating expenses but before interest and tax.

Option 4 is incorrect because QW's ROCE would be higher, as the investment in associate will have reduced capital employed. There would be no impact on QW's operating profits as associates are excluded from profit before interest and tax when calculating ROCE. Furthermore, the associate was acquired on the last day of the year and therefore no share of profit in the associate would have been included in QW's profit in the first place.

60 The correct answer is: Reduces both ROCE and gearing

By holding property, plant and equipment under the revaluation model, RC would have higher capital employed due to the revaluation surplus in equity and lower profit due to a higher depreciation charge. This would cause a decrease in ROCE.

The increase in equity would also reduce the gearing ratio of RC.

Appendix: Maths tables and formulae

PRESENT VALUE TABLE

Present value of 1.00 unit of currency, that is $(1+r)^{-n}$ where r = interest rate; n = number of periods until payment of receipt.

Periods (n)	1%	2%	3%	4%	5%	6%	7%	8%	9%	10%
1	0.990	0.980	0.971	0.962	0.952	0.943	0.935	0.926	0.917	0.909
2	0.980	0.961	0.943	0.925	0.907	0.890	0.873	0.857	0.842	0.826
3	0.971	0.942	0.915	0.889	0.864	0.840	0.816	0.794	0.772	0.751
4	0.961	0.924	0.888	0.855	0.823	0.792	0.763	0.735	0.708	0.683
5	0.951	0.906	0.863	0.822	0.784	0.747	0.713	0.681	0.650	0.621
6	0.942	0.888	0.837	0.790	0.746	0.705	0.666	0.630	0.596	0.564
7	0.933	0.871	0.813	0.760	0.711	0.665	0.623	0.583	0.547	0.513
8	0.923	0.853	0.789	0.731	0.677	0.627	0.582	0.540	0.502	0.467
9	0.914	0.837	0.766	0.703	0.645	0.592	0.544	0.500	0.460	0.424
10	0.905	0.820	0.744	0.676	0.614	0.558	0.508	0.463	0.422	0.386
11	0.896	0.804	0.722	0.650	0.585	0.527	0.475	0.429	0.388	0.350
12	0.887	0.788	0.701	0.625	0.557	0.497	0.444	0.397	0.356	0.319
13	0.879	0.773	0.681	0.601	0.530	0.469	0.415	0.368	0.326	0.290
14	0.870	0.758	0.661	0.577	0.505	0.442	0.388	0.340	0.299	0.263
15	0.861	0.743	0.642	0.555	0.481	0.417	0.362	0.315	0.275	0.239
16	0.853	0.728	0.623	0.534	0.458	0.394	0.339	0.292	0.252	0.218
17	0.844	0.714	0.605	0.513	0.436	0.371	0.317	0.270	0.231	0.198
18	0.836	0.700	0.587	0.494	0.416	0.350	0.296	0.250	0.212	0.180
19	0.828	0.686	0.570	0.475	0.396	0.331	0.277	0.232	0.194	0.164
20	0.820	0.673	0.554	0.456	0.377	0.312	0.258	0.215	0.178	0.149

Periods (n)	11%	12%	13%	14%	15%	16%	17%	18%	19%	20%
1	0.901	0.893	0.885	0.877	0.870	0.862	0.855	0.847	0.840	0.833
2	0.812	0.797	0.783	0.769	0.756	0.743	0.731	0.718	0.706	0.694
3	0.731	0.712	0.693	0.675	0.658	0.641	0.624	0.609	0.593	0.579
4	0.659	0.636	0.613	0.592	0.572	0.552	0.534	0.516	0.499	0.482
5	0.593	0.567	0.543	0.519	0.497	0.476	0.456	0.437	0.419	0.402
6	0.535	0.507	0.480	0.456	0.432	0.410	0.390	0.370	0.352	0.335
7	0.482	0.452	0.425	0.400	0.376	0.354	0.333	0.314	0.296	0.279
8	0.434	0.404	0.376	0.351	0.327	0.305	0.285	0.266	0.249	0.233
9	0.391	0.361	0.333	0.308	0.284	0.263	0.243	0.225	0.209	0.194
10	0.352	0.322	0.295	0.270	0.247	0.227	0.208	0.191	0.176	0.162
11	0.317	0.287	0.261	0.237	0.215	0.195	0.178	0.162	0.148	0.135
12	0.286	0.257	0.231	0.208	0.187	0.168	0.152	0.137	0.124	0.112
13	0.258	0.229	0.204	0.182	0.163	0.145	0.130	0.116	0.104	0.093
14	0.232	0.205	0.181	0.160	0.141	0.125	0.111	0.099	0.088	0.078
15	0.209	0.183	0.160	0.140	0.123	0.108	0.095	0.084	0.074	0.065
16	0.188	0.163	0.141	0.125	0.107	0.093	0.081	0.071	0.062	0.054
17	0.170	0.146	0.125	0.108	0.093	0.080	0.069	0.060	0.052	0.045
18	0.153	0.130	0.111	0.095	0.081	0.069	0.059	0.051	0.044	0.038
19	0.138	0.116	0.098	0.083	0.070	0.060	0.051	0.043	0.037	0.031
20	0.124	0.104	0.087	0.073	0.061	0.051	0.041	0.037	0.031	0.026

Cumulative present value table

This table shows the present value of $1 per annum, receivable or payable at the end of each year for n years $\frac{1-(1+r)^{-n}}{r}$.

Periods (n)	Interest rates (r)									
	1%	2%	3%	4%	5%	6%	7%	8%	9%	10%
1	0.990	0.980	0.971	0.962	0.952	0.943	0.935	0.926	0.917	0.909
2	1.970	1.942	1.913	1.886	1.859	1.833	1.808	1.783	1.759	1.736
3	2.941	2.884	2.829	2.775	2.723	2.673	2.624	2.577	2.531	2.487
4	3.902	3.808	3.717	3.630	3.546	3.465	3.387	3.312	3.240	3.170
5	4.853	4.713	4.580	4.452	4.329	4.212	4.100	3.993	3.890	3.791
6	5.795	5.601	5.417	5.242	5.076	4.917	4.767	4.623	4.486	4.355
7	6.728	6.472	6.230	6.002	5.786	5.582	5.389	5.206	5.033	4.868
8	7.652	7.325	7.020	6.733	6.463	6.210	5.971	5.747	5.535	5.335
9	8.566	8.162	7.786	7.435	7.108	6.802	6.515	6.247	5.995	5.759
10	9.471	8.983	8.530	8.111	7.722	7.360	7.024	6.710	6.418	6.145
11	10.368	9.787	9.253	8.760	8.306	7.887	7.499	7.139	6.805	6.495
12	11.255	10.575	9.954	9.385	8.863	8.384	7.943	7.536	7.161	6.814
13	12.134	11.348	10.635	9.986	9.394	8.853	8.358	7.904	7.487	7.103
14	13.004	12.106	11.296	10.563	9.899	9.295	8.745	8.244	7.786	7.367
15	13.865	12.849	11.938	11.118	10.380	9.712	9.108	8.559	8.061	7.606
16	14.718	13.578	12.561	11.652	10.838	10.106	9.447	8.851	8.313	7.824
17	15.562	14.292	13.166	12.166	11.274	10.477	9.763	9.122	8.544	8.022
18	16.398	14.992	13.754	12.659	11.690	10.828	10.059	9.372	8.756	8.201
19	17.226	15.679	14.324	13.134	12.085	11.158	10.336	9.604	8.950	8.365
20	18.046	16.351	14.878	13.590	12.462	11.470	10.594	9.818	9.129	8.514

Periods (n)	Interest rates (r)									
	11%	12%	13%	14%	15%	16%	17%	18%	19%	20%
1	0.901	0.893	0.885	0.877	0.870	0.862	0.855	0.847	0.840	0.833
2	1.713	1.690	1.668	1.647	1.626	1.605	1.585	1.566	1.547	1.528
3	2.444	2.402	2.361	2.322	2.283	2.246	2.210	2.174	2.140	2.106
4	3.102	3.037	2.974	2.914	2.855	2.798	2.743	2.690	2.639	2.589
5	3.696	3.605	3.517	3.433	3.352	3.274	3.199	3.127	3.058	2.991
6	4.231	4.111	3.998	3.889	3.784	3.685	3.589	3.498	3.410	3.326
7	4.712	4.564	4.423	4.288	4.160	4.039	3.922	3.812	3.706	3.605
8	5.146	4.968	4.799	4.639	4.487	4.344	4.207	4.078	3.954	3.837
9	5.537	5.328	5.132	4.946	4.772	4.607	4.451	4.303	4.163	4.031
10	5.889	5.650	5.426	5.216	5.019	4.833	4.659	4.494	4.339	4.192
11	6.207	5.938	5.687	5.453	5.234	5.029	4.836	4.656	4.486	4.327
12	6.492	6.194	5.918	5.660	5.421	5.197	4.988	4.793	4.611	4.439
13	6.750	6.424	6.122	5.842	5.583	5.342	5.118	4.910	4.715	4.533
14	6.982	6.628	6.302	6.002	5.724	5.468	5.229	5.008	4.802	4.611
15	7.191	6.811	6.462	6.142	5.847	5.575	5.324	5.092	4.876	4.675
16	7.379	6.974	6.604	6.265	5.954	5.668	5.405	5.162	4.938	4.730
17	7.549	7.120	6.729	6.373	6.047	5.749	5.475	5.222	4.990	4.775
18	7.702	7.250	6.840	6.467	6.128	5.818	5.534	5.273	5.033	4.812
19	7.839	7.366	6.938	6.550	6.198	5.877	5.584	5.316	5.070	4.843
20	7.963	7.469	7.025	6.623	6.259	5.929	5.628	5.353	5.101	4.870

Formulae

DVM

$$k_e = \frac{d_1}{P_0} + g$$

$$g = r \times b$$

$$g = \sqrt[n]{\left(\frac{\text{latest dividend}}{\text{past dividend}}\right)} - 1$$

$$IRR = L + \left[\frac{NPV_L}{NPV_L - NPV_H}(H-L)\right]$$

Cost of Irredeemable Debt

$$K_d = \frac{I(1-t)}{P_0}$$

WACC

$$WACC = k_{eg}\left[\frac{V_E}{V_E + V_D}\right] + k_d[1-t]\left[\frac{V_D}{V_E + V_D}\right]$$